Literature
of
Belief

THE RELIGIOUS STUDIES MONOGRAPH SERIES

NIBLEY ON THE TIMELY AND THE TIMELESS
Classic Essays of Hugh W. Nibley

DEITY AND DEATH
Selected Symposium Papers
edited with an introduction by Spencer J. Palmer

THE GLORY OF GOD IS INTELLIGENCE
Four Lectures on the Role of Intellect in Judaism
by Jacob Neusner

REFLECTIONS ON MORMONISM
Judaeo – Christian Parallels
edited with an introductory essay by Truman G. Madsen

THE WORDS OF JOSEPH SMITH
Contemporary Accounts of the Nauvoo Discourses
compiled and edited by Andrew F. Ehat and Lyndon W. Cook

Literature
of
Belief

Sacred Scripture and Religious Experience

Edited with a Preface by
Neal E. Lambert

VOLUME FIVE
IN THE RELIGIOUS STUDIES MONOGRAPH SERIES

Introduction by
M. Gerald Bradford

Religious Studies Center
Brigham Young University

Lithographed in the United States of America
PUBLISHERS PRESS
Salt Lake City, Utah

To Spencer J. Palmer.
The vision behind this book is his.

Contents

LATTER-DAY SAINT SCRIPTURE

Preface

As a people who derive their identity from a sacred book, Mormons have a natural interest in religious texts and narratives. Indeed, they are in a significant way a "people of the book," for the Book of Mormon as a religious text is both a keystone of the Latter-day Saint church and an expression of the deepest matters of faith for each member. Along with that book the often-told story of Joseph Smith's 1820 theophany in the woods of upstate New York has become a sacred narrative of the highest significance as it both identifies and narrates the beginnings of this new religious tradition. This interest in religious expression is of course at least as inclusive as it is exclusive. That is why the suggestion of a symposium at Brigham Young University devoted to the literature of belief met with such an immediate and enthusiastic response when it was first proposed almost two years ago.

We knew, of course, that any attempt to be either comprehensive or exhaustive with such a vast subject as religious literature would be foolhardy. From the *sutras* of Buddhism and the epic tales of the *Bhagavad Gita* to the ancient creation narratives of Moses and the modern warnings of approaching apocalypse, the array of forms and modes and subject matters of religious literature both written and spoken make the whole field infinitely vast and complex. So we knew to begin with that any symposium could offer only tantalizing bits and pieces at best. But the idea itself was so appealing that we could not resist making an attempt. We were fortunate in this regard in being able to have the support of two important organizations on campus, the Center for International and Area Studies and the Religious Studies Center. Drawing on the impressive backgrounds of our own colleagues in these centers, we were able to bring together their combined resources in a remarkable effort of mutual support and unselfish cooperation quite unusual even for a college campus. With this support we were able to invite scholars from within the borders of our own country and others from halfway around the world as participants in the conference.

As the acceptances began to come back, we could tell that our highest hopes for the symposium were being realized. Not only would the topics be exciting and varied, but the speakers would, without question, be some of the most significant scholarly voices of our time.

When sessions got underway that Thursday and Friday, March 7-8, 1979, the enthusiastic reaction of the audiences demonstrated that the symposium was everything we had hoped for. From the exotic and stimulating presentation of Joseph Campbell, through the dance-like lecture of Wing-tsit Chan, to the enchanting narratives of the charismatic P. Lal, the different sections of the symposium presented us all with a varied and unusually appealing intellectual feast.

But if good luck and good management of car pools, room assignments, and microphones can make a good symposium, far more is needed to make a good book. While we had hoped all along to be able to publish the proceedings of the symposium, we recognized as the program went on that we had before us an array of presentational modes that fit the symposium format splendidly, but were less easily set down in cold print.

It was at this point that we received unusual help, not just from the symposium participants themselves in shaping their manuscripts, but from two remarkable and capable people, Lavina Fielding Anderson and M. Gerald Bradford. Lavina has helped us not only with the preparation of the copy for the book itself, she has helped find appropriate manuscripts to cover some of the obvious gaps which the symposium itself, because of the limits of time, had simply to acknowledge and pass over. Gerald, out of his own scholarly background and sense of friendship to BYU, stayed with us throughout this whole project as advisor, editor, and as an essential guide, steering those of us less knowledgeable away from the pitfalls of our own ignorance. If errors persist, they are ours, not his. Anyone who reads the introduction which follows will sense the contributions that Gerald has made to this volume.

Many others deserve thanks as well: A. Terry Schiefer, JoAnn Allen, Cloma E. Callahan, Lillian M. Osborne, and my colleagues in the Center for International and Area Studies who were the originators and organizers of many of the sessions where these materials were first presented. I especially want to acknowledge the substantial assistance given to the symposium and this volume by the World Religions area of the Religious Studies Center and by the general director of the Center, Ellis T. Rasmussen. Dean Rasmussen has been impressively patient and supportive as the effort to get these pages prepared has moved slowly along since the original symposium in the spring of 1979. His unflagging interest kept alive a project that, given the difficulty, may have otherwise quietly expired.

Finally, no one knows more than those of us who have worked on it how eclectic, even fragmented, this collection of papers may seem. However, like a collection of fine crystals, each piece casts a particular hue that considered along with the others creates for the observer a rich and pleasing experience. Seeing each of these pieces in the context of the rest will, we believe, be a rewarding experience.

Neal E. Lambert
Brigham Young University

Introduction

Brigham Young University's symposium on "The Literature of Belief" focused, as does this volume, on that great body of literature best referred to as sacred literature or holy scripture. The goal was to learn more about the nature of religious experience by examining its expressions in the sacred texts of a number of the world's religious traditions.

Both the papers written originally for the symposium and five additional studies prepared under other auspices address the theme of the conference. Several different religious perspectives and academic backgrounds are represented in the different essays, yet all of the scholars involved share a keen interest in the study of religion, particularly the study of sacred literature.

In appreciation of these differing viewpoints and interests, no attempt was made to structure the symposium beyond asking the participants to address the experiences of the sacred as recounted in the religious texts they selected for study. Hence this collection manifests a broad range of approaches. Some are very personal, even autobiographical; many come at the task using the tools of the literary critic, the historian, the philosopher, and even the theologian. Some of the essays are clearly introductory; others speak chiefly to specialists. The result is an impressive undertaking, a cooperative endeavor to understand the religious dimension of our common human heritage.

A major objective of those who planned the symposium and this volume has been to provide an occasion for studying some of the scriptures of The Church of Jesus Christ of Latter-day Saints in a broad comparative setting. Consequently, this anthology includes not only reflections on Jewish, Christian, and Islamic texts, and on writings held sacred by Hindus, Buddhists, and Taoists, but also studies of the Book of Mormon, the Articles of Faith, and the Prophet Joseph Smith's account of his first vision. Here the goal is to consider what the structure and content of these Mormon scriptures can tell us about things of the spirit and to emphasize the stature of these writings in the context of world religious literature.

Obviously in treating such an extensive subject as "the literature of belief," no attempt has been made to be comprehensive. Rather these essays must be seen as individual insights into aspects of some of the world's major scriptures. By bringing these viewpoints together, we hope that the reader will learn more about this kind of writing and better appreciate the varieties of religious experience and their dynamic nature.

Of all the aspects of religion, none is more important, because none is more foundational, than the experiential dimension. William James, for one, makes "the feelings, acts, and experiences of individual men in their solitude, so far as they apprehend themselves to stand in relation to whatever they may consider the divine," the very center of his definition of religion. It is from this base — from relationships with the divine expressed in rituals, beliefs, moral affirmations, and even physiological and psychological states — that, according to James, "theologies, philosophies, and ecclesiastical organizations" emerge.[1]

One has only to consider a number of classical incidents in the lives of several religious figures to appreciate this observation. For instance, a main theme in the earliest of the Buddhist sacred texts centers on how the Buddha sought for and achieved enlightenment while sitting beneath the Bo Tree. The singular visions of the Hebrew prophets taught them something profoundly important about God and emboldened them to teach others in his name. Muhammad's own experiences prompted him to preach the unity of Allah and, in the course of time, to be instrumental in bringing forth the divine teachings known as the Qur'an. Surely the climax of the most popular of all Indian holy texts, the *Bhagavad Gita,* is the terrifying theophany granted to Arjuna, leaving him filled with awe and promising unstinting love and devotion to Lord Krishna. The Book of Mormon narrative recounts experiences which radically transformed the lives of the prophets and others — Lehi's dream, Enos's answer to prayer, the conversion of Alma the Younger, and the Nephites' encounter with the Savior. And as with the prophets, so with the Master. Christ's temptation in the desert, his transfiguration, and the ministrations and manifestations that accompanied his prayer convey the intimate relationship he enjoyed with the Father; divine himself, his experiences with the divine informed his teachings and marked him "as one having authority" (Matt. 7:29).

It is experiences such as these — expressed in mythic accounts, in epics, stories, and poems about the gods and cultural heroes, in historical narratives highlighting the intervention of God in the course of events, in sacred laws and ritual instructions, in teachings and expositions of venerated spiritual authorities and dialogues of seers and sages, in moral anecdotes and philosophical and theological discussions, and in countless hymns and prayers — that make up much of what is spoken of as sacred scripture. This is the subject matter of this book.

Part One deals with the sacred literature of the West. Judaism, Christianity, and Islam share not only a common heritage of belief in one God, but are spoken of as "religions of the book" in deference to the indispensable role the Hebrew Bible, the Old and New Testaments, and the Qur'an play in these respective traditions.

For generations the teachings and ways of the Hebrews were transmitted orally. In time, sacred lore became sacred writ, and the books of scripture were divided into the Law (Torah), the Prophets (Nevi'im), and the histories, psalms, and lessons called the Writings (Ketubim). The entire collection is often referred to as Torah or the Hebrew Bible. Herbert Schneidau's presentation calls attention to the characteristic style of the Hebrew Bible and suggests that this style not only illuminates how the ancient Israelites may have experienced their world and the things of God but also that it eventually produced Western literature.

In so arguing, Schneidau grapples with the age-old confrontation between two ways of experiencing the world — the historical and the mythological. He demonstrates that the Hebrew way of thinking is historical — there is no *logos* in the biblical narrative, God can remain hidden and yet still not be inscrutable, and for the Jews, the historical and social order of things has no status beyond contingency. This thesis well illustrates the distinctive Hebrew world perspective and simultaneously helps us to grasp important differences that separate this tradition (and to an extent that of Christianity and Islam) from other religions of the world.

Gerald N. Lund also deals with the scriptural material contained in the Hebrew Bible, coming at his task from a Christian perspective. The term *Old Testament* means "old covenant" and describes the dealings of God with the Jews under the Mosaic law. Christians reading the Old Testament find Christ foreshadowed there and thus regard the New Testament or the "new covenant" as the fulfillment of the Old.

Lund illustrates this cardinal point in detail, focusing on the Old Testament's rich trove of ritual instruction and dramatic historical narrative. He describes sacrifice, circumcision, the cleansing of lepers, and important days of worship: the Sabbath, the Feast of Weeks, and the Days of Atonement and the Feast of Tabernacles. He concludes by considering the meaning of such epic events as Abraham's near-sacrifice of Isaac, Moses' liberation of the children of Israel from Egypt, the establishment of the ritual of Passover, and the Jews' wandering in the wilderness and their final entry into the Promised Land. All of these acts and events, Lund argues, can only be fully understood when interpreted, with the aid of latter-day scripture, as symbolically pointing to Jesus Christ and his atonement.

Turning to the New Testament, Richard L. Anderson examines experiences of divine revelation as recounted in this holy text, convincingly demonstrating that Paul's letters contain records of the same events written in the later synoptic Gospels. Recorded soon after the events described, the letters validate historical events and thus function as checks on their authenticity.

Correctly pointing out that these letters record events as

understood by the first generation of those who knew the Lord, Anderson finds a pattern of revelation in Paul's letters to the Corinthians. From the foundational level of spiritual gifts to personal visions of Jesus Christ, the pattern instructs the Corinthian Saints in the Resurrection, not only its reality as a historical event but also as a revelation of the personality of the Father. Anderson concludes that Paul's letters teach, intentionally and elaborately, that God is a divine personality. Thus, later generations of scholars and theologians who quarrel with this definition of God deny "the living revelation of God that constitutes the New Testament witness and fired the zeal of the early Christians."

The remaining article in Part One is Fazlur Rahman's consideration of Islam's sacred scripture, the Qur'an. No other religious tradition is so wedded to a single book of scripture. Many authors produced the books of the Bible, but from the mouth of Muhammad alone sprang the Qur'an.

Qur'an comes from the Arabic verb meaning "to read, repeat aloud." Thus, according to Muslim tradition, Muhammad did not write the Qur'an but was taught by a spirit usually identified as the angel Gabriel, and recited it. The text itself was composed later by scribes and other hearers as it was recited. The scripture read in the original Arabic is said to move listeners to tears because of the elegance of its powerful, rhythmic prose. For all Muslims, the Qur'an is *the* book, a divinely dictated scripture, unique and incomparable. Furthermore, for Muslims, God's revelation is the *book* itself. In contrast, Jews seek for God in the events of history, and Christians see God revealed in Jesus Christ.

In outlining what he sees as the Qur'an's essential teachings, Rahman looks to the religious experiences in Muhammad's life and especially the social and economic conditions that prevailed in Muhammad's Mecca. The result is a concise, fascinating introduction to the world of Islam.

Over the course of twenty-three years, Muhammad, struggling against the injustices in his society and the powerful influence of tribal polytheism, proclaimed the radical oneness of

Allah and the need to abolish economic and social disparities. These two principles, along with the assurance that God will yet judge the world, anchor all other teachings in the Qur'an.

Rahman underlines the Qur'an's teaching that human beings, unlike the rest of creation, are free to obey or disobey the will of God. Still, he points out, the holy book also emphasizes that individuals are invariably short-sighted, selfish, and narrow-minded, inclined, in times of prosperity and acclaim, to forget their responsibility to others and God, a theme familiar in the Bible and the Book of Mormon too. Given self-deception, human beings think they do good, judged by the standards of the world, but more often than not misjudge themselves and their deeds. The Qur'an teaches that for persons to be righteous they must not simply desire the good but actively pursue it, judging their deeds according to divine, not human, standards. And herein, Rahman stresses, the Qur'an brings its teachings about human nature full circle. "So long as man acts only on the basis of immediate consequences, there is not much possibility of his producing deeds that will be consequential in the long run. So to cultivate *taqwa* (the fear of God), to clear the earth of corruption and to reform the earth — to create on earth a social order based on ethically valid principles — is the message of the Qur'an."

Part Two is devoted to the sacred literature of India and the Far East and deals with representative scriptures of Hinduism, Buddhism, and Taoism.

Composition of India's wondrously diverse scriptures may have begun as early as A.D. 2000 and, following Hindu custom, are considered to be either *shurti* ("that which is heard") — the most sacred and hence most authoritative — or *smriti* ("what is remembered"). *Shurti* includes the ancient Vedas or sacrificial hymns; the Brahmanas that explain them; the Aranyakas or Forest Books; and the Upanishads that transform the earlier ritual narratives into deeper philosophical and theological insights. All four are also collectively called the Vedas. *Smriti* embraces the great epics, the Mahabharata and the Ramayana, and the Puranas — tales of gods and ancient beings — as well as philosophical and sectarian texts. Of all the Vedas, Western thought has tended to focus on the Upanishads as Hinduism's most important and typical literature even though a section of the Mahabharata known as the *Bhagavad Gita* ("The Song of God") is clearly best known and most loved by Hindus.

One could not ask for a better guide into the world of Indian sacred writings than P. Lal of Calcutta. He chooses to deal indirectly with these texts, telling us of his personal quest for enlightenment and thus enabling us to better understand how a Hindu might experience and interpret the world. Implicit in his parables is the Hindu belief that all beings are subject to *samsara* — the seemingly endless cycle of birth, death, and rebirth — and that they are trapped in this condition by virtue of *karma,* the cosmic law of cause and effect which holds that what we did in prior lives accounts for the circumstances of our present life and along with our present conduct determines our future circumstances. Both good and evil result in rebirth; hence, for the Hindu, the ultimate goal of life is to be freed from *samsara* altogether. This theme, introduced in Lal's parable of the wish-fulfilling tree, lies at the very heart of the teachings of the Upanishads, the *Bhagavad Gita,* and other sacred Indian texts. According to these scriptures, the aim of life, the goal of all worship and ritual, the point of service to others and the gods is liberation from the cycle of rebirth and union with Brahmin — the One, the All, the Absolute.

The moral of Lal's story for us, then, is our need to recognize that the meaning of life lies in performing "pure acts" — deeds of compassion done wholly without regard to the consequences. Lal thus advocates the tradition of *karma marga* (the way of works and performance), one of four classical means of liberation. (The others are *jnana marga,* the way of knowledge, *raja yoga,* the way of mental discipline, and *bhakti marga,* the way of love and devotion to God.) But regardless of the path, the message is always the same: just as all mountain streams eventually empty into the sea, so all paths lead to the Universal One, the Absolute.

No theme is more readily identified with the religions of the East than is *yoga,* a term derived from the Sanskrit *yuj* (to link, join, or unite). While most westerners associate it only with physical control and discipline of the body (properly hatha yoga), each of the four *margas* just mentioned are also called yogas. So is the tradition of practices known as tantra or kundalini explicated in this symposium by Joseph Campbell.

In his *The Masks of God: Oriental Mythology*, Campbell observes that both *yoga* and *religion* (from the Latin *religio*) mean "to link back, or bind" but that this linguistic resemblance masks profound theological and spiritual differences. Religion refers to a *historical* linking of man and the divine by way of a covenant, a sacrament, or, in the case of Islam, a holy scripture. Yoga implies a *psychological* linking of the mind to that superordinate principle "by which the mind knows." In yoga, what seems to be two is in reality one, whereas in religion, what is linked are God and man, which are not the same.[2] Though both yoga and religion imply man's distance from the divine in his normal secular life, "yet the arguments radically differ, and therefore support two radically different civilizations," Campbell points out. "For, if man has been removed from the divine through a historical event [the Fall], it will be a historical event that leads him back, whereas if it has been by some sort of psychological displacement that he has been blocked, psychology will be his vehicle of return. And so it is that in India the final focus of concern is not the community, . . . but yoga."[3]

Campbell calls kundalini yoga India's great gift to us as a "highly developed *psychological* science." Reaching back to pre-Aryan times in India, it is suggested in the earliest of the Upanishads and has influenced not only Hinduism and Buddhism but Jainism as well. The tradition suddenly reemerged in the fourth century B.C. in India and ever since then has "shaped and informed every significant development of Oriental doctrine." Campbell takes us up "the jeweled tree" of the kundalini centers, in what amounts to a *tour de force* in exposition and interpretation of the rich symbolism of its seven *chakras* (circles).

As the techniques of yoga remind us, it is not death but rebirth that is the enemy in Hinduism and Buddhism. In the older tradition of India, liberation from this ceaseless round comes in the uniting of self with the Self. Buddha built on this old faith but developed its doctrine into a new doctrine, a new code of life, a new way. Buddha showed his followers a way to end rebirth, through right conduct and mindful concentration. His path leads to peace of mind, to knowledge, to enlightenment — to Nirvana.

The *dharma* (teachings) of the Buddha are often compared to a raft that carries believers across the river of *samsara* to Nirvana on the further shore. Theravada Buddhism ("the way of the Elders"), is sometimes known as the "lesser vehicle"; it involves joining the *sangha* (order of monks) and hence attracts fewer followers. A monk who reaches Nirvana becomes an *arhant* (saint). In this school, Buddha is merely one who has attained this goal and whose example shows others the way.

The sacred scriptures of Theravada Buddhism (the Pali Canon) is called the *Tripitaka* because it is divided into three sections. This canon, not counting its thousands of commentaries, is estimated at twice the length of the Bible. The most popular anthology of Buddha's original teachings is the *Dhammapada*.

Mahayana Buddhism, also known as the "greater vehicle," offers the ultimate goal to both the pious monk and the layman. Its followers strive not only for Nirvana but for a godly existence of self-sacrifice and compassion. This tradition's ideal is not the *arhant* but the *bodhisattva* — one who embodies the buddha-nature and in compassion vows never to cross the river "until every living being, every blade of grass is liberated." In this tradition, Buddha is more than "one who shows the way." Buddha is a universal principle, neither one Buddha nor many, but the origin and source of buddhahood itself.

Mahayana scriptures include not only translations of the Sanskrit *Tripitaka* but thousands of original works in Chinese, Tibetan, Japanese, and other languages. Two of the most important are the *Vaipulya Sutras* containing the *Saddharma Pundarika* ("Lotus Sutra") and the *Prajnaparamita Sutras* ("Discourses on the Perfections of Wisdom").

Richard Mather's paper traces the influence of one of these sacred texts, the *Nirvana Sutra*, in the development of Mayayana Buddhism in China. He shows how, in the fifth century B.C., the Buddhist ideal of the *bodhisattva* contributed to southern China's idea of an eternal Buddha as the sole means of liberation. This belief in turn nurtured an intellectual and spiritual climate favorable to the radical teachings of the *Nirvana Sutra,* which challenged conventional Buddhism by positing a "real self" which even Nirvana does not destroy. Since everyone contains the buddha-nature, buddhahood is within everyone's reach. Mather illustrates the kind of theoretical controversies which this text ignited (for instance, is enlightenment sudden or gradual?) but is more interested in showing how this scripture eventually helped popularize *ahimsa* (the practice of nonviolence) among Chinese Buddhists as the ultimate expression of belief in the compassionate Buddha.

Whether the basic texts of Taoism or Confucianism should be called sacred is open to question. They were originally viewed as human wisdom books, written by men for men. In time, these writings acquired added authority and were accorded profound reverence, thus becoming, in effect, sacred texts. The *Tao-te-Ching,* the topic of the last paper in Part Two, is an example.

Wing-tsit Chan, the patriarch of Chinese scholars in this country, is interested in showing how this Taoist classic determined the course of Chinese philosophy and religion centuries before the time of Christ.

He focuses on the *Tao-te Ching's* central theme, the idea of the Tao, explores its various meanings, traces the influence of Taoism on Confucianism and, even later, on Buddhism in China, and shows how Taoism was, in turn, changed by these contacts. The Taoist effort to promote life, their search for the means to prolong life, and even achieve immortality, and their teaching of the inherently mysterious nature of the *Tao,* are, according to Chan, elements which transformed Taoism into a religion and hence into a major factor in the religion of ancient China.

The standard works of The Church of Jesus Christ of Latter-day Saints include ancient works (the Bible and the Book of Mormon), the modern Doctrine and Covenants, and the Pearl of Great Price with both ancient and modern writings. Part Three explores certain of these sacred texts.

The Pearl of Great Price, probably the least-known Mormon scripture outside the Church is the focus of Adele McCollum and Steven Sondrup. McCollum discusses Joseph Smith's account of his first vision while Sondrup examines the Prophet's summation of the central tenets of Mormonism in the Articles of Faith.

In her paper, McCollum traces some theological implications of the First Vision, coming to some startling conclusions. She considers this inaugural vision as a classical instance of a numinous experience: a revelation that by its very occurrence threatens established ways of thinking and dealing with the world.

To appreciate the implications of an experience with two Gods, she reaches back to the polytheism of the ancient Greeks and argues that Mormonism's polytheistic theology symbolizes the multiple-faith experiences of Latter-day Saints who, in their practice of religion and in their acts of worship, focus their commitment on *one* God. In this respect Mormonism is in the vanguard of the future of religion since, for McCollum, any religion which is to survive in today's pluralistic culture must be polytheistic.

Steven Sondrup examines another central document in the Pearl of Great Price, the Articles of Faith. Creedal statements have played a vital role in the religious traditions of the West. While there is no single, simple creed for Jews, the most famous of the Jewish scholastics, Moses Maimonides, produced a twelfth-century statement of Jewish beliefs known as the "Thirteen Articles of Faith," each prefaced, in time, by "I believe." In the Christian tradition, early ecumenical councils produced, for instance, the Apostles' Creed and the Nicene Creed, codifying Catholic doctrine. The Westminster Confession of Faith represents Protestantism in this respect. Islam's formal creed is very short: "There is no god but Allah, and Muhammad is his Prophet."

Sondrup compares the Articles of Faith with other Christian creeds, not in content but in form and as a means of confessing the faith. He shows how the linguistic distinctions between

"believing that" and "believing in" not only communicate intellectual assent but more importantly profess trust and commitment. Furthermore, Sondrup finds that professing belief in this
manner also means to act in a way that contributes to one's salvation. Here Sondrup compares the performative function of
the Articles of Faith with the Mormon tradition of publicly confessing one's faith in "testimony meetings." He argues that the
testimonial formula "I know" and the creedal "we believe" are
complementary, not antithetical and that, in fact, the dynamic
relationship between the individual and the communal modes of
expressing belief energizes the tradition.

1980 is the sesquicentennial anniversary of the publication of
the Book of Mormon, historically the Church's most significant
scripture. Object of countless studies both within and, increasingly, outside the LDS tradition, it has only recently been dealt
with as a literary text. The three remaining papers in Part Three
each view the Book of Mormon from this vantage point, not
only illuminating the structural integrity of the book but employing a tool that the authors hope will better enable readers to
understand the experiential dimension of the text and appreciate
its spiritual depth.

Bruce Jorgensen follows the lead of such literary critics as
Northrop Frye and Erich Auerbach in applying a typological
approach to a literary investigation of the Book of Mormon.
Furthermore, he asserts, the Book of Mormon, like the Bible,
invites this mode of interpretation through its prophetic and
messianic nature.

Armed with this structural insight, Jorgensen not only discovers types that foreshadow the end of times, the Church,
ritual ordinances, and the Christ, but also an archetype which
subsumes all the rest into one unifying image — Lehi's dream of
the Tree of Life or Jacob's parable of the tame and wild olive
trees. He argues that all of God's actions in the world — creation,
conversion, covenant, and redemption — are one act of transformation, a move from darkness into light. The Book of Mormon, by this reading, testifies that only this change, required of
us individually and collectively, will let us experience life as
God wishes and be in the world in a truly sanctified state.

Richard Dilworth Rust extends this approach by focusing on the numerous occasions where Book of Mormon prophets themselves teach the gospel typologically. He particularly notes Alma's instructions to his son Helaman, Moroni's teachings from the prophecies of Ether, the sermon of King Benjamin, and, of course, the discourses of Lehi and Nephi. For them, understanding and teaching the gospel typologically was, according to Rust, so natural as to be almost taken for granted.

George S. Tate continues this line of interpretation and finds a unifying type for the Book of Mormon in the exodus of the Israelites from Egypt and their settlement in the land of promise. This type not only ties together the narrative of the Old Testament but, according to Tate, unifies the Old and New Testaments. Hence, he argues, we ought to expect this typology in the Book of Mormon. In fact, he finds the Exodus figure in greater concentration in the Book of Mormon than in the Old Testament and sees Book of Mormon prophets who look back to Moses and forward to Christ employing it consciously and skillfully.

Mormon readers in particular will find this book, fifth in a series sponsored by BYU's Religious Studies Center, a worthy successor to its predecessors. Like *Deity and Death* and *Reflections on Mormonism: Judaeo-Christian Parallels,* it is the result of the combined efforts of a number of individuals — Mormon and non-Mormon — who have sought to learn more about the dimensions of religion. This volume's focus on the sacred scriptures of the world adds a distinctive contribution to what can be discerned about religious belief and experience by carefully studying the structure and contents of the "literature of belief."

No attempt has been made in this introduction or by individual authors to come to any final conclusions other than to make this plea: whether in the *sutras* of Buddhism, the revelations on the banks of the Jordan, or the prophetic experiences in the Sacred Grove of New York, there are voices that need to be heard and understood.

The alert reader will no doubt detect areas of similarity or even agreement in these voices. But comparative efforts such as this also highlight important differences on issues like the meaning and purpose of life, the nature of God and man, and their proper relationship. As Latter-day Saints we are taught to seek continually for greater insight and knowledge on these matters.

Studies such as this can obviously assist us and need to be evaluated both for their helpfulness and for their scholarly contributions. In fact, we look to the scriptures for sanction in pursuing such projects. The Doctrine and Covenants records the Lord's admonition to "study and learn, and become acquainted with all good books, and with languages, tongues, and people" (D&C 90:15). But in the same scriptures, he also cautions us that if we are to learn the truth about such matters we need to "seek learning, . . . by study and also by faith" (D&C 88:118). Simply put, study such as this not only teaches us about other people, places, and things but directs our attention to the deeper things, to questions and concerns that can have eternal value for us. To paraphrase the Prophet Joseph Smith, the issues raised and dealt with in this book are "of deep import; and time, and experience, and careful and ponderous and solemn thoughts can only find them out."[4]

For those who will make the effort, the rewards can be great indeed.

M. Gerald Bradford
The University of California at Santa Barbara

NOTES

1. *The Varieties of Religious Experience* (New York: New American Library for Mentor Books, 1962), p. 42.

2. *The Masks of God: Oriental Mythology* (1962; reprint ed., New York: Penguin Books, 1977), pp. 13-14.

3. *Ibid.*, p. 13.

4. *Teachings of the Prophet Joseph Smith*, sel. Joseph Fielding Smith (Salt Lake City, Ut.: Deseret Book Co., 1938), p. 137.

JEWISH, CHRISTIAN, AND ISLAMIC SCRIPTURE

Transliterations of Arabic, Hebrew, Sanskrit, and Chinese are styled throughout this volume to omit diacritics.

1

Herbert N. Schneidau

Biblical Style
and
Western Literature

Professor of English at the University of Arizona, Dr. Schneidau has linked his interest in literature to his fascination with Biblical studies and has long been recognized as a scholar on the literature of the Bible as well as a leading authority on Ezra Pound. His most recent book is Sacred Discontent: The Bible and Western Tradition.

In his presentation on "Biblical Style and Western Literature," he argues that Biblical thinking produced Western literature and that the shape of this thinking was persistently and resistantly nonmythic, unlike the literature being produced by Israel's neighbors during the time the Hebrew Bible was being shaped. He traces characteristic manifestations of this nonbiblical style in the manifestations of Yahweh to the children of Israel, the "identity crisis" precipitated when Israel demanded a human king instead of retaining its loyalty to its divine king, Yahweh, and the profound differences thus developed between

the Hebraic point of view and the Greco-Roman worldview,
differences now obscured by traditions of classical education.

———————

I am going to be talking about a tradition which is defiantly parochial in some senses — a tradition that stresses uniqueness rather than universality and, of course, proceeds precisely by means of words and meanings rather than seeking the "word beyond meaning" or seeking through the ladder of images to achieve the state of the sound beyond meaning and so on. Specifically, also, I am going to be concerned more with written things — with the emphasis on what happens when oral traditions turn into written traditions; and that, of course, is something that can be a very fateful change.

This meditation is going to take, as its basis and its epigraph, a passage from Erich Auerbach's magisterial work, *Mimesis*. In the well-known first chapter, he contrasts the style of Genesis with that of Homer, using the text in which God commands Abraham to sacrifice Isaac. Auerbach asks:

> Whence does [God] come, whence does he call Abraham? We are not told. He does not come, like Zeus or Poseidon, from the Aethiopians, where he has been enjoying a sacrificial feast. Nor are we told anything of his reasons for tempting Abraham so terribly. He has not, like Zeus, discussed them in set speeches with other gods gathered in council; nor have the deliberations in his own heart been presented to us; unexpected and mysterious, he enters the scene from some unknown height or depth and calls: Abraham! It will at once be said that this is to be explained by the particular concept of God which the Jews held and which was wholly different from that of the Greeks. True enough, but this constitutes no objection. For how is the Jewish concept of God to be explained? Even their earlier God of the desert was not fixed in form and content, and was alone; his lack of form, his lack of local habitation, his singleness, was in the end not only maintained but developed even further

in competition with the comparatively far more manifest gods of the surrounding Near Eastern world [the mythological world, I call it]. The concept of God held by the Jews is less a cause than a symptom of their manner of comprehending and representing things.[1]

To my mind this passage, especially that last sentence, repays careful and repeated study. *"The concept of God held by the Jews is less a cause than a symptom of their manner of comprehending and representing things."* This sentence announces what might be a major theme of this conference especially — that the processes of mind that lie behind a people's religion will also be seen in the style of its literature. But even more, it suggests that, at least in this case, the argument can be extended. The concept of Yahweh might, in a sense, be the *result* of the style — the biblical style.

Just to give a totally secular sidelight on this, I could make an example of Oscar Wilde's argument that nature imitates art, that a London fogscape is never seen again in the same way after one has viewed impressionist paintings, that style in key ways is creative of content.[2] I always thought that Wilde's point was very well taken — irrefutable, in fact. I remember very vividly going to the Museum of Modern Art in New York and how different New York looked when you came out of that museum. The forms which the artists represented in that museum deal, in a very clear connection — a very intrinsic relation — with the architecture of New York City; what you do is experience something that can only be called an education in form. It immediately strikes you when you come outside. You do not look at the city the same way: at least I did not.

In the case of the Bible, what I want to argue is that Auerbach was right, and right not only about those qualities he was concerned to explain — those ways in which Yahweh, to use Auerbach's words, "is not comprehensible in his presence, as is Zeus; it is always only 'something' of him that appears, he always extends into depth."[3] As Auerbach suggests, the Hebrew style as represented in the Bible is a possible explanation of the singular fact that as Yahweh grows more competitive with the gods of the ancient Near East, he grows not more like them, but

less. His lack of form, his lack of local habitation, grow even
more marked. His lack of what I call mythological manifestation is more pronounced. But I would go still further and say
that Auerbach gives us a key, not only to the Bible, but to a link
between the way Yahweh's appearances are recorded and the
very shapes and matrices of Western literature.

In short, I assert that biblical thinking produced our literature, and furthermore, that this kind of thinking, which was so
very different from the thinking of cultured people in the
ancient era of the Egyptians and the Mesopotamians, cannot be
taken for granted as normative. It is, in fact, a very different
kind of thinking, very possibly an aberrant form of thought, if
you add up all the ways human beings have had in which to
think. What are ultimately the characteristics of this biblical
style and the kind of thinking it bespeaks?

In order to extend Auerbach's superb description of it, I will
make a quick survey of biblical literature and its recordings of
the manifestations of Yahweh. The picture I draw is taken mostly from recent biblical scholarship; and though it will need to be
updated in some respects, I hope it will be acceptable in the
main.

What came before the Bible itself? No doubt there were various creeds, sagas, and collections of traditions. Perhaps the
most important for our purposes are the kinds of collections
quoted in several passages in the Bible, one of which bears the
significant name, "the Book of the Wars of Yahweh" (see Num.
21:14; RSV used throughout). What was in it? The title suggests
that it consisted of poems like those we now have in the Songs
of Miriam and Deborah (see Exod. 15; Judges 5). "[Yahweh] is a
man of war; [Yahweh] is his name" (Exod. 15:3). This, in turn,
suggests that the Exodus and Conquest traditions, during which
the conception of Yahweh was powerfully reshaped and reaf-
firmed (if not, in fact, created for the first time), originally displayed the centrality of Yahweh the warrior, probably to be
understood as literally present at the forefront of the militia
horde that used his name as a battle cry. We have several broken
and garbled traditions from the books of Exodus through Joshua
that speak of manifestations of just what it was that went in

front of the army: the famous pillar of cloud by day and fire by night, the angel or messenger, the hornet (sometimes plural), the fear or terror, the panic, and, of course, the Ark. (See, for example, Exod. 13:21; 14:19; 23:23-28; Deut. 1:33, 7:20; Num. 10:33; Josh. 24:12.) I'm suggesting simply that all of these are variant memories of what once was Yahweh himself manifest in various signs. The Ark as throne would be probably a later reconstruction or a hypostatization of that presence.[4]

Two things are important to note: one, that in later writings there is no developed nostalgia for this "presence" of Yahweh. The prophets speak of the wilderness period as a honeymoon because it manifested a simple faith of the Israelites in Yahweh and because it was a period lacking in external forms and ceremonies — not because the proximity of the presence guaranteed any metaphysical superiority. Two, the traditions of Yahweh's presence and guidance are prefaces to the Hebrew conception of history itself, which is, at first, a recording of the signs and wonders of the "mighty hand" and the "outstretched arm," to use the language of Deuteronomy 4:34; 26:8. The biblical style may be said, then, to evolve from these celebrations. And later the visions of the prophets recreate them in the future tense, with important differences, of course.

Moreover, though Yahweh's role as warrior is clear, his agency at any given moment may take a variety of forms, none of which are him in his essence but only signs. Thus, from these very earliest of biblical texts, we have the tradition which is central to Auerbach's contentions, namely, that biblical narratives always demand interpretation, whereas Homer positively resists it. Homer puts everything — including all the intentions and inner thoughts of Zeus — into a "uniformly illuminated" foreground,[5] everything present and accounted for. Homer's text is, in some ways, like the art desired by certain primitives who are wary of perspective, foreshortening, and such devices because these sometimes hide parts of the bodies represented. They worry if a hand or a leg is missing. The Bible writers don't know Homer's certainties and they use a style with background, with built-in perspective. They begin with texts referring to great but mysterious acts that are signs, the meaning of which must be constantly sifted, probed, and recounted. In spite of expectations to the contrary, nothing is ever established as a certainty by act of God. History from its beginnings is a process, not simply of recording but of interpreting. And this produces not only the condition that Auerbach calls being " 'fraught with background' "[6] but also the demanding, problematic, ultimately parabolic nature of Western literature.

This quality is thrown into even higher relief in the texts we have next to take up — those dealing with the great identity crisis of Israel that led to the establishment of the monarchy. According to current theory, the Court History of David (2 Sam. 9-20; 1 Kings 1:2) was the first extended part to be written down, and the rest of the text accrued around it. This may well be true, but the key is that the parts dealing with the Judges, with Samuel, and with Saul, even if written later, are testimony to a precondition without which the significance of David's reign cannot be understood: namely, that in accord with a tradition of Yahweh as warrior, Israel maintained itself in the Judges's period as a theocracy with no human king. Thus, the proposal to establish one presented them with what I have called an identity crisis. The king, in Semitic usage in this time, was a warrior who "go[es] out before us and fight[s] our battles" (1 Sam. 8:20). A human warrior-king is what the people ask for because they want to be like all the nations, the gentiles. They want to have what the other people have. "I will not rule over you, neither shall my son rule over you: [Yahweh] shall rule over you," Gideon is supposed to have replied to an earlier temptation to make himself a king (Judg. 8:23). But we may suspect this text of being a whitewash since Gideon has a son whose name is Abimelech, meaning "my father is king."

In any case, the tradition is clear that would indicate powerful religious opposition to dynastic kingship. That is the major reason why the acts of Samuel, Saul, and David must be so scrupulously recorded and interpreted. Parts of this story were undoubtedly written down in the belief that in allowing David to succeed where Saul failed, Yahweh was validating and endorsing the monarchy. But other parts, such as 1 Samuel 8, were written to show that in allowing a king Yahweh was simply giving the people enough rope to hang themselves. In verse 7, Yahweh, with grim foreboding, says to Samuel, "They have not rejected you, but they have rejected me from being king over them." The prophets, of course, take up this latent opposition to the monarchy and to the Canaanitish syncretism that it led to after Solomon, with some kings going so far as to put male prostitutes in the temple. They interpret the disasters looming ahead for Israel as divine punishments for such faithlessness. They even denounce the military efforts and alliances of the kings as merely further examples of men putting their trust in man instead of God and of entangling in foreign alliances the one nation that should not have been like all the other nations, that should have remained an unsophisticated and uncorrupted theocracy. The prophetic denunciations of economic exploitation, of perversions of justice — even of weights and measures — must be understood as part of this opposition to the kings and to the upper classes who supported the monarchical program of importing idolatrous foreign ways and practices. Certainly they were linked together in the prophetic mind.

Thus, the record shows that history, for early Israel, entailed putting into writing the train of events that manifested Yahweh's special and mysterious purposes for the nation. He, himself, is hidden behind his acts and behind events — hidden, though not inscrutable. We can do no better for purposes of comparison than to bring up Shakespeare's history plays where the Wars of the Roses parallel the history of Israel and in which the recurrent question is: "Who has God's mandate?" The Henrys are technically usurpers like David, and the Richards are, in some ways, like Saul. They once had the mandate but they forfeited it through arrogant presumption, through facile claiming of religious prerogatives. In *Henry V*, the king kneels down and prays to the "God of battles" (Yahweh Sabaoth) to forgive him for the sins of his fathers and to show it by giving him victory against all the odds at Agincourt (see 4. 1. 306-22). One of the reasons he does not want any more men with him is that he has contrived this battle as a test of precisely that question. After he has been given this great victory, he instructs his soldiers to sing *Non Nobis* and *Te Deum*, "not to us, but to you,

O God, shall this triumph be ascribed" (4. 8. 127-28). This is the climax of these plays, although chronologically — that is, in terms of what Shakespeare was dealing with — it comes in the middle of the sequence. However, in dramatic terms, it provides a spectacular answer to the recurrent problem of lawful rule and I have always thought that is why he wrote it last. This answer is couched insistently in biblical terms.

Shakespeare's plays are fundamentally different from Greek tragedies, only partially for the reasons eloquently argued by Helen Gardner, who says that Greek tragedy presents crisis whereas Elizabethan tragedy presents process.[7] What I would say distinguishes them is the same mark that distinguishes Hebrew history from the dominant modes of thoughts of the ancient Near East as well as from Greek thought: in neither Shakespeare nor the Bible is there a sense of what the Greek philosophers sometimes call the *logos.* This term is notoriously hard to define in Greek usage, but here I take it to mean the concept that the whole cosmos has an order, an essential structure which is ultimately apprehensible by reason, hence speakable in some ideal way if certain clouds of misapprehension that may be obscuring the reason are swept away. This concept of an eternal and immutable order on which all possible changes in the world are merely variations is, of course, found very widely in ancient thought and has close relations to the Egyptian concept of *ma'at* and to the Sumerian *gish-khur* and to many other manifestations. In Greek thinking, it is the concept that allowed Aristotle to assert that poetry is a higher and more philosophic thing than history, for history represents the actualizing of only a small part of the infinite world of potentialities of what anything might be; and poetry, which can represent the impossible but probable (to use Aristotle's term) can therefore represent the *logos,* being tied, as it is, not to events but to reason.[8] Obviously these standards are at variance with the Yahwist belief in which there is no sense of an eternal order of things that somehow stands beyond Yahweh's will.

The important point is that Shakespeare doesn't believe in the *logos* either. (I am, of course, not referring to the Christian adaptation of that term.) What makes a true English king is not his place in some immutable order but rather God's mysterious election. Richard II believes in the *logos*. He thinks that his person is intrinsically sacred and that when his soldiers desert, angels will replace them (see *Richard II*, 3. 2. 58-62). Once the king always the king. But the Henrys know it is not so. They will surely be tested by God, i.e., by history, and must prove worthy. Shakespeare does not repudiate the medieval concept of the king's two bodies. In fact, he follows it in believing that God's election may light on any man as it once did on the humble shepherd boy.

In Egypt, only the changeless was truly significant, remarks Henri Frankfort.[9] Changes are insignificant, being at best minor and transient rearrangements of the cosmic kaleidoscope in an ideology of the *logos*. But changes are, of course, the very stuff of history, and change in Hebrew thought has very much the significance and the enabling power that Jacques Derrida ascribes to difference, or *differance*,[10] as we can call it, although when he spells it with his *a* he does not mean it to be pronounced any differently. Not to be reified or made into a metaphysical concept, it yet is that which permits all significance and all concepts to be brought into being. Indeed, historical change is simply difference in a certain context; therefore, it makes a great difference whether a people's literature is founded on the concept of the *logos* or on the idea of history that Aristotle would call lower — the idea of history which I define as the search for meaning in a world without the *logos*.

History presupposes no fixed order, no pattern to which all things will sooner or later return no matter how wide the pendulum of events swings. Hence the phrase "the laws of history" is a contradiction in terms, which may explain why no historians have ever been able to find any. The modern historian may think he is searching for them but his activities taken as a whole do not suggest this. In fact, they rather suggest the Hebrew sense of recording and interpreting everything, because you never know which facts will be messages. The modern historian has, of course, no conscious thought of God, but the form of his work still suggests a search for somebody calling the shots.

To make the point in another way, let us turn to Lévi-Strauss.[11] If what he says about myth is valid, it evokes a world view which is essentially that of the cosmos as *logos*—which is to say, of course, that myth and history are poles apart. This is hardly a new point, but perhaps it needs repeating now when structuralism and other philosophies can accuse us with much justice of mythologizing history. The kind of society Lévi-Strauss studies and favors uses myth as a powerful element in its constitution. One might say, in fact, that myth provides the DNA of these cultures, passing on much of the information needed for their self-replication. Surely it is characteristic of the ideology of these societies, as Lévi-Strauss implies in his analysis of the Oedipus myth, that in them social structure and cosmology verify and reinforce each other. The cosmos is seen as having a structure to which human life must relate, and social order must reproduce it. In Yahwist thinking, this is manifestly impossible. The social order like the historical order has no status beyond contingency, and it draws no sacredness nor any other form of validation from cosmic order, since the latter does not really exist in Yahwist thought. As many have noted, the Bible seems to take positive delight in challenges to the social order. We could take tests as various as the Song of Hannah—"The bows of the mighty are broken, . . . He raises up the poor from the dust; . . . to make them sit with princes. . ." and so on —to the New Testament motto, "the last shall be first" (1 Sam. 2:4, 8; see Matt. 19:30). Although it is unfashionable to say so, mythological societies are far more conservative, tradition-bound, and deferrent to their own social orders than those in the biblical or Western tradition. This is a concept that Lévi-Strauss particularly has trouble dealing with because of his intrinsically revolutionary bent.

It is equally true, of course, that the Bible can be used as a mythos, as in Byzantium or Europe in the Middle Ages; and also it does not mean that mythological societies are not creative (witness Sumer and Egypt)—but these do identify the social order with the cosmos and both with some kind of *logos*; hence, their literature would be of the kind to suit Aristotle as philosophic while their histories remain those of annals and chronicles and king lists. Take Gilgamesh, for example. Though most scholars now believe he really existed, the epic about him can hardly be said to be even historical fiction. It has no trace of the historical texture of the story of Abraham, to say nothing of that of King David. It may be that the story's attitude toward the *logos* is mournful or rebellious, but the *logos* is there anyway in forming the eternal truths that the story illustrates. Gilgamesh almost sees the secret of immortality, but now snakes have it and men do not. This is a Just-So Story, like that of Adam, no doubt; but the story of Adam is not really typical of the Bible whereas the story of Abraham is. We might think here of Lévi-Strauss's phrase, "What gives the myth an operational value is that the specific pattern described is timeless; it explains the present and the past as well as the future."[12]

A further corollary: according to Lévi-Strauss the order of events in a myth is relatively insignificant. By this method, which is to lay out the mythemes, or shortest possible statements of the myth's events, on a kind of grid, the meaning is found by explicitly ignoring the narrative order and concentrating on the relations of the mythemes — arranged, if possible, in parallel columns. Were we to tell the myth, says Lévi-Strauss, we would disregard the columns and read the events in the order in which they occur. But if we want to understand the myth, then we must disregard the so-called diachronic arrangement of the events and look for the hidden relationships in and between the columns.[13] This is from his famous essay, "The Structural Study of Myth," which I call "the Oedipus essay."

This flat and absolute contrast between telling and understanding is thus a major feature of the structuralist method, corresponding to their assertion that the anthropologist can slice through the images that the native uses to present his society to himself. But for our purposes, the key point is that for Lévi-Strauss the narrative is merely a vehicle, merely a medium, for the presentation of the myth's true meanings. The narrative itself can hardly be intrinsically involved with these meanings if one has to ignore it in order to understand the myth. One could say that the narrative for Lévi-Strauss is like Plato's poet in the *Ion* — it doesn't know anything of the truths it has to convey.

Here let us go back again to Auerbach for the contrast which the biblical style presents — not only God, he points out, but all the biblical personages have background, and it is precisely their biographical pasts, or what has happened to them earlier in the narrative, of which this background consists:

> Abraham's actions are explained not only by what is happening to him at the moment, . . . but by his previous history; he remembers he is constantly conscious of what God has promised him and what God has already accomplished for him. . . . Such a problematic psychological situation as this is impossible for any of the Homeric heroes, whose destiny is clearly defined and who wake every morning as if it were the first day of their lives. . . . Herein lies the reason why the great figures of the Old Testament are so much more fully developed, so much more fraught with their own biographical past, so much more distinct as individuals, than are the Homeric heroes . . . [who] have no development, . . . [and who] appear to be of an age fixed from the very first. Even Odysseus, in whose case the long lapse of time and the many events which occurred offer so much opportunity for biographical development, shows almost nothing of it. Odysseus on his return is exactly the same as he was when he left Ithaca two decades earlier. But what a road, what a fate, lie between the Jacob who cheated his father out of his blessing and the old man whose favorite son has been torn to pieces by a wild beast! — between David the harp player, persecuted by his lord's jealousy, and the old king, surrounded by violent intrigues, whom Abishag the Shunnamite warmed in his bed, and he knew her not! [14]

In one of his best strokes, Auerbach disposes of the objection that the historical texture in the biblical stories sometimes arises from the combination of several legendary personages into one, as with Jacob and also David, since the Goliath story is certainly a legend. This does not matter, as Auerbach shows, because so strong is the historicizing character of biblical style that even where its raw material is legend, the stories are transmuted into a continuous narrative with historical texture. The very lacunae and joins in the text evident to the specialist only add to the background effect described by Auerbach.

Even by such a modern criterion as historical reliability we find the Bible amazingly nonlegendary. The point, of course, is not the truth of the Bible but the character of its style and of the thought processes which caused certain Hebrews to preserve their traditions in certain ways. I do not see how there can be a much more important stylistic feature than this point: that in the Bible the narrative — the order of events — is not merely a vehicle but is itself crucial to the meaning. And this, in turn, implies why structuralist methods, designed to elucidate myth, work so poorly on the Bible. We must give Lévi-Strauss credit; he himself is notoriously hesitant to apply his techniques to the Bible, though not all his followers are so cautious. History and myth no doubt mix in many ways. But my point is that the literature that draws its inspiration from the one is likely to seem almost antithetical to the other.

As a footnote I may add that whereas by Lévi-Straussian standards myth might as well be totally episodic, Aristotle prescribed that such loose-jointedness was not to be tolerated in tragedy. But his reason is the key. He rejects episodic plots because they offend our sense of the rational necessity of the *logos*. Once fully disclosed, the events of the tragedy must be seen as having been inevitable. In biblical narratives, on the other hand, the reasons for rejecting episodic qualities have to do with historical fact and sequence, not with the *logos*. There is no true inevitability, given Yahweh. Many myths are in fact episodic, so much so as to be deeply puzzling to us. In at least one version of the Gilgamesh epic, Enkidu, whose death precipitates Gilgamesh's epic journey, is spoken of at the end as if he were alive, which goes to show that Auerbach's contrasts are relevant not only to the Greeks but to all the ancient world vis-à-vis the Hebrews.

It seems to me that the character of literature in the West follows the biblical pattern in much more important respects than it follows the Homeric or mythological. Someone has remarked that all the great Western writers are realists in their own terms; that is, they define themselves as realists against any romanticism or idealism or other mythologizing tendency in their predecessors or contemporaries. Even so visionary a poet as Blake felt himself to be asserting a kind of realism against the illusionism of Sir Joshua Reynolds and other purveyors of the false classics. Blake's preference for biblical prophetic visions as against imitation Augustanism is well known.

But my point has to do not only with conscious preferences but also with unconscious models. This realism preferred by our great writers is very much the result of that historicizing that Auerbach shows to be the hallmark of biblical style. Even the visions of the prophets and the anguished meditations of the Psalmist are historically situated and full of realistic touches in a sense utterly foreign to Homer and to most myth with which I am familiar. It may well be that there are other cultural traditions in which historical quality is found in the literature. But as Auerbach goes on to show in subsequent chapters of *Mimesis,* the Greco-Roman world was not much interested in these.

For a long time now, Western critics have assumed that the so-called classics, that is, the literary works of the Hellenistic world, were the matrix and nurturer of our literature. These critics seem not to have read Auerbach. Frankly, I suspect that the English public school tradition, in which knowledge of Greek and Latin was the mark of a gentleman, may have been an efficient cause of this misleading identification. English social snobbery would also explain something of the neglect of the Bible, for close knowledge of the scriptures was often the mark of the dissenter, the charity boy, the nonuniversity man like Blake or D. H. Lawrence. The kind of realism I am talking about here is that which derives from taking the historical to be the real so that the texture of the work (Joyce's *Ulysses* would be the supreme example) must be full of gritty actualities. Notice that by these standards even Dante's *Commedia* is realistic. If he had simply rhapsodized about the structure of the world beyond or made his epic journey through it meeting only allegorical beasts, as in the first cantos, and not meeting any of the historical characters that he does meet, then the work would be something else; it would be a fable, let us say. But Dante's work, like that of Chaucer, Shakespeare, Cervantes, Molière, et al., is rooted in historicism, even when mythic archetypes are invoked, for these are always subordinated, as they are even in such a grandiose and supposedly timeless work as *Paradise Lost*, to the realities of the time as the author sees them. Who was more embroiled in the issues of his day than Milton or, for that matter, Dante? The notion of the artist in the ivory tower is, of course, a fallacy.

My point here is to lead up to the assertion that historicizing produces many different kinds of historical texture, that there need not be an obvious historical setting for a work to be realistic in this sense. Some strategies have different requirements. Let me quote Hugh Kenner, who says in his book, *The Counterfeiters:*

Consider an anecdote from the German occupation of France:

> Two men have been sent into the country to make a rendezvous with a third, whom they have never seen and know only by a code name. They work hard at making their presence and movements seem natural, an especial challenge since they seem to have no cover story. They scrounge vegetables, sleep in ditches, submit like tramps to indignities and beatings: and at the appointed spot no one meets them. Should they move on or stay? It seems best to stay; the normal prudence of the underground has withheld from them any clue to the significance of their rendezvous, but they cannot assume its significance is slight. So they set about the business of waiting, on a country road, at evening, not too obtrusively. The tax on their resources is enormous. A refugee passes, his servant loaded with belongings; they are so relieved to see anyone at all that they almost give their mission away. Then a boy runs up with a message, "Mr. Godot told me to tell you he won't come this evening but surely tomorrow:" and they are committed to a second time of waiting, more deadly than the first.

As Kenner says, "It seems reasonable to guess that Beckett's play had some such germ," especially since Beckett was involved in the Resistance. But "the anecdotal specificities" have been withdrawn. Kenner notes that "a few references to Germans and sector chiefs would have told us to say that the play is 'about the Occupation.' As things are, it is difficult to say what

it is about, except about waiting, and so powerful is the experience of a play about waiting, once we have experienced it, that
no adduction of Occupation detail will distract us. We have
meaning, then, without specific content."[15] In short, the play
derives its power from a historical situation, even where the
detail that would specify that situation is missing. The detail
would have made the play a lesser work, a kind of thriller. But
there is no appeal to the *logos* by Beckett, not in Aristotle's
sense. History produces far stranger things in heaven and earth
than are dreamed of in Aristotle's philosophy.

That such a strategy is ultimately biblical I hope to persuade
you by pointing to the example of Job. At first glance the book
of Job seems to violate biblical style. It seems to be a self-
conscious fable. It even begins with the Hebrew equivalent of
"once upon a time." (I'm ignoring for the moment most of the
problems about the text.) But there are many theories about the
date of composition and so on, and the book would seem to
have no more determinable historical setting than the early
chapters of Genesis. Yet I believe that it does have one. I base
my case entirely on a reading of the twenty-eighth chapter of
Deuteronomy. This chapter purports to be an exhortation by
Moses, listing the blessings that Yahweh will send for keeping
the law and curses for not keeping it. The list of curses is far
more significant and longer and more detailed. Manifestly, it is
not a prediction, but a memory of the horrors of the Assyrian
invasion. Let me just read nine consecutive verses from this long
chapter:

> The Lord will smite you with the boils of Egypt, and
> with the ulcers and the scurvy and the itch, of which you
> cannot be healed. The Lord will smite you with madness
> and blindness and confusion of mind; and you shall
> grope at noonday, as the blind grope in darkness, and
> you shall not prosper in your ways, and you shall be only
> oppressed and robbed continually, and there shall be
> none to help you. You shall betroth a wife, and another
> man shall lie with her; you shall build a house, and you
> shall not dwell in it; you shall plant a vineyard, and you
> shall not use the fruit of it. Your ox shall be slain before
> your eyes, and you shall not eat of it; your ass shall be

violently taken away before your face, and shall not be restored to you; your sheep shall be given to your enemies, and there shall be no one to help you. Your sons and your daughters shall be given to another people while your eyes look on and fail with longing for them all the day; and it shall not be in the power of your hand to prevent it. A nation which you have not known shall eat up the fruit of your ground and of all your labors; and you shall be only oppressed and crushed continually; so that you shall be driven mad by the sight which your eyes shall see. The Lord will smite you on the knees and on the legs with grievous boils of which you cannot be healed, from the sole of your foot to the crown of your head (Deut. 28:27-35).

I have selected this passage so as to highlight the boils, but even without these I cannot but believe that this catalogue of pains and humiliations, this mental landscape of anguish and helplessness, was very much in the mind of the Job writer. Deuteronomy 28 is the pre-text for Job in all senses of the word. The Job poet had only to transmute the disasters suffered by fallen Israel into horrors that may come into any life, no matter how guiltless the individual, and his work was before him. He may have done something very like what Beckett did with his play. The lack of specifying detail is not a sign of the lack of a historical framework. There are other biblical examples of this: the Songs of the Servant of Yahweh, for instance (see Isa. 42:1-4; 49:1-6; 50:4-9; 52:13; 53). By common agreement the book of Job contains no real structuring of a theodicy, no successful attempt to answer the monumental questions about the suffering of the innocent. We must endure our plagues; and after our cries are wrung from us, we must be silent. There is no attempt to say that partial evil is universal good, no appeal to such a *logos*.

The book of Job is not a fable; but it is very like a parable, that form which finds ultimate flowering in the New Testament. Some parables may be simply homely attempts to set down common truths, but the form is capable of more than that. The great New Testament parables — I would instance particularly the laborers in the vineyard (see Matt. 19:30-20:16) and those like it — are those that make it clear that common truths do not answer the real problems, indeed, that the real problems are so hard we can barely understand or frame them, let alone answer them. Parables are a form of literature whose very existence is itself a parable, a parable about the immense labors of soul-searching and mind-searching needed for understanding. "This is a hard saying; who can listen to it?" (John 6:60) so many hearers have said.

The parable returns us to Auerbach's final formulation of biblical style: "certain parts brought into high relief, others left obscure, abruptness, suggestive influence of the unexpressed, 'background' quality, multiplicity of meanings and the need for interpretation, universal-historical claims, development of the concept of the historically becoming, and preoccupation with the problematic."[16] Those are among the concluding words of Auerbach's chapter in defining that style. And I believe that these are the qualities that gave continuity to the Bible and to Western literature in its image.

NOTES

1. Erich Auerbach, *Mimesis: The Representation of Reality in Western Literature,* trans. Willard Trask (1953; reprint ed., Garden City, N. Y.: Doubleday Anchor Books, 1957), pp. 5-6.

2. "The Decay of Lying," in *The Complete Works of Oscar Wilde,* 12 vols. (New York: Wm. H. Wise & Co., 1927), 5:47-48.

3. Auerbach, *Mimesis,* p. 9.

4. See Thomas Mann, *Divine Presence and Guidance in Israelite Traditions* (Baltimore: Johns Hopkins University Press, 1977).

5. Auerbach, *Mimesis,* p. 5.

6. *Ibid.,* p. 9.

7. Helen Louise Gardner, *Religion and Literature* (London: Faber, 1971), p. 74.

8. Aristotle, *On Poetics,* 9:1451^b 5-10.

9. Henri Frankfort, *The Birth of Civilization in the Near East* (New York: Anchor Books, n.d.), p. 9.

10. "Differance," *Speech and Phenomena,* trans. David B. Allison (Evanston, Ill.: Northwestern University Press, 1973).

11. Claude Lévi-Strauss, "The Structural Study of Myth," *Structural Anthropology,* trans. Claire Jacobsen and Brooke Grundfest Schoepf (New York: Basic Books, 1963), pp. 206-31.

12. *Ibid.,* p. 209.

13. *Ibid.,* p. 214.

14. Auerbach, *Mimesis,* pp. 9-10, 14.

15. *The Counterfeiters* (Bloomington: Indiana University Press, 1968), pp. 159-60.

16. Auerbach, *Mimesis,* p. 19.

2

Gerald N. Lund

Old Testament
Types
and Symbols

*An employee of the Church Educational System of The
Church of Jesus Christ of Latter-day Saints for the past fifteen
years, Gerald N. Lund currently serves as director of its college
curriculum department. Author of two books,* The Coming of
the Lord *and* This is Your World, *he graduated from Brigham
Young University with bachelor's and master's degrees in soci-
ology and has also been involved, at various times, with preparing curriculum material for adult Sunday School classes.*

*His interest in typology stems from teaching a class on the
book of Revelation in the institute system some years ago. In*

This paper was originally delivered at the Third Annual Church Educational System Religious Educators' Symposium on the Old Testament at Brigham Young University August 16-18, 1979, and is printed in *A Symposium on
the Old Testament,* August 16, 17 and 18, 1979 (Salt Lake City: Corporation
of the President of The Church of Jesus Christ of Latter-day Saints, 1979), pp.
182-93.

this paper, he reevaluates the commonly held idea that the religion of the Old Testament was a primitive or even semipagan system. Modern revelation asserts that Israel had "the preparatory gospel" and Gerald Lund specifies in three areas — ordinances, festivals, and historical events — some of the ways in which this preparatory gospel mirrored the dominant image of Christ as faithfully as the "fulness" restored to Joseph Smith.

In addition to giving some useful guidelines for the beginning student on how to tell if a given event should be interpreted typologically, the author selects examples from the rich treasury of the Old Testament that will arouse curiosity and desire for further investigation on the part of anyone who has read through the Old Testament in mingled bewilderment, excitement, and challenge.

M any in the world and even some in the Church think of the Old Testament as reflecting a pregospel culture centered around the Mosaic covenant which was given in place of the gospel laws. And it is true that the Israelites, when they rejected the higher law, were given a lesser law. But note what the Lord said about it: "And the lesser priesthood continued, which priesthood holdeth the key of the ministering of angels and the *preparatory gospel; which gospel is the gospel of repentance and of baptism, and of the remission of sins, and the law of carnal commandments*" (D&C 84:26-27; italics added). They did not receive the *fulness* of the gospel but they did receive a *preparatory* gospel, dealing with the basic principles of the gospel of Jesus Christ. As Paul taught the Galatian Saints, this was done so that they could be brought to Christ: "Wherefore the law was our schoolmaster to bring us unto Christ, that we might be justified by faith. But after that faith is come, we are no longer under a schoolmaster" (Gal. 3:24-25).

In short, the Old Testament is not pregospel but primary gospel; and we can expect that the Old Testament, especially in its types and symbols, will richly reflect that gospel, the gospel of preparation for faith in Christ. It can be a preparation of value to every person including those who have access to, though possibly not complete understanding of, the fulness of the gospel. Therefore, as Elder Bruce R. McConkie suggests, "It is wholesome and proper to look for similitudes of Christ everywhere and to use them repeatedly in keeping him and his laws uppermost in our minds."[1]

When is an act or object recorded in scripture to be taken literally and when should it be interpreted figuratively? Symbols can be taken too literally and their true meaning lost in a grotesque parody of reality. On the other hand, sometimes one can explain away the actual meaning of a passage by saying it is only figurative. The following guidelines may be helpful as one tries to decide how to interpret correctly the symbols used in the Old Testament:

1. Look beyond the symbol for its intended meaning.

2. Look for the interpretation of the symbol in the scriptures themselves.

3. Look for Christ in the symbols and imagery of the scriptures.

4. Let the nature of the object used as a symbol contribute to your understanding of its spiritual meaning.

5. Seek the reality behind the symbol. One author used this interesting analogy:

> The most perfect representation of a steam-engine to a South-sea savage would be wholly and hopelessly unintelligible to him, simply because the reality, the outline of which was presented to him, was something hitherto unknown. But let the same drawing be shewn to those who have seen the reality, such will have no difficulty in explaining the representation. And the greater the acquaintance with the reality, the greater will be the ability to explain the picture. The savage who had never seen the steam-engine would of course know nothing whatever about it. Those who had seen an engine but know nothing of its principles, though they might tell the general object of the drawing, could not explain the details.

But the engineer, to whom every screw and bolt are familiar, to whom the use and the object of each part is thoroughly known, would not only point out where each of these was to be found in the picture, but would shew what others might overlook, how in different engines these might be made to differ.[2]

The reality behind the Old Testament is Jesus Christ and his teachings of salvation. The better we understand him, the more clearly we will see the meaning of the symbols.

The preliminary exploration of Old Testament types and symbols which follows deals with three areas: ordinances, festivals, and historical events. Of course, space does not permit more than a sampling of the full range of symbols available in the Mosaic covenant.

ORDINANCES

Sacrifices and Offerings. Sacrifices and offerings represent the very center of the Mosaic law. Though they varied in the manner of offering, the requirements, the item offered, and the time of offering, all of the sacrifices and offerings had three general things in common: an offerer, the offering, and the priesthood. Adam was taught that the law of sacrifice was instituted as "a similitude of the sacrifice of the Only Begotten of the Father" (Moses 5:7). The similitude of Christ's sacrifice carries through all three aspects. One author explained the typology of all three aspects in this manner:

What, then, is *the offering*? what *the priest*? what *the offerer*? Christ is the offering, Christ is the priest, Christ is the offerer. Such and so manifold are the relations in which Christ has stood for man and to man, that no one type or set of types can adequately represent the fulness of them. . . . As man under the law, our substitute, Christ stood for us towards God as offerer. . . . Thus His body was His offering: he willingly offered it; and then as priest He took the blood into the holiest. As *offerer*, we see Him *man under the law*, standing our substitute, for us to fulfil all righteousness. As *priest*, we have Him presented as the *mediator,* God's messenger between Himself and Israel. While as *the offering* He is seen *the innocent victim,* a sweet savour to God, yet bearing the sin and dying for it.[3]

Nephi taught that we are to follow the example of the Son of God (see 2 Ne. 31:10, 12-13, 16). Jesus asked, "What manner of men ought ye to be?" and then answered his own question by saying, "Even as I am" (3 Ne. 27:27). If Christ becomes our model for living, then in the three aspects of the law of the offerings, we too should be typified. In other words, just as all three objects and persons involved in the sacrifices were types of him, they should also serve as types of us. Thus, the offering becomes a type or symbol of our lives, our acts, our works, our being — our all — offered to God on the altar so that it becomes a sweet-smelling savor to him. The Saints are to become "kings and priests," or as Peter said, "a royal priesthood" (Rev. 1:6; 1 Pet. 2:9). Further, like Jesus they are to become the saviors of men by sharing the principles of his teachings and sacrifice with others (see D&C 103:9-10). In this manner they are typified by the priest. And the offerer also typifies us as well as Christ, for, like him, we must willingly yield ourselves to come into the proper relationship with God.[4]

Circumcision. Abraham was specifically commanded by the Lord to institute circumcision upon himself and all the males of his household as a token of the covenant made with God (see Gen. 17:9-14). In the Joseph Smith Translation of the Bible of this passage, we learn that circumcision was instituted as a token of the covenant; but the token was given because the people were in a state of apostasy, had lost sight of the true meaning of the ordinance of baptism, and were washing their children and sprinkling them with blood so that they would be free from sin. Circumcision reminded the people that while children were born in the covenant they were not to be held accountable until they were eight years of age (see JST, Gen. 17:4-11).

Other scriptures provide additional clarification that it was not circumcision itself but what it stood for that gave it its greatest significance. In many places the Lord speaks of the true circumcision as being that of the heart or, in other words, loving God and being obedient to the Spirit. The "uncircumcised of heart" are the wicked, proud, and rebellious (see Deut. 10:16; 30:6; Jer. 4:4; Ezek. 44:7; Acts 7:51; Rom. 2:25-29; Col. 2:11). Though a person may have the token of circumcision in the flesh, unless he is righteous the covenant is invalidated and the circumcision becomes profitless. Thus, circumcision was only a sign or token of what needed to happen to the inward man. If the inward change had not taken place, then circumcision was virtually meaningless. Following the atonement of Christ, the token of circumcision was no longer required of God's covenant people since it was replaced by baptism, the symbol of Christ's own death and resurrection (see Jer. 9:25-26; Acts 15:22-29; 1 Cor. 7:19; Gal. 5:1-6; 6:12-15; Phil. 3:3-4).

The Abrahamic covenant makes frequent reference to one's seed, as for example, Genesis 17:6-12. The organ of the male body that produces seed and helps bring about physical birth is the very part of the body which bears the token of the covenant. However, the organ of spiritual rebirth is the heart (see 3 Ne. 9:20). Thus, when a person was circumcised it signified that he, like a child, was born into the covenant but need not be baptized until he became accountable before the Lord. But spiritual circumcision, or the circumcision of the heart, must take place once one becomes accountable, or one is not considered as true Israel. As Paul said so aptly, "For he is not a Jew, which is one outwardly; neither is that circumcision, which is outward in the flesh: but he is a Jew, which is one inwardly; and circumcision is that of the heart, in the spirit, and not in the letter; whose praise is not of men, but of God" (Rom. 2:28-29).

Cleansing of the Leper. In Leviticus 14 we have a detailed description of the ritual that was to take place when a person's leprosy had been healed. Because of the nature of the ritual, many people have seen it as a primitive, superstitious, and abhorrent rite which makes the Israelites barely more than pagan. However, when we apply our guidelines for interpreting symbols, we find that the ritual is a beautiful representation of gospel truths. This case is worth examining in some detail in its twelve major aspects:

1. *The leper.* Leprosy in its various forms was a loathsome disease that involved decay and putrefaction of the living body; it required the sufferer to be ostracized and cut off from any fellowship with the rest of the house of Israel. Because of these characteristics, leprosy was also an appropriate type or symbol of what happens to a man spiritually when he sins. Sin introduces decay and corruption into the spiritual realm as leprosy does into the physical. Also, a sinful person was cut off from fellowship with spiritual Israel and could not be part of the Lord's covenant people. So the leper himself provided a type or similitude of what King Benjamin called the "natural man" (see Mosiah 3:19).

2. *The priest.* The priest served as the official representative of the Lord, authorized to cleanse the leper and bring him back into full fellowship. As we have seen earlier, the priest was also a type of Christ.

3. *The birds.* The birds symbolized the candidate. Because of the two truths to be taught, two birds were required. The first bird was killed by the shedding of its blood, signifying that the leper (the natural man) had to give up his life. The second bird, after being bound together with other symbols, was released, signifying that the man had been freed from the bondage of sin.

4. *The cedar wood.* The cedar wood is still used today because of its ability to preserve surrounding objects from decay and corruption; its meaning is obvious.

5. *The scarlet wool.* The word *scarlet* (Lev. 14:4) really meant a piece of wool dyed bright red, a reminder of blood, which is the symbol of life and also of atonement (see Lev. 17:11).

6. *The hyssop.* Though we are not sure exactly why, we do know that in Old Testament times the herb hyssop was associated with purification (see Exod. 12:22; Ps. 51:7; Heb. 9:19).

7. *The basin of water.* Notice that the blood of the bird was mixed with water. In Moses 6:59 we learn that blood and water are the symbols of birth, both physical and spiritual. Also, we know that the baptismal font, the place of spiritual rebirth, symbolizes the place where the natural man is put to death (see Rom. 6:1-6; D&C 128:12-13). Over the basin of water the first

bird was killed, symbolizing the death of the natural man and the eventual rebirth of the spiritually innocent person. The release of the second bird symbolized the release of the man from the bondage of sin.

8. *The washing of the leper.* Both physically and spiritually, the washing was a symbol of cleansing.

9. *The shaving of the hair.* This act, including even the eyebrows, would make a person look very much like a newborn infant, who is typically virtually without hair. Thus, after going through the process of rebirth symbolically, the candidate graphically demonstrated on his own person that he was newborn spiritually.

10. *The sacrifice of the lamb.* The typology of the sacrifice of the lamb is clear, since the lamb offered had to be the first-born male without spot or blemish. It symbolized the offering of the Son of God himself.

11. *The smearing of the blood on the parts of the body.* In Hebrew the word which is usually translated *atonement* literally means "to cover." Thus, when the priest touched something with the blood, his action suggested the sanctification of, or atonement made for, that thing. In this case we find the blood of the lamb sanctifying the organ of hearing or obedience (the ear), the organ of action (the hand), and the organ of following or walking in the proper way (the foot). Thus, every aspect of the person's life was touched and affected by the atonement of Christ.

12. *The oil.* "The olive tree from the earliest times has been the emblem of peace and purity."[5] Modern revelation further instructs us that olive oil symbolizes the Holy Ghost (see D&C 45:55-57). To touch with oil suggests the effect of the Spirit on the same organs of living and acting that had previously been cleansed by the blood of Christ. Thus, every aspect of the candidate's life was purified and sanctified by both the Atonement and the Holy Ghost.

FEASTS AND FESTIVALS

Special holidays and festivals were a common part of everyday life during biblical times. Moreover, unlike modern times, most of the feasts and festivals had religious significance and were an inseparable part of worship.

The Sabbath. Certainly the most frequent festival among the Hebrews was the weekly day of rest, instituted in similitude of what God had done during the creation of the earth when, we are told, the Lord "sanctified" the Sabbath and rested (Gen. 2:2-3).

In Exodus 31:13 the Lord revealed the basic key to understanding the significance of the Sabbath: "Verily my sabbaths ye shall keep: *for it is a sign* between me and you throughout your generations; *that ye may know that I am the Lord that doth sanctify you*" (italics added). In other words, the Sabbath is the day that man ceases his labors so that God can work his own work — the work of sanctification — on man. The requirement of a sabbatical year, that the land be left untilled, required man to exercise tremendous faith in God's ability to sustain his people both temporally and spiritually (see Lev. 25:1-7, 18-22). The promises for those who keep the Sabbath are beautifully outlined by Isaiah and in modern revelation (see Isa. 58:13-14; D&C 59:9-24).

The Feast of the Passover. Passover (which included the Feast of Unleavened Bread) was one of the festivals which most clearly offered typologies of Christ and his atoning sacrifice. (See "Actual Historical Events," below.)

The Feast of Weeks. On the fiftieth day after Passover (a period of seven weeks of seven days, or a sabbath of weeks) a second major festival was held, though it lasted only one day. Christians are more familiar with this feast by its Greek title, Pentecost, which means "fiftieth." Elder McConkie explains in detail its important typology:

> It is not without significance that the Lord chose the Pentecost, which grew out of the final Passover, as the occasion to dramatize forever the fulfillment of all that was involved in the sacrificial fires of the past. Fire is a cleansing agent. Filth and disease die in its flames. The baptism of fire, which John promised Christ would bring, means that when men receive the actual companionship of the Holy Spirit, then evil and iniquity are burned out of their souls as though by fire. The sancti-

fying power of that member of the Godhead makes them clean. In similar imagery, all the fires on all the altars of the past, as they burned the flesh of animals, were signifying that spiritual purification would come by the Holy Ghost, whom the Father would send because of the Son. On that first Pentecost of the so-called Christian Era such fires would have performed their purifying symbolism if the old order had still prevailed. How fitting it was instead for the Lord to choose that very day to send living fire from heaven, as it were, fire that would dwell in the hearts of men and replace forever all the fires on all the altars of the past. And so it was that "when the day of Pentecost was fully come, they were all with one accord in one place. And suddenly there came a sound from heaven as of a rushing mighty wind, and it filled all the house where they were sitting. And there appeared unto them cloven tongues like as of fire, and it sat upon each of them. And they were all filled with the Holy Ghost" (Acts 2:1-4).[6]

The Day of Atonement. The Day of Atonement, which took place each autumn, was the most sacred and solemn of all Israelite festivals. In it, the typology or symbolism of Christ's work for Israel fairly shines. A day of national fasting, it signified that the sins of Israel had been atoned for and that the nation and its people were restored to fellowship with God. The feast included the following major items as detailed in Leviticus 16:

1. The high priest had to go through meticulous preparation to be worthy to act as officiator for the rest of the house of Israel. He made sacrifices for himself and his house, as well as washing various objects in the tabernacle and purifying them through the sprinkling of sacrificial blood.

2. The high priest put off the official robes he normally wore and clothed himself in simple, white linen garments, signifying "the righteousness of the saints" (Rev. 19:8).

3. Two goats were chosen by lot. One was designated as the goat of the Lord, and one was designated as the scapegoat or, in Hebrew, the goat of *Azazel.* The goat of Jehovah was offered as a sin offering, and the high priest took its blood into the Holy of

Holies of the tabernacle and sprinkled it on the lid of the ark of the covenant (called the "mercy seat"), thus making atonement for the sins of Israel.

4. The other goat, *Azazel,* was brought before the high priest, who laid his hands upon its head and symbolically transferred all of the sins of Israel to it. Then it was taken out into the wilderness and released where it would never be seen again. Commentators explain the significance of *Azazel* by saying that it represented "the devil himself, the head of the fallen angels, who was afterwards called Satan; for no subordinate evil spirit could have been placed in antithesis to Jehovah as *Azazel* is here, but only the ruler or head of the kingdom of demons."[7]

The apostle Paul in the book of Hebrews drew heavily on the typology of the Day of Atonement to teach the mission of Christ. In that epistle he pointed out that Christ is the great "High Priest" who, unlike the high priest of the Aaronic Priesthood, was holy and without spot and did not need to make atonement for his own sins before he could be worthy to officiate for Israel and enter the Holy of Holies (Heb. 3:1; 7:26-27). His perfect life was the ultimate fulfillment of the symbol of wearing white garments.

Furthermore, the true tabernacle (or temple, or house of the Lord) in which the priest officiated is in heaven, and the earthly tabernacle made by Moses was a "shadow" or type of the "heavenly" one (Heb. 8:2-5; 9:1-9).

Christ, as Lamb of Jehovah as well as High Priest, shed his own blood to enter the heavenly Holy of Holies where that blood ransomed from their sins those who would believe in him and obey his commandments (see Heb. 9:11-14; 24-28; 10:11-22; D&C 45:3-5).

The Feast of Tabernacles. The third of the national feasts requiring the attendance of all males was the Feast of Tabernacles (Hebrew *Sukkoth*), which took place five days after the Day of Atonement. It was a celebration of the completion of the harvest and was a time of great joy and thanksgiving. During the week of the festival, Israel was required to live in homemade tabernacles rather than in their homes, a reminder that they had dwelt in tents or tabernacles (King James *booth*) when the Lord brought them out of Egypt (see Lev. 23:42-43).

Elder McConkie points out that this will be the only Mosaic feast reinstituted in this gospel dispensation:

> In the full sense, it is the Feast of Jehovah, the one Mosaic celebration which, as part of the restitution of all things, shall be restored when Jehovah comes to reign personally upon the earth for a thousand years. Even now we perform one of its chief rituals in our solemn assemblies, the giving of the Hosanna Shout, and the worshipers of Jehovah shall yet be privileged to exult in other of its sacred rituals. . . . The fact that it celebrated the completion of the full harvest symbolizes the gospel reality that it is the mission of the house of Israel to gather all nations to Jehovah, a process that is now going forward, but will not be completed until that millennial day when "the Lord shall be king over all the earth," and shall reign personally thereon.[8]

ACTUAL HISTORICAL EVENTS

Nephi taught that "all things which have been given of God from the beginning of the world, unto man, are the typifying of [Christ]" (2 Ne. 11:4). One cannot read far into the Old Testament without discovering that Nephi's phrase, "all things," even includes actual historical events. We know that God raises up men for special purposes and uses nations to bring about his will. He calls Assyria "the rod of mine anger" (Isa. 10:5-7), Cyrus of Persia the "anointed" of the Lord (Isa. 45:1), and Nebuchadnezzar's kingdom a gift from "the God of heaven" (Dan. 2:37). But many people do not look beyond that kind of direct intervention in historical events to see that the Lord may also influence events in such a way that they take on symbolic significance. This does not, of course, suggest that the events did not happen as described. Rather, it means that in the reality of the events we also find the Lord's hand at work, giving history symbolical as well as historical significance.

The Testing of Abraham. Most people immediately see the symbolism of the divine Father offering his only Son in Abraham's test, but many miss the precision of detail which God used to show what he himself would have to do in the future with his own Son.

Abraham obviously was a type or similitude of the Father. Interestingly enough, his name, *Abram,* means "exalted father" and *Abraham* means "father of a great multitude" (Gen. 17:5).

Isaac was a type of the Son of God (see Jac. 4:5). Note that, like Jesus, he was the product of a miraculous birth. Though not the literal son of God, like Him Isaac was conceived through the intervention of God. Paul called Isaac "his [Abraham's] only begotten son" when he referred to this event (Heb. 11:17).

Not only did the Lord ask Abraham to perform the act which would mirror his own future actions, but he also designated a specific place, Moriah — "upon one of the mountains which I will tell thee of" (Gen. 22:2). Mount Moriah today is one of the three major hills of Jerusalem. The traditional site where Abraham offered Isaac is one occupied today by the Dome of the Rock, a beautiful Arab mosque. A few hundred yards to the north on that same hill system is another world-famous site known as Gordon's Calvary. Its Hebrew name was Golgotha. The specific location further strengthens the symbolism and echoes between the two sacrifices.

When they arrived at Moriah, the Genesis account says that Abraham "took the wood of the burnt offering, and laid it upon Isaac his son" (Gen. 22:6). The Joseph Smith Translation is even more specific: "laid it upon his back" (JST, Gen. 22:7). Some have seen here a similarity to Christ's carrying of the cross upon his shoulders on the way to the crucifixion.[9] Note also that both Christ and Isaac were "bound" (Gen. 22:9; Matt. 27:2).

One important aspect that is often overlooked is Isaac's voluntary submission to Abraham. The Old Testament does not give us enough detail to determine exactly how old Isaac was at the time of this event, but it is very likely that he was an adult, since, immediately following the account of the sacrifice on Mount Moriah, we are told that Sarah dies at the age of 127 (see Gen. 23:1), which would have made Isaac thirty-seven at the time of her death. Even if this journey to Moriah had happened several years before her death, Isaac would have been in his thirties. But the exact age is not really important. What is significant is that Abraham was well over a hundred years old and Isaac, almost certainly no child, could have put up a fierce resistance had he chosen to do so. Instead, he submitted willingly to his father, as did the Savior.

Once the intended sacrifice had been accepted, Abraham named the place *Jehovah-jireh,* which the King James Version translates as "in the mount of the Lord it shall be seen" (Gen. 22:14). Adam Clarke, citing other scholars, says the proper translation should be "on this mount the Lord shall be seen." Clarke then concludes: "From this it appears, that the sacrifice offered by Abraham was understood to be a *representative* one, and a tradition was kept up, that Jehovah should be seen in a sacrificial way on this mount. And this renders . . . more than probable . . . that Abraham offered Isaac on that *very mountain,* on which, in the fulness of time, Jesus suffered."[10]

Two other scholars, C. F. Keil and F. Delitzsch, note not only the significance of the site for the sacrifice of Jesus himself, but also point out that it relates to the site of Solomon's temple: "The place of sacrifice points with peculiar clearness [to] Mount Moriah, upon which under the legal economy *all the typical sacrifices were offered to Jehovah; . . . that by this one true sacrifice the shadows of the typical sacrifices might be rendered both real and true.*"[11]

The Exodus. In the events of Israel's deliverance from Egypt and its eventual return to the promised land, we see great and significant typology and many similitudes. This is true not only of the night of Passover but in subsequent events as well.

First, it should be noted that the very situation which led to the Exodus is a type of the children of God. Israel, the Lord's chosen people, was in bondage to an evil power. Note how Egypt, like Babylon, is used as a symbol of the world or spiritual wickedness (see Rev. 11:8). Also note how frequently sin is compared to bondage and how consistently Satan's power is acknowledged (see, for example, Rom. 6:12; 7:15; 2 Ne. 1:18; 2:29; 28:22-23; Alma 12:11; 34:35).

In spite of the great power demonstrated by Moses, again and again Pharaoh hardened his heart and refused to let Israel go. Finally, in the spring, the time when all nature seems to be coming to life again, the Lord revealed to Moses the final steps they must take to be delivered from bondage. This remarkable event, known as Passover, involved numerous items, all of which have typological significance, especially when one remembers that Israel's state of slavery was itself a type of our bondage to sin and Satan.

The Lord indicated that Israel's calendar was to begin its cycle from this event and was to be the beginning of the year (see Exod. 12:2). Symbolically speaking, the deliverance from the bondage of sin marks a new beginning, a new time, a new life, as it were.

A lamb, chosen on the tenth day of the month, was sacrificed in the evening of the fourteenth day (see Exod. 12:3-6). The lamb's typology is obvious. It had to be a male without any defects or blemishes. Each household in Israel was to take such a lamb, signifying that the coming deliverance from the angel of death applied to every household of the covenant.

Moses specified that each householder must place the blood on the door frame using the herb hyssop, a symbol of purification, as a brush or dauber (see Exod. 12:7). These instructions suggest two things: since the doorway to the home is the entry to be guarded if enemies are to be kept out, the blood not only kept out the angel of death (see Exod. 12:13), but also, the blood of the lamb on the lintels and sideposts would overshadow every entrance and exit of an individual — every thought, word, and action. Is this not related to the modern commandment that all of our ingoings and outgoings should be in the name of the Lord? (see D&C 109:17-18)

The family would then roast the entire lamb and consume it with unleavened bread and bitter herbs. Anything left of the lamb (the inedible parts, such as bones, feet, and so on) were to be burned with fire (see Exod. 12:10; also see Elder McConkie's statement above on the significance of fire). As the Lamb of God gave himself wholly to be sacrificed for the sins of the world, so must the *paschal* lamb (from *pesach*, the Hebrew word for passover) be wholly consumed. When food is eaten, it goes into the body and literally becomes part of us, sustaining life and giving us strength. So with the atoning sacrifice of the Savior; it must be partaken of and absorbed entirely so as to provide spiritual life and strength.

The Jews saw the bitter herbs as a reminder of the bitterness of their bondage in Egypt. The unleavened bread has its own significance. Leaven is a symbol of corruption because of its tendency to spoil. Christ warned the disciples about the leaven of the Pharisees and the Sadducees, defining it as the false teachings and the hypocrisy of these men (see Matt. 16:6-12; Mark 8:15; Luke 12:1). Following the actual Passover, the Israelites were commanded to observe the Feast of the Unleavened Bread, not only abstaining from any leaven for seven days, but also purging it out of their houses (see Exod. 12:18-19). Knowing that leaven is a type or symbol of corruption helps us see the beauty of this requirement. After deliverance from death and bondage by the blood of the Lamb, we are to purge all wickedness, pride, and hypocrisy from our lives. Paul also drew on the typology of leaven to teach about Christ (see 1 Cor. 5:7-8).

The feast was to be eaten hastily, with loins girded, shoes on the feet (which was contrary to normal custom), and staff in hand (see Exod. 12:11). The typology here is quite obvious: when the Lord delivers us from the bondage of sin there must be no tarrying, no delay.

At midnight the angel of death smote all the firstborn of the land but "passed over" the houses of the children of Israel marked by the blood of the lamb (see Exod. 12:29). Our deliverance from the angel of spiritual death comes only when we have partaken of the "flesh and blood" of the Lamb of God and have metaphorically placed his blood on the doorposts of our lives so that it overshadows all we do. We note also that Pharaoh (the type of Satan) absolutely refused to let Israel go free. The only thing which changed his mind was the death of the firstborn son (see Exod. 12:30-32).

The symbolic significance of the Passover night is clear and beautiful, but that did not end the Lord's teaching device. As noted above, he can influence history so that the events themselves take on the nature of a similitude and provide us with important symbols and types. Note the following events which became part of the Exodus experience.

At the command of the Lord, Moses stretched out his hand and the Red Sea parted, making a way for the Israelites to pass through the water and escape destruction (see Exod. 12:15-31). The only way any person can escape spiritual death and the bondage of sin is to demonstrate faith in Christ to the point of true repentance so that he can be "buried" in the waters of baptism and be born again by being drawn forth from those waters (see Rom. 6:1-6; John 3:3-5; Mosiah 27:24-25).

In the Exodus, the angel of God went before the Israelites in the form of a pillar of fire and smoke which overshadowed them by night and day (see Exod. 13:20-22; 14:19). Being baptized of water is not sufficient to save a person; he must also receive the Holy Ghost, whose influence and presence are symbolized, among other things, by fire and burning (see, for example, Acts 2:3-4; D&C 9:8-9). Receiving the Holy Ghost after baptism is likened unto being baptized by fire (see Matt. 3:11; 2 Ne. 31:17). As part of their deliverance from the slavery of Egypt, the Israelites were saved both by passing through the water and by being overshadowed by the fire (see 1 Cor. 10:1-4).

In the wilderness, the Israelites were sustained by the manna God sent forth, specifically called "bread from heaven" (Exod. 16:4). In the great "Bread of Life" sermon, Jesus pointedly taught that he was "the living bread which came down from heaven"; and John the Revelator promised certain faithful Saints that they could eat of "hidden manna" (John 6:51; Rev. 2:17).

In the wilderness, God provided Israel with his law and instructed Moses to build a tabernacle, or portable temple, so that the Lord could dwell in their midst (see Exod. 19-31). But rebellious Israel demanded that Aaron make them false gods to worship (see Exod. 32). For this and repeated rebellions, many Israelites were destroyed, a law of carnal commandments was given, and they were denied the full power of the priesthood (see D&C 84:24-27). Later, for further lack of faith, all adults but two were denied access to the promised land and made to wander in the wilderness for forty years (see Num. 14:30).

Clearly, these events teach us that deliverance from the bondage of sin through baptism and receiving the Holy Ghost are not enough. We must maintain faith in the Lord and hearken to his commandments or lose the promised blessings. As Nephi taught, baptism is only the gate to the straight and narrow path, and we must "press forward with a steadfastness in Christ" if we are to achieve eternal life (2 Ne. 31:17-20).

In the wilderness of Zin, the Israelites ran out of water to drink and once again began to murmur to Moses. By command of the Lord, Moses and Aaron gathered the people before a rock, Moses smote it, water came forth, and Israel lived (see Exod. 17:1-7). At the well in Samaria, Jesus told the woman of the "living water" he could give, which, if partaken of, would become "a well of water springing up into everlasting life" (John 4:14). In the closing parable of the Sermon on the Mount, Jesus likened his teachings to a rock. Moses and other Old Testament prophets called Jehovah the Rock of salvation (see, for example, Deut. 32:4, 15, 18; 2 Sam. 22:3, 47; Ps. 18:2, 31, 46). Thus we see that when Israel hungered they were fed the bread that came down from heaven and when they thirsted they received the waters of life from the Rock. Paul synthesized these events when he said, "Moreover, brethren, I would not that ye should be ignorant, how that all our fathers were under the cloud, and all passed through the sea; And *were all baptized* unto Moses *in the cloud and in the sea;* And did all eat the same spiritual meat; And did all drink the same spiritual drink; for they drank of that spiritual Rock that followed them: *and that Rock was Christ*" (1 Cor. 10:1-4; italics added).

While wandering in the wilderness, the Israelites were also afflicted with a plague of fiery serpents, and many died. The Lord told Moses to make a brass serpent and place it on a pole so that if a person were bitten he could look upon the brass serpent and he would live (see Num. 21:6-9). How can one miss the typology of that event? The covenant people, wandering in the wilderness (notice the similarity to Lehi's dream, 1 Ne. 8:4) because of rebellion were being bitten by serpents (a symbol for Satan) and were suffering death. To be saved, they looked to a figure lifted up on a pole and death was averted. Again, the evidence is clear that this event had more than mere historical coincidence (see John 3:14-15; 2 Ne. 25:25; Alma 33:19-21; Hel. 8:14-15).

Finally, the children of Israel crossed over Jordan and entered the promised land. Obviously, the ultimate promised land is the celestial kingdom, but one also enters a new land (or life) when he is born again through baptism (see Alma 37:45). With that in mind, notice the following interesting items associated with that event. The person who led Israel into the promised land was Joshua, whose Hebrew name is *Yehoshua* or *Yeshua.* When Greek became the dominant language of the Middle East, the name *Yehoshua* was transliterated into *Hee-ay-sous,* which in English became *Jesus.* But Jesus' Hebrew name was *Yehoshua* or *Joshua,* which interestingly enough means "God is help" or "Jehovah saves." Notice that twice in the New Testament the name Jesus is used when the speaker obviously means Joshua (see Acts 7:45; Heb. 4:8). So "Jesus" led Israel into the promised land.

Anyone who rebelled against the leadership of Joshua and refused to cross over Jordan was to "be put to death" (Josh. 1:18). Anyone who refuses to follow Jesus into the celestial kingdom will suffer some degree of spiritual death. That is, he will be separated from the presence of God.

Joshua called upon the people to "sanctify" themselves so they would be worthy to go into the promised land (Josh. 3:5). One must be sanctified, or cleansed from sin, in order to enter a new life with God.

The ark of the covenant, which symbolized the presence of Jehovah, went before the camp of Israel and led the way into the new land (see Josh. 3:11). Like the passing through the Red Sea, Israel again passed through the midst of the waters to enter the promised land (see Josh. 3:15-17). The Lord specifically connected the two events by asking that a memorial be built (see Josh. 4:20-24).

The crossing of Israel into the new land was done on the first day of Passover (see Josh. 4:19; Exod. 12:2-3), again invoking the typology of deliverance from bondage and death.

Once they entered into the promised land, Joshua was commanded to perform the ordinance of circumcision among the Israelites (see Josh. 5:2-7). While wandering in the wilderness, this token of the Abrahamic covenant had not been performed. Now that they had sanctified themselves and followed Jesus (seen in the types of Joshua and the ark of the covenant) into the promised land, they were once again the true covenant people and therefore the token was reinstituted.

Thus we see that while the Passover itself has great typological significance, in actuality the whole exodus from slavery to entry into the promised land provides a type or similitude of what must happen to each individual if he is to "[put] off the natural man and [become] a saint through the atonement of Christ the Lord" (Mosiah 3:19).

One does not go to a great museum like the Smithsonian in Washington, D.C., and fully explore its treasures in an hour or two. Similarly, one does not exhaust the typology of the Old Testament in so brief a presentation as this. A lifetime of exploration and pondering is required; the Lord revealed to what extent he has filled the treasure house when he said, "And behold, all things have their likeness, and all things are created and made to bear record of me, both things which are temporal, and things which are spiritual; things which are in the heavens above, and things which are on the earth, and things which are under the earth, both above and beneath: all things bear record of me" (Moses 6:63).

NOTES

1. *The Promised Messiah: The First Coming of Christ* (Salt Lake City: Deseret Book Co., 1978), p. 453.

2. Andrew Jukes, *The Law of the Offerings* (1966; reprint ed., Grand Rapids, Mich.: Kregel Publications, 1976), pp. 14-15.

3. *Ibid.*, pp. 44-45.

4. For a more detailed discussion of the typology of Old Testament sacrifices and ordinances, see Richard D. Draper, "Sacrifice and Offerings: An Ordinance Given by Jehovah to Reveal Himself as the Christ," *A Symposium on the Old Testament,* August 16, 17, 18, 1979 (Salt Lake City: Corporation of the President of The Church of Jesus Christ of Latter-day Saints, 1979), pp. 71-78.

5. Joseph Fielding Smith, *Doctrines of Salvation,* comp. Bruce R. McConkie, 3 vols. (Salt Lake City: Bookcraft, 1954-56), 3:180; italics omitted.

6. McConkie, *Promised Messiah,* pp. 431-32.

7. C. F. Keil and F. Delitzsch, *Commentary on the Old Testament in Ten Volumes,* "The Pentateuch, Three Volumes in One" (Grand Rapids, Mich.: William B. Eerdmans Publishing Co., 1973), 1 (The Third Book of Moses): 398.

8. McConkie, *Promised Messiah,* pp. 432-33.

9. Adam Clarke, *The Holy Bible . . . with Commentary and Critical Notes,* 6 vols. (New York: N. Bangs and J. Emory, for the Methodist Episcopal Church, 1827-31), 1:134; John 19:17.

10. Clarke, *Holy Bible,* 1:146.

11. Keil and Delitzsch, *Commentary,* 1 (The First Book of Moses): 253, italics added.

3

Richard L. Anderson

Types of
Christian Revelation

Professor of ancient scripture and history at BYU, Professor Anderson has trained himself academically in law, in Christian texts, and in early Mormon history, combining his linguistic and analytical backgrounds to produce groundbreaking works, especially in the field of Mormon history.

In this presentation, he challenges the underlying theory of form criticism: that the Gospels of the New Testament are basically oral tales, elaborated as proof texts to serve the theological needs of a later generation. In the New Testament epistles themselves he finds the "raw Gospels" that predate the actual composition of the evangelical Gospels and testify to the existence of preexisting source materials.

A second evidence is the unity of purpose that ties both Gospels and epistles together: both testify — repeatedly, persuasively, and insistently — to the reality of Christ's resurrection. In cataloguing only the revelations Paul mentions in his letters to

the Corinthians, those rich sources of basic Christian doctrine,
Professor Anderson points out a variety of types of revelation
that includes gifts of the Spirit, direct manifestations of the
Lord, the ministry of angels, and guidance by the Holy Spirit.
Yet for all their richness, these manifestations show "a certain
economy" that, to him, "adds significantly to the integrity and
impressiveness" of Paul's testimony. Paul testifies of Christ;
Christ testifies of the Father. And that witness to the personality
of God has a vitality that has withstood generations of critical
depersonalization.

N ew religions and new offshoots typically start with a creative or inspired founder, followed by a later definition of the
new teachings — the stage of canonization. Primitive Christianity differs distinctly from this pattern in the length of its first
generative stage, continuing roughly from the annunciations of
Jesus and John the Baptist to the closing ministry of John on
Patmos and his subsequent letters to the churches of Roman
Asia. Thus there is a century of revelation that founded the religion rather than a single originator. Without serious question
Jesus of Nazareth is the founder of Christianity. Yet there is a
valid point in the gross simplification that Jesus established the
religion but the apostle Paul created its theology. The valid
point lies in the continuity of Christian creativity from Jesus to
Paul.

Scholars who study Jesus follow an inverse procedure from
Christianity's own chronology. They typically begin with the
assumed latest writings, the Gospels, and work to the earliest,
the letters. However, in studying Joseph Smith, I have worked
from journals of those who recorded his life and his pronouncements, plus his own occasional handwritten letters. With such
firsthand records, going to the Brigham Young period for light
on the earlier Mormon founder would be an inferior approach.
But in the case of Jesus, I am assured by many scholars that

there are no authentic records from his time, that the Gospels are traditional stories, repeated orally and theologized. This is essentially form criticism, the hypothetical study of how Gospel episodes were expanded. The majority of vocal scholars today see the Gospels as overlays of successive traditions about Jesus —early stories modified during a period of oral transmission, imaginatively expanded with theological purposes in mind. In short, there is widespread professional skepticism on the general validity of the Gospels as sources for Jesus' life and teachings.

But one can be just as skeptical of form criticism as form criticism is of the Gospels. Investigating how the Gospel accounts have changed begs the question of *whether* they have changed. The Gospels present parallel stories of Jesus' life with occasional contradictions in details, but each Gospel represents a rich supplement to the information on the life of Jesus available in any other Gospel. Form criticism assumes a creativity on the part of the early Christian community different from the "continuity of revelation" creativity I spoke of; it is, instead "invention" creativity—the assumption that the early Christian community adapted these stories to their preaching needs at any given time. Then form criticism "recovers" the doctrinal issue that influenced the metamorphosis of the particular story being transformed. If Pauline Christianity was combating Jewish works, for instance, then an anonymous preacher supposedly added useful proof texts to the episodes of Jesus' life.

Such a theory contradicts all that the early Christians said about the integrity of their texts. Form criticism is just one hypothesis to explain the differing detail of an incident in two or three Gospels. It attempts to line up the accounts in sequence and construct a development in the story. But Gospel variation can be the natural differences of accounts written with knowledge but with different personality interests of the authors. For instance, similar variations are found in journals known to be contemporary reports of a discourse of Joseph Smith's—here a case of simultaneous and partial reporting rather than add-on evolution. Or look at current newspapers. One news service will report details unrecorded by a rival news service, and a third source, a correspondent, will confirm parts of each story, adding other details uncovered by his diligence or stressed by his interests as a responsible reporter. Thus instead of two additional reports being evolving forms of a proto-story, contemporary journalists regularly show simultaneous diversion — not a linear development of a changing episode but concurrent selection of differing relevant details.

In my view, form criticism is also badly out-of-date in its assumption that there was a period of oral transmission of the stories of Jesus. The recovery of hundreds of fragments and of books from Qumran shows an intense religious creativity accompanied by an equally intense fanaticism for the writing of commentaries and handbooks of community living. The Qumran community is, of course, a slightly pre-Christian reformation movement of Judaism. Just the other side of the first century we have the letters of the apostolic fathers, the orthodox bishops of the early second century. We also have the fertile inventions of Gnostic dissidents which developed and continued a tradition from the same time period.

We also have twenty-one letters of the New Testament, proving the capability and inevitability of writing output in the earliest Christian Church. With such impressive evidence of writing among Jewish reformists, orthodox Christians, and sectarian Christians, why should one assume a period of oral transmission divorced from the stability of written records?

Our best evidence indicates that Paul began writing his letters beginning about A.D. 50, but the extant letters suggest even earlier letters. For example, he ends 2 Thessalonians by personally inscribing his salutation which he says is his "token" in every epistle (2 Thess. 3:17). Even the Gospels bear clear traces of being worked up from preexisting written records, since their common material is not just generally parallel but verbally identical in many cases. Thus, for a long time, liberal and conservative New Testament scholars have accepted some form of the Q-document or documents (derived from abbreviating the German *Quelle*, source), a collection behind the present Gospels. So at this time, the height of the influence of form criticism, there are weighty reasons to reexamine its assumption and challenge its orthodoxy.

Our ability to reconstruct early Christian revelations lies in the New Testament letters, particularly those of Paul. All that we have can be dated with fair precision between A.D. 50 and 68, thus beginning within twenty years of the death of the Master. And Paul's letters are not propaganda for outsiders. They are spontaneous and candid responses to Christian problems. They report the sins of early Christians with no attempt to gloss them over; they are filled with far more sarcasm and irony than most readers catch in the stately King James translation; they abound with historical allusions to Christian personalities, including Christ. In effect, they are raw gospels preceding the writing of formal Gospels. Good historians like letters for many of these same characteristics. As the editors of Mary Todd Lincoln's letters said: "Like all letters, these have far greater value as evidence than the most candid diary or autobiography. Each one was written on a particular day under a specific impulse, with no thought that it would be judged in a larger context, or, for that matter, read by anyone other than the person to whom it was addressed."[1] I'm not willing to concede that we can hold on to Christian history in the New Testament only by selecting a canon of "reliable" letters. But any letters accepted become validations of the history recounted in the Gospels because they furnish historical controls dated extremely close to the events that the Gospels describe.

The comparative quality of these letters as historical sources measures well in terms of our general demands from ancient history — which are not the same restrictions as the demands on modern history. A scholar of American history asked in wonder when introduced to several ancient historians: "Where are your archives?" It would be wonderful to have them, but we don't. History, like politics, is the art of the possible. To sit in the ivory tower and demand perfection from early Christian writers becomes a game.

Early Gospel authors produced documents and records that compare well with those of the great historians of Greece and Rome, Thucydides and Tacitus. These Christian authors all wrote after the fact but were eyewitnesses or were able to check with survivors of events, and all were men of clear intellect and ruthless honesty. If that seems too high an estimation, remember that they risked their lives — and gave their lives — for what they said and wrote.

Luke, Paul, and John emerge in the New Testament as personalities seen through adequate literary samples. The first two, Luke and Paul, have extensive vocabularies, state clearly a philosophy of reliance on historical truth, and demonstrate the judgment of skilled intellects at work in their writing. Both of them knew well the apostles who walked with Jesus. Paul said that he first met Peter three years after his conversion and spent two weeks with the senior apostle who had walked with the Lord (see Gal. 1:18). Here is historical contact with a major source for the history of Jesus. Luke also insists that he went to the sources. Books were available to him, Luke says in his Gospel preface, from the "eyewitnesses, and ministers of the word" (Luke 1:2). These King James version phrases have historical importance: *eyewitness* in Greek is just that, and "ministers of the word" were, in application, the officials of the Church, that is, the founding apostles. As Paul's companion, Luke had access to these men who spoke of Jesus' life and resurrection firsthand. Thus, both Luke and Paul used historical controls on the Gospels.

Historians of stature have seen Luke as a historian of stature, a proposition which I think must stand despite much prestigious skepticism. And Paul's letters are also an excellent historical control on Luke, giving verification of missionary events and Christian interchange described in Luke's Acts of the Apostles. A recent opinion is helpful from a scholar who has taken the incredible trouble to digest all major works, including the skeptical treatments, ever written on Acts. After such study Ward Gasque concludes: "There is no reason to doubt the essential reliability of the narrative of Acts."[2] This historian of the critics faults the theologians who have refused to learn from their fellow scholars who are experts in the history, literature, and archaeology of the ancient world. He feels that Luke passes these tests, ignored by too many analysts of Luke's apostolic history.

With all these preliminary remarks on our sources, we can go to the records of Christian revelation, realizing that they are records of events as the generation understood them which experienced them. I will work from the base of Paul's most voluminous body of correspondence to any branch of the Church, that is, his letters to the Corinthians. The two long letters were sent to the major Christian center in southern Greece in the years A.D. 56 and 57. The letters are brilliant. The Corinthians had departed from the faith in several major areas under the counter-leadership of, in Paul's sarcastic phrase, "super apostles," or in the more stately King James translation, "false apostles" (2 Cor. 11:13).

These letters are such a rich source precisely because the Corinthians had departed so far from Christian basics. Paul here penned his fullest compendium of doctrine to correct them. His goal was to reconvert, and he restates his original Corinthian preaching. Paul says that the Corinthians will be "saved" if they remember the gospel (1 Cor. 15:1-2), implying, of course, that they do not remember it; and so he addresses himself to the issue of what the gospel is. In the opening of his letter he attacks the formation of parties following Cephas, Apollos, and himself (see 1 Cor. 1:12). Paul insists throughout that the issue isn't a question of which party you follow but a question of following the gospel. He is adamant in insisting that there is only one gospel. "Whether . . . I or they [meaning Peter and the other apostles], so we preach, and so ye believed" (1 Cor. 15:11).

That one verse suggests a great deal, not only for the proposition that Paul and the other apostles taught the same message, but that they agreed because they all obtained that message from historical truth. The great facts of Christ's death for sins and of his resurrection are prefaced by Paul's insistent words: "I delivered unto you first of all that which I also received" (1 Cor. 15:3). The independence and quality of that historical information can then be assessed because Paul next lists five resurrection appearances as examples of what he had shared with the Corinthians from his knowledge from the eyewitnesses. Three of these are also detailed in the Gospels — the appearances to Peter, the first appearance to the apostles, and the last appearance to the apostles (see 1 Cor. 15:5-7). The other two appearances are not found in the canonical Gospels — the appearance

ance to James and to "five hundred brethren" — though the appearance to James is detailed in a very early and surprisingly reliable source, the Gospel of the Hebrews.[3] So when Paul insists that he is giving accurate information from his contact with reliable sources, his information shows the characteristics of reliable sources in general — basic agreement, plus the individual supplemental knowledge that is the hallmark of an independent source.

Another Corinthian controversy is settled by Paul with impressive historical knowledge of the earthly ministry of Jesus. The problem is chaos in the Christian feast accompanying the Lord's Supper. Paul finds it terribly inconsistent for "brethren" to discriminate against each other in eating together and shameful that some turned their religious and social association into a time of revelry. Thus Paul calls to mind what the Lord did on the night before he was crucified, narrating Jesus' breaking, blessing, and offering the bread, "in remembrance of me," and similarly blessing and offering the wine. Again Paul prefaces this historical recital with the words: "For I have received of the Lord that which also I delivered unto you" (1 Cor. 11:23-24). And this account unquestionably recorded in a document some years prior to the writing of Luke's Gospel, agrees with what was later written in Luke's Gospel. Thus the intermediate history is the same as the final form of Christian history (see Luke 22:17-20). Paul's pattern of undergirding doctrine by citing realities from Christ's life is why I say that these letters are gospels before the Gospels. Because of these two Corinthian instances of authentic historical information given before the writing of the Gospels, we must treat similar references as valid historical samples from the large body of material known, stabilized, and formally presented for outsiders in another literary form when the Gospels were later written. Thus 1 Corinthians is both a letter and an early example of Christian history at work.

In that letter, Paul inventories the type of revelations common in his own life and common among the Corinthian Christians, a fascinating description of their weaknesses and strengths, Paul supplementing their weaknesses with his strengths. Chapter 12 is virtually a catalogue of various types of

Christian revelation, despite much overlapping. Yet without going into all the nuances of each spiritual gift, let me stress that Paul's central issue is still the problem that the letter began with: divisions within the Church deepened by a pseudo-intellectualism that revises Christian basics.

Paul's list of spiritual gifts includes a "word of knowledge" and a "word of wisdom" given by the Holy Ghost (1 Cor. 12:8). The informed reader stops short, recalling that Paul criticized both knowledge and wisdom in the early chapters. He condemned the Greeks for seeking after wisdom (see 1 Cor. 1:22) and later said that he would rather speak "five words with my understanding [literally, by my mind] . . . than ten thousand words in an unknown tongue" (see 1 Cor. 14:19). So *mind* is a positive term, but *wisdom* and *knowledge* are frowned upon? There is a greater issue here. *Mind,* which is translated *understanding* quite often in the New Testament, nearly always has positive connotations, whereas both *knowledge* and *wisdom* have a double use. The ambivalence is not only Paul's; he sees men in their "sophistication" (related to *sophia,* wisdom) using their own egotistical perspectives on the amount of knowledge that they have. So Paul is actually developing a contrast between man-made achievements and spiritual revelations. But as he does so, we see that it's more a matter of supplement than contrast — more a matter of man's being humble enough (with all the wisdom that he can get) to reach out for higher things. That eloquent passage on the Holy Ghost in 1 Corinthians 2:10-16 says that man may understand the things of a man by "the spirit of man," but he understands the things of God by the Holy Ghost. The very fact that Paul uses *wisdom* and *knowledge* both positively and negatively, shows me that revelation is a process of supplemental knowledge rather than an anti-rational procedure. Even the revelation is judged by its coherence, by its capacity to make sense somehow to both the spirit and the mind. That is the burden of the message of 1 Corinthians 14: "The spirits of the prophets are subject to the prophets" (14:32).

When we see Paul talking about gifts of discernment or prophecy or tongues, he is describing processes that went on in the Christian meeting. In 1 Corinthians, we walk right into the door of the Christian church — even though it is not a chapel but rather Crispus's home adjoining the synagogue. (Some of you who have been to Corinth may have actually seen the lintel from the synagogue, probably dating from this first century because it's so badly written.) Paul takes us right into those early Christian testimony meetings. One person stands up and speaks in tongues; another person interprets. Paul says that's fine, but don't speak if you don't have anything intelligent to say — something that will appeal to the mind of the nonmember who walks in. Go ahead and say it to God sometime when you're privately with him. But if you're with other people, reach their minds while reaching their souls (see 1 Cor. 14:23-28).

In short, Paul specifies other gifts that are controlled by the "word of knowledge" and "word of wisdom" as we see them in context. Obviously prophecy and tongues are gifts given for Christian meetings, but "word of knowledge" and "word of wisdom" seem to be private gifts until we realize that Paul uses *word* (*logos*) in a far more specific context than we're accustomed to. "My speech [word] and my preaching was not with . . . man's wisdom," he says in describing his manner of speech (see 1 Cor. 2:4). So the "word of knowledge" is your inspired capacity to explain knowledge; the "word of wisdom" is the wisdom that you speak. The Revised Standard Version correctly translates these phrases as "utterance of knowledge" and "utterance of wisdom," which communicates to us better than *word*.

All religions meet on the ground of claiming some enlightenment. The early Christians, like the Mormons, claimed exclusive access to enlightenment from the Holy Ghost. Of course, neither group claimed that they were the only people God inspired; early Christians acknowledged inspiration as a worldwide, ongoing process, as Latter-day Saints do. However, they felt that their method of enlightenment, the Holy Ghost, was unique in its directness, even though an outsider might not see that distinction as basic. It would be possible for the outsider to see the Holy Ghost simply as the Christians' name for the spirit working with all men's minds and enlightening those in many religions.

However, it is precisely at that point that Christianity goes beyond other religions. They may all start from the same base, but Christianity goes on to erect a pyramid consisting of additional patterns of revelation. The next level beyond the spiritual gifts that we have mentioned is visions. Paul's discussion of visions occurs in the highly personalized and aggressive second letter to the Corinthians. Putting down the people who were a thorn in his side, whom he called "super apostles," he demanded to know what they had given comparable to his sacrifices for the Church. He then catalogued his sufferings: "Thrice I suffered shipwreck, a night and a day I have been in the deep; in journeyings often, in perils of waters . . ." (see 2 Cor. 11:13, 23-27). And he goes on and on. Every conceivable peril that could have happened to Paul did happen.

Then he says, still contrasting himself to the false apostles, "I will come to visions and revelations of the Lord" (see 2 Cor. 12:1). And here, surprisingly, the account suddenly shifts to understatement. After a dozen or more examples of dramatic persecution, we might expect a half a dozen episodes of dramatic revelation just to drive his point home. Instead, Paul's awe, humility, and gratitude for having received those revelations turn him from aggressiveness to reverence—even reticence. The fact that he describes the vision as happening to "a man in Christ" is such an evidence of that humility, though he is obviously speaking of himself. The passage makes no sense if it isn't his own revelation, since he's reminding the Corinthians of his credentials contrasted to those of the "false apostles." Immediately after suggesting his glorious vision, Paul returns to the first person of admitting his need to glory in revelations but acknowledging, "I shall not be a fool." Yet he has made his point with a single example of what he calls his own "abundance of . . . revelations" (2 Cor. 12:2, 5-7).

He describes that vision as being "caught up to the third heaven" (see 2 Cor. 12:2). The phrase, "third heaven," will immediately ring bells with those who study Christian and Jewish apocryphal literature. R. H. Charles's compilation of apocalypses in his *Pseudepigrapha* volume is studded with references to twelve heavens, seven heavens, and occasionally three heavens.[4] They're always numbered from the bottom up, so the third heaven, if you follow that cultural pattern, ought to be the highest heaven. Thus Paul clearly believed that there were three heavens.

Even more important than Paul's description is what he hints at but doesn't say. He says that he saw and heard things that were unlawful to be uttered: "unspeakable words, which it is not lawful for a man to utter" (2 Cor. 12:4). I immediately ask myself, "But what about his other visions? He not only alludes to his vision of Christ on the road to Damascus in Galatians, 1 Corinthians, and other letters, but Acts describes and details it three times." This "third heaven" vision of "unspeakable" things, then, was so overwhelming that it superseded even seeing Christ! Such sacredness again shows that this "third heaven" is for Paul the highest heaven. "Whether in the body, or out of the body, I cannot tell," he adds, letting us know it was far more than an intellectual process or meditative enlightenment (2 Cor. 12:3).

I stress this vision because it was obviously the high point of Paul's spiritual life, but his "first vision" of Christ was hardly unimportant. He had earlier reminded the Corinthians: "Am I not an apostle? . . . have I not seen Jesus Christ our Lord?" (1 Cor. 9:1) Again, the material in these early letters acts as a check on the later book of Acts. To the Corinthians, he had testified that the apostles saw the Lord, that Peter saw the Lord, that five hundred brethren saw the Lord all at once, and then he added: "Last of all he was seen of me also, as of one born out of due time," a tactful English translation for his very vivid Greek word, by which he compares himself to an aborted fetus, a premature, misshapen mass (1 Cor. 15:5-7). So in Paul's humility he admits that he saw later, but *really* saw. It was an actual, objective experience. The book of Acts reinforces its reality by asserting that this vision was partially experienced by those nearby (see Acts 9:7; 22:9). Thus, the experience spilled over into the objective world, not only for Paul but for his companions.

Paul stresses the vivid reality of this revelation because he is teaching his converts the history of Christianity, especially the reality of its central event: the resurrection of Christ. As soon as he has catalogued the appearances of the resurrected Christ, he says essentially: "If you don't believe in the resurrection of Christ, you have made us false witnesses" (see 1 Cor. 15:15). The ground of Christian commitment to the resurrection is experience and knowledge — not meditation but sight, hearing, and touch. That, of course, is also the testimony of the Gospels. We can see the letters as headlines, with the details given in the closing chapters of each Gospel.

In addition to spiritual gifts and visions, there is another form of revelation — the ministering of angels, indirectly mentioned in the Corinthian letters. It is interesting that Paul does not mention angels very often. Viewed strictly from the point of view of function, angels are simply messengers (the literal meaning of the Greek term), and in function their message could come from the voice of the Spirit or from an audible voice without a vision. But angels are crucial in other portions of the biblical record. Their presence adds authority to the content of messages that could come by other means. Mary sees Gabriel. So does Joseph. Angels minister to the Lord. Cornelius learns about Peter from an angel. John's guide during his great revelation is an angel, who has to keep telling John not to worship him because "I am thy fellowservant" (Rev. 22:9). Paul mentions angels in his letters in explaining doctrine, but his history mentions a message from an angel only once, before the shipwreck on the way to Rome (see Acts 27:23).

We have been talking about the types of revelation in the New Testament, but let us look at another element in that pattern. How frequently did Paul receive revelations? It is not a matter of simply adding them up. We cannot count revelations by the Holy Spirit because he was obviously led by the Spirit regularly, even when our records take that for granted. Being told not to go preach in Asia and Bithynia is one example of spiritual direction (see Acts 16:6-7). Yet we can catalogue the visions mentioned by Paul or Acts: his conversion on the road to Damascus (Acts 9:3-18); the Lord's appearance to him in the temple, confirming his assignment from the Twelve to go to Tarsus (Acts 9:30; 22:17-21); Paul's magnificent vision of the third heaven at approximately the time that he was called to the gentile mission (2 Cor. 12:1-6); and the vision of a man from Macedonia, asking him to "come over . . . and help us" (Acts 16:9). After Paul arrived at Macedonia, he was persecuted out of three cities, and we can empathize with Paul's probable need for the next revelation, just after being excluded from the synagogue at Corinth, the fourth city where he encountered major opposition. There the Lord appeared in vision and assured him: "Be not afraid, but speak, and hold not thy peace; for I am with thee, and no man shall set on thee to hurt thee: for I have much people in this city" (Acts 18:9-10). That is the fifth recorded vision. Afterward Paul went to Jerusalem, and after persecution, rejection by his own people, and dramatic debate in the Sanhedrin, he received another appearance of the Lord, assuring him that he would eventually go to Rome (see Acts 23:11). Enroute he saw the angel already mentioned, promising him safety in the midst of the fearful storm and coming shipwreck (see Acts 27:23).

Thus the total is seven known visions. Paul certainly was not converted any earlier than A.D. 30. If we place his death at A.D. 68, we have a maximum ministry of thirty-eight years. Probably Paul's ministry lasted from about A.D. 33 to about A.D. 67 or A.D. 68, or, in round numbers, about thirty-five years. Seven known visions in thirty-five years averages a vision every five years. Thus I see a certain economy in the Christian pattern of revelation, which is deeply consistent with Paul's rationality in teaching the Corinthians about spiritual gifts. Paul's calling entitles him to direct manifestations from God, but he receives them in serious and unusual circumstances. They are not debased in value by being claimed for every casual question in his life. Of course, we are talking about visions from God, whereas Paul's directions by the Spirit are a constant and daily matter of direction, corresponding to his daily outreach of thought and soul. But Paul does not cheapen revelation by vision by broadening his definition any further than necessary. And that, to me, adds significantly to the integrity and impressiveness of his testimony.

There is a sort of pyramid of increasingly direct Christian revelations. The broad base rests on the common gifts of the Spirit, moving upwards to prophecy, which Paul designates as more important (and less common) than speaking in tongues (see 1 Cor. 14:5). Then we build up to visions. At the apex is the personal sight of Christ and of God the Father. And in this pyramid frequency appears to be in inverse ratio to directness. The New Testament contains a limited use of theophany. Stephen and John see Christ long after the resurrection — perhaps John also saw the Father as Stephen did (see Acts 7:55-56). Paul, as we have noted, saw Jesus Christ on at least four occasions. But the most impressive appearance for all the apostles was before Paul's conversion. All of the New Testament letters describing revelation highlight the resurrection experience. Yes, the Lord continually directed the Church afterwards, but the apostles were not inventing new visions to justify their actions or to rationalize their problems. We see this in examining their answer to the greatest problem that the Church experienced: the directive to Jewish Christians not to impose circumcision on the gentile converts. Why didn't the apostles claim a vision at that point? Peter had in fact had a vision earlier when the gentiles were to receive the gospel — a very dramatic one (see Acts 10:10-16). But when the apostles revoked the law of circumcision, and hence the Mosiac law of the Old Testament for the gentiles, there was no appearance of the Lord, but only: "It seemed good to the Holy Ghost, and to us" (Acts 15:28). That one example, it seems to me, proves an authentically careful use of theophanies. When they come, they are spectacular; but they don't come often. The great event that everyone goes back to is not a continuing presence of Christ, but his resurrection. It was historical and unique in that his apostles touched his physical body; but it was an experience not thereafter repeated. Occasional direct visions paralleled the apostles' experience to the end of the first century.

Paul is persistent and consistent in asserting that the resurrection must be taken seriously, not only because of his own vision but because of the witnesses who saw Christ right after his death. "We stand together," he basically says, "but I am not even in their category" (see 1 Cor. 15:1-11). So the historically resurrected Christ constitutes the ultimate revelation: the revelation of the Father. The epistles testify that the resurrection of Christ is the revelation of the Father. By Christ's own witness, if you have seen me, you have seen the Father (see John 14:9). This is a Johannine teaching, and it is also a Pauline teaching: Christ is "the image of the invisible God" (Col. 1:15). *Invisible*, incidentally, is a very unfortunate translation since it implies that God could never appear. *Unseen* is better, implying the possibility that God will appear — that he is temporarily unseen but not permanently unseeable. Thus for Paul, Christ's physical form is closely similar to the form of the Father who shall be seen in eternity, for John and Paul thus preach the same message: Christ is indeed the representation and the likeness of the Father.

As Edmond Cherbonnier pointed out in his paper presented at BYU in 1978, a Christian ought to be able to be orthodox and also believe in an anthropomorphic God because that is the way God is represented in the scriptures.[5] And this is where the types of revelation in the New Testament lead us: to the revelation of the personality of God. In the last few years we have certainly seen a revitalization of attempts to define God as personal. It's too bad that Hugh Nibley doesn't give his class on Christian creeds anymore, but my old class notes show the pattern he laid out: the modification by Christian creeds of earlier understandings of God as personal — the application of philosophic abstractions to God that were unknown by the generation of Christians that knew God. After fifteen hundred years of saying that God is impersonal, an invisible spirit, we now see creeds like the creed of the United Church of Canada terming him an infinitely loving, personal spirit. Why did God ever become an abstraction? I remember the day Hugh Nibley lectured on Origen and read us that marvelous passage where Origen really struggles with the nature of the Incarnation. Origen was a Christian who studied Greek philosophy, a tremendously honest man, a compulsive worker, and a powerful writer of the third century. He puzzles how Christ — God, and Son of God —

could come to earth, be laid in a cradle, how he could need food, cry as a baby, later walk among us, and then be cruelly murdered but resurrected with a physical body. "I don't understand," says Origen, and adds, "I think that it surpasses the power even of the holy apostles; nay, the explanation of that mystery may perhaps be beyond the grasp of the entire creation of celestial powers."[6] Now Origen was honest enough, or should I say informed enough, to admit that you cannot be a Christian according to New Testament standards and deprive Jesus Christ of a real body, either before or after the resurrection. Yet Origen lived in the generation that was at work in depersonalizing God because of a philosophical premise that a perfect God must be nonmortal and therefore nonmaterial.

Early medieval generations defined Christianity more mystically, more abstractly. Here is a typical statement. It's from Arnobius, a fourth-century father, but you can virtually reach into the theological pool and randomly pick whom you wish. Here is his philosophical, nonintimate approach to God: "For thou art the first cause, the place and space of things created, the basis of all things whatsoever they be. Infinite, unbegotten, everlasting, eternal alone art thou, whom no shape may represent, no outline of body define; unlimited in nature and in magnitude unlimited; without seat, motion, and condition, concerning whom nothing can be said or expressed in the words of mortals."[7]

Needless to say, in contrast to this praise of an undefined and undefinable God, the New Testament revelation of God is empirical, experimental, observational, and personal. Succeeding theologians, in abstracting possible characteristics of God, thus removed from him his greatest attribute — personality. And in so doing, they denied the living revelation of God that fired the zeal of the early Christians and became the New Testament witness.

NOTES

1. Justin G. Turner and Linda Levitt Turner, *Mary Todd Lincoln: Her Life and Letters* (New York: Alfred A. Knopf, 1972), pp. xxi-xxii.

2. W. Ward Gasque, *A History of the Criticism of the Acts of the Apostles* (Grand Rapids, Mich.: William B. Eerdmans, 1975), p. 309.

3. See Jerome in M. R. James, *The Apochryphal New Testament,* corrected ed. (Oxford: Clarendon Press, 1953), pp. 3-4.

4. See *The Apocrypha and Pseudepigrapha of the Old Testament,* 2 vols. (Oxford: Clarendon Press, 1963-64), vol. 2.

5. See "In Defense of Anthropomorphism," in *Reflections on Mormonism: Judaeo-Christian Parallels,* ed. Truman G. Madsen, Religious Studies Monograph Series, no. 4 (Provo, Ut.: Religious Studies Center, Brigham Young University, 1978), pp. 155-73.

6. *de Principiis,* bk. 2, ch. 6, sec. 2 in *Ante-Nicene Fathers,* eds. Alexander Roberts and James Donaldson, 3 vols. (Grand Rapids, Mich.: William B. Eerdmans, 1968), 4:281-82.

7. Cited in Johannes Quasten, *Patrology,* 3 vols. (Westminster, Md.: Newman Press, 1964), 2:388.

4

Fazlur Rahman

Elements of Belief in the Qur'an

Dr. Fazul Rahman, originally from West Pakistan and currently a professor at the University of Chicago, has served with distinction on the faculties of universities in four countries: his own Pakistan, Canada, England, and the United States. Admired and respected by his colleagues and students, he is a recognized authority on the culture and religion of Islam. His most recent book, published in 1979, is entitled simply, Islam.

In discussing "Elements of Belief in the Qur'an," he performed the difficult task of making an ancient, complex, and unfamiliar religion intelligible and coherent to an audience almost entirely unacquainted with it. Using the Qur'an itself as the key to understanding the Muslim world, Professor Rahman discusses the historical context for the appearance of the religion itself, Muhammad's role as its prophet, and its key beliefs. The topics he discusses with such deceptive simplicity include the nature of God, the nature of man, the origin of evil, the rela-

tionship between the Creator and his creations, sin and salva-
tion, individual responsibility, and collective accountability.
All of these factors are organized by the two great messages of
the Qur'an: the sovereignty of God and the need for social
justice, lofty and noble ideals that have seen their working out
in the hundreds of cultures that have embraced Islam.

T he Qur'an, as you know, is for Muslims the revealed scripture of God. In what I am going to say to you, I will therefore
try to present the general structure of the main ideas of the
Qur'an.

Muhammad, the founder of Islam, was born in Mecca in
northern Arabia around A.D. 570. His father had predeceased
him and his mother died when he was a child. He was brought
up by his uncle, Abu Talib. Mecca was a purely commercial
town. The Meccans several generations back had been Bedouins
in the desert; but some generations before the advent of Muhammad, they settled in this place and mediated the trade
between India and the Indian Ocean and throughout the Byzan-
tine Empire. It was, therefore, on the whole quite a prosperous
community. There were in this community, however, despite its
prosperity, or rather because of its commercial prosperity, certain darker sides to the picture: a fairly large-scale exploitation
of the poor, of the disenfranchised, of the have-nots. There was,
in short, a very considerable socio-economic disparity.

Muhammad, just before the age of about forty, was disturbed by two problems in this city. One was the socio-
economic disparity, and the other was the Meccan polytheism.
In their sanctuary, the Ka'ba, and around it there was a multiplicity of gods, usually a god representing a tribe. This polytheism therefore to Muhammad was not just polytheism; it
symbolized the division of mankind into different tribes at
loggerheads with one another. Socially and economically, the
richer classes were exploiting the poor.

When he was disturbed, he resorted to a cave, called Hira Cave, in the north of Mecca in the mountains. It is a very small cave; I have seen it. Two men can barely sit there, or one person can lie there. Muhammad used to go to that cave and sometimes stay for long periods, in contemplation and praying to God for a solution of these problems. The echo of this disturbance and of the solution that he ultimately received from God is recorded in the early chapters of the Qur'an: "Have we not now opened up your heart [i.e., to the truth], and we have removed from you that burden which was breaking your back?" (*sura* [chapter] 94:1-3)

Muhammad, when he came out of his cave, summoned his fellow Meccans to accept two things: to accept one god — to discard the multiplicity of gods representing the multiplicity of tribes — and to remove the ugly socio-economic disparity that existed in the society.

The Meccans, of course, had vested interests in both of these things because the Meccans were in charge of the pagan Arabian religions at that time. They were the priests. Therefore they rejected his call for monotheism and, of course, they rejected his invitation to social justice. A struggle ensued that lasted for twenty-three years.

Having spent ten years in Mecca where he had a small band of devoted followers who understood his message, Muhammad moved to Medina where he was invited by the Medinese.

The Qur'an is a document which is a collection of the messages that came to Muhammad during these approximately twenty-three years of his prophetic life, answering questions as they arose in the struggle. In order, therefore, to understand the Qur'an properly, it is absolutely imperative to understand first of all that background in Mecca which provoked this message in the first place, and then to understand the background of almost every passage. Without this background, the Qur'an seems to be a jumble of heterogeneous passages addressing heterogeneous questions. When people study the Qur'an as a book, they get frustrated because it is not a book in the usual sense. It is a collection of these passages. It is extraordinarily eloquent; its language is extraordinarily expressive; but in order to be understood properly, this background needs to be kept in mind.

Now with this brief introduction, let us come to what the Qur'an has to say to us. Because the Qur'anic message is also a social message, it is a message heavily laden with an invitation for socio-economic justice. Some Western scholars have thought that the Qur'an is essentially a body of socio-political teaching; that it somehow, by accident, became a religion. Whatever the interpretation, the fact remains that Muhammad felt, and felt it in his inmost being, that he had been called by God.

Let us spend a few moments on this God. God is one and unique, the only being who is infinite. Everything else, everything other than God that has been created by him, is finite. The hallmark of a creature is its essential finitude. Creatures of God have potentialities, have powers to act, but nevertheless are limited and finite. When God creates a thing, at the same time he puts the law of its behavior in it. Because of this inborn law, everything fits well into the entire pattern we call the universe. The universe is, for the Qur'an, a well-knit, formally created structure in which there are no gaps, no dislocations, no ruptures. It is an extraordinarily well-built working machine, which acts or works according to the laws that God has put into it. The Qur'an, therefore, calls the universe and everything in it *muslim,* which is an active participle derived from the root *islam* and means "surrender to God's law or to God's will." And because the universe obeys God's laws that are engrained in it, the Qur'an frequently calls the whole universe *muslim.* Man is invited to be *muslim.* Whereas the rest of the universe automatically obeys God, man has been given the choice to obey or disobey. And for this obedience or disobedience, the risks and rewards are high.

The Qur'an tells the story of the creation of Adam and says that when God wanted to create Adam, God said to his angels, "I am going to put on the earth a live spirit," and the angels did not like this. They said to God, "We glorify you and sing your praises and carry out your commands. Are you putting on the earth a creature who will sow corruption and shed blood?" God does not deny that man will sow corruption and shed blood. He simply says, "I know what you know not." And thereafter God summons both the angels and Adam and commands the angels,

"Name these things." The angels express their inability to name things: "We only know what you have taught us. Beyond that we do not know anything." But Adam was able to name things. (The Qur'an is quite clear that man possesses a tremendous capacity for creative knowledge whereby he is distinguished from the rest of the universe and indeed from angels.) When the angels lost the battle in this competition, God asked them to prostrate themselves to Adam and to honor him. They all did except one. That one, who refused because of sheer pride, became Satan (see *sura* 2:20-32). There was, therefore, no Satan before Adam appeared. Satan and Adam are coevals; they take their birth together. This points to a very deep-seated fact about human nature.

God then said to Adam and Eve, "All right, I will send you my guidance from time to time, so those of your progeny who listen to my call will be successful" (see *sura* 2:37-38). (The Qur'an does not use the word *salvation*. Its term is *success*.) "Those who will not listen to my call will fail; the successful will enjoy paradise and the others will burn in fire."

Now this God who is infinite, in his infinite mercy, just as he has given laws to the universe, so has he given his law through his messengers to mankind. This is called moral law, and man is invited to accept this moral law, to be good, to be *muslim*. The Qur'an's basic critique of human nature is that man is very short-sighted. He doesn't look at the end; he looks at the immediate all the time, is extremely selfish, has a petty narrow mind and a very limited vision. When he is asked to sacrifice for the poor, he thinks he is going to be impoverished. This is Satan whispering in man's mind. Whereas God promises prosperity in exchange for this compassion (see *sura* 30:38), man, because of his narrow vision, finds it very difficult to get outside of this nature that God has made.

The Qur'an insists that God is both outside nature because he is infinite and inside nature because nature is his handiwork (see *sura* 88:16-20). Nature is autonomous because it works through laws that were given to it by God, but it is not autocratic because it points to some infinite being beyond itself and because it is finite. God is thus both outside nature and inside nature; but man, when he is inside nature, cannot see God; he sees only nature. And because of this shortsightedness, he forgets God. When man forgets God, he forgets himself because the principle of the integrity of every being, including human beings and human societies, *is* God. Once God is left out, the being of man, individually and collectively, disintegrates. This is why God is necessary for man—to keep the integrity of his own being and to develop. The Qur'an complains repeatedly that it is only when natural causes fail man that he discovers God. When a ship is sailing in the sea with favorable winds and calm waters, man is liable to forget God. But when suddenly a storm brews and angry waves strike against the ship, then man remembers God. Therefore the Qur'an calls upon man essentially to remember God because it is this constant keeping in mind of something beyond him—something that has created him and that sustains him—it is this constant being on watch that will keep him intact.

The first idea that appears in the Qur'an after these two initial invitations to monotheism and social justice is the idea of the last judgment. "If you do not mend your ways," says the Qur'an to the Meccans, "then there will be a day when you will all be called to account for your deeds. Every individual will be called to account for his or her deeds. Alone you will come to us, just as we created you alone" (see *sura* 34:45).

A little later, another theme appears which can be called judgment in history. The final judgment will be passed on individuals for their individual performances. But there is a judgment in this world which is passed, not on individuals as such, but on collectivities—on nations, on peoples. And the Qur'an then begins to tell and retell the stories of past nations that were destroyed when they went astray. Messengers of God had come, but they had refused to accept the messengers. God saved good people in these societies but only those who were *actively* good. The Qur'an asks, "Why did the virtuous and knowledgeable people in those societies not actively try to reform those societies? Why did they not actively try to call them to goodness?" (see *sura* 17:12). Being passively good by yourself doesn't help. And therefore those people who were passively good were destroyed along with those who were actively bad because God does not forgive those who know what ought to be done and yet don't do anything about it. Maybe they themselves are good, and on the day of judgment maybe they will be successful in giving account of their individual deeds. But in this judgment in history, only those people are saved who actively call others to goodness.

Now in part of the Qur'an, biblical figures appear beginning with Adam and Noah, through Abraham, through Moses, through biblical prophetic personalities to Jesus. All these men God has sent from time to time to warn people against their evildoing and to invite them to do good. These men are called prophets or messengers of Allah. But this prophetology is not entirely biblical. Certain Arabian names are associated with it. Two Arab tribes that were destroyed, the tribes of Ad and Themoud of ancient Arabia, are also constantly mentioned, and the two prophets which had been sent to them (see *sura* 7:63-70). The Qur'an says, "God's guidance is not limited to Jews and to Arabs. God has been sending these messages all over the world to all peoples in all nations. There is no nation in the world to which guidance has not been given. Every people has had an invitation to goodness and a warning against evil." It is on this ground that Muhammad and the Qur'an severely criticized the claims of Jews and Christians that they were proprietors of truth, that they were proprietors of God. The Qur'an says, "These people claim that if you want to get guidance you must become a Jew or become a Christian. But guidance is God's guidance, not Jewish or Christian guidance. God is at work everywhere" (see *sura* 2:103-09, 129). His guidance is universal. And all proprietary claims to God are, in fact, negations of the divine truth. No nation, no people, no community in the world may claim exclusive rights over God. Now this message which has at its center this unique God and also this doctrine of socio-economic justice — what is its purpose? The purpose of this endeavor, we are told, is to remove "corruption from the earth."

Somehow after a few generations, every people begins to decay unless it keeps a very constant vigil over its state of heart and mind. Every people, after it achieves greatness and after it, as the Qur'an puts it, "inherits the earth," begins to decay. And that is the perilous stage where it must be able to keep watch over itself. If it does not, it will go down the drain just as others have gone down the drain. The Qur'an has a long catalogue of earlier peoples who have been "harvested out."

No nation, no people on earth has an irrevocable passport to eternal life and success. The end of man's endeavor on earth is to reform the earth and to remove corruption from it. But here is the catch: man is a creature who is particularly liable to self-deception. When he acts in history and thinks he is doing good, he more often than not misjudges himself. This self-deception is something on which the Qur'an spends a great deal of attention, a great deal of effort. It warns: "Whenever it is said to them, 'Please don't sow corruption on the earth,' they say 'We are only reformers' " (see *sura* 2:7-10). Beware, these are the corrupters of the earth, but they are not aware — they don't know it.

The Qur'an insists that deeds have weight. We are told that this weighing of deeds comes from the commercial background of Muhammad, which is, of course, true. Mecca was a market where things were weighed. But those merchants weighed commodities, gold, and silver; they didn't weigh deeds. Yet the Qur'an insists on the weighability of deeds. There are deeds which look very weighty to the doer but in the end have no result, are inconsequential. So the Qur'an says, "Say to them, shall I tell you of those people who are the greatest losers in terms of their deeds? These are the people whose endeavors are lost in the images of the world. They think they are achieving great deeds, that they are doing prodigies" (see *sura* 101:5-6; 83:1-5). It is, therefore, extremely important to be able to weigh one's deeds.

How do I weigh my deeds? How do I know that I am not being deceived, that I am not in a mirage created by myself? The Qur'an suggests a remedy called *taqwa,* a state of mind every human being must cultivate. This term *taqwa* has been translated often into English as "fear of God," which is not incorrect. But, you see, fear is of different types — we fear wolves, criminals fear the police — at least they used to — and children fear their parents and teachers if they are naughty — at least they used to. And a person who does wrong and then becomes aware that he has done wrong also fears. But he fears the consequences that might follow upon the wrong that he has done. *Taqwa* may be defined as an "inner torch" whereby a person is able to distinguish between right and wrong, provided he is also convinced that there is a criterion of judgment which lies outside him, not inside him. What he is doing will be judged, but judged by a criterion which he has not made. He must come up to the standard of this criterion of judgment. He must try. *Taqwa* does not guarantee that man always succeeds, but it guarantees that he will try. Without this instrument of *taqwa* there is no hope that man will even try to do the right. And to do the right is imperative if man is to succeed, if man has to do that which will be consequential in the long run. The Qur'an criticizes the Meccan merchants who are very proud of their wealth — their short-term effects — but are unaware of the long-term effects, of the final ends of their lives, hence this concept of the day of judgment, whenever that day is. It becomes central to the teaching of the Qur'an. So long as man acts only on the basis of the immediate consequences, there is not much possibility of his producing deeds that will be consequential in the long run. So to cultivate *taqwa*, to clear the earth of corruption and to reform the earth — to create on this earth a social order based on ethically viable principles — that, in summary, seems to me to be the message of the Qur'an.

HINDU,
BUDDHIST,
AND TAOIST
SCRIPTURE

5
P. Lal

The Hindu Experience: An Examination of Folklore and Sacred Texts

Purushottam Lal, a native of India and professor of English at the University of Calcutta, is an internationally recognized poet and scholar. In 1958 he founded the Writers Workshop of Calcutta, an association of writers committed to translating the best of Indian literature into English and to promoting English as a creative force in Indian writing. For the past twenty years Professor Lal has edited this association's scholarly journal, Miscellany. *He has written and edited dozens of books, including works of his own poetry and translations of much of the sacred literature of India. His current task is a "transcreation" of one of the world's longest epic poems, the* Mahabharata. *To date he has published at least 132 volumes of the proposed 180-volume project.*

In his remarks, Professor Lal denies that India has a "literature" of belief as such, and instead gives us both explanation and experience through the deceptive simplicity of narrative

*and parable, the oral tradition that has preserved and trans-
mitted India's sacred literature throughout the vast sweep of her
history and across the vast expanse of her subcontinent. The
counterpoint of his own half-ironic, half-puzzled commentary
underlines the listener's responsibility to derive his own meaning from these tales, although by anchoring them to crisis points
in his own autobiography — his coming of age paralleling that
of India's — Professor Lal lets the audience experience vicari-
ously his or her own search for meaning.*

*Part of the warmth of his presentation lies in that personal
sharing. Part of it also lies in the flashes of wit that make his
telling of these stories unique and idiosyncratic — similar to but
not identical with their written forms. In his own way, he keeps
the oral tradition alive. And in his questioning of his own culture, he also brings us face-to-face with the half-submerged
questions we have always sensed about the links between our
own society and our religious tradition.*

There's a poem by Rabindranath Tagore which he wrote on
27 July 1941 on his deathbed in Calcutta. It's called "Poem Thirteen." He numbered these poems because he was so afraid he
was going to die. In fact, two days after he wrote the poem he
became unconscious and he never recovered; a week later he
died. (He's the only Asian poet to have received the Nobel
Prize. That was in 1913, and since 1913 no one seems to have
found an Asian poet worthy to receive the Nobel Prize.) This
man believed, and believed deeply. Never in his life did he ever
think there was no answer; and yet in those last days, he was
very worried, terribly worried. He'd started losing faith. The
poem is called "The First Sun," or "The First Day's Sun." And
here it is — very brief, very telegraphic. There's not much to say
when you're going to die. (It's something, I think, perhaps
speakers and lecturers should learn.)

The first sun asked the world's first life,
"Who are you?"
No answer. Years passed. The last sun asked the last question
From the western ocean on a songless evening,
"Who are you?"
No answer.[1]

You can see what he's getting at. The sun rises in the east and sets in the west — somewhere in Utah. And the East thought it had an answer when the sun first rose. No way. It isn't that easy. And the West tried its best, too — much later, with technological and other revolutions, yet as the sun set, the question was the same. There was no answer. As Tagore says, " 'Who are you?' No answer."

So please don't expect any answers today. Some confusions, some illuminations, some suggestions on this problem of belief, of how to live, of who I am, of what I learned and what I hope I can communicate.

I was born in 1929 in the Punjab but I've lived all my life in Calcutta. (That's forty-nine years.) My father left Punjab when I was one year old, put a thousand miles between us and it, and never went back. It was difficult. I was a Punjabi coming into a Bengali environment. I was a Hindu. And as my introducer remarked, I got sixteen years of Catholic training. (I had no choice in this. Various things were decided for me.)

It was a time of uncertainty and terror and mystery because, in 1939, it just happened that somebody declared war on somebody and it was the Second World War. Every morning, a young boy of ten, I would open the newspapers and find these pictures of killing, of destruction. Every day.

And I had a question. (I've always had questions and never had answers.) There was no one to go to except mother. In fact, that's my point. That's the way the "literature of belief" operates in India. We have no texts. We don't go to temples. There are no sermons. We don't study it in the university. If I had a problem, I would go to her. It is the oral tradition. It sustained me up to a point, and beyond that point it didn't. But whatever answers came came that way. I will try and give them to you.

So when all this happened—the mystery and the uncertainty and the terrors of growing up in an alien environment—and because the Catholics had some answers which didn't fit into my way of looking at life, I went to mother and said, "What is this? What is going on? Why do people kill each other? What are we here for? What are we doing?" She's a very devout worshipper of Krishna and has a god-room in which she worships. (My father is not a believer. My father says that when she goes to heaven he'll hang on her sari and he'll manage to get there.) She came up with a parable. (*This* is the literature of belief. There are no set statements, nothing definite, clear, written down.)

She said, "Have you heard the story of the parable of the drop of honey?" And I said no. It's a parable that's found its way into Christian doctrine too. In the *Gesta Romanorum,* it is retold in a very Christian way by John of Damascus, but he changes it. And this is the parable—in the context of World War II, people killing each other, India being pulled into the war, Indian soldiers fighting too, and a young boy just questioning and wondering why this should be.

It's about a Brahmin who is walking through a forest. Darkness falls in the forest, and he doesn't know exactly where he's going, but he sort of knows the road. (We all sort of know the road yet do not know that this is a very tricky kind of world in which we live—a jungle, sometimes called the cement jungle.) In any case, he walks; and without warning, suddenly there's a well overgrown with creepers. He thinks it's the road, and he falls in. As he falls, knowing he is falling, he reaches out and grasps at a root that is protruding from the side and he hangs on. And then he wonders what to do. So he looks up and there's the sky, and all around him is grass of all kinds and creepers and shrubs, and this root. He says, "I can get out. It's not that difficult." But as he tries, the root weakens and loosens. "Oh no," he says, "no, I'd better hang on." So he wonders, he looks around, and he sees there's nothing else to do, no hope, no rescue. And then he finds that on his left is a grass blade; and on that grass blade, for some mysterious reason, there is a drop of honey. So, hanging on with one hand to his root, he reaches out—very gingerly because the least effort he makes is going to create problems for him. (The least effort we make is a movement towards the grave.) But he reaches out, he lifts that drop of honey with one finger, and very slowly, very artistically, very happily, he tastes it — puts it on his tongue — and says, "How sweet."

And that was the metaphor I was told, the parable that was supposed to explain to me the existential predicament of man, why people did what they did in the well in which they had fallen, why people killed each other, why they worried. And of course, the idea was that you must keep looking for the drop of honey. I believed that and I kept looking.

I grew older and went to school at Saint Xavier's College which is a Catholic Jesuit institution. Every morning they taught us the New Testament — we had to learn it by heart — and Bible history and moral instruction and catechism. Four periods a day went into that. And it was now 1943. I was a young boy of fourteen. India was still at war and a great deal of the wealth in India was going to feed the army and the battle effort. So every morning we prayed (this was compulsory): "Our Father, which art in heaven, Hallowed be thy name. Thy kingdom come. Thy will be done. . . . Give us this day our daily bread" (Matt. 6:9-11). Daily bread? 1943? Does anyone know that date? Does it have any meaning? The Bengal famine? Three million people who died in the streets of Calcutta while we were chanting our prayer?

"And forgive us our debts, as we forgive our debtors. And lead us not into temptation, but deliver us from evil: For thine is the kingdom, and the power, and the glory" (Matt. 6:12-13).

It just so happened that the kingdom happened to be England's, and the British were ruling us. And so there was a problem. We had all the lovely, beautiful ideals in front of us. And everything was in books, and in books at least it was all right. God *was* in his heaven, but all was not right with the world. The world was out of joint. O cursed spite that ever we were born to set it right.[2] Three million people. This is a matter of historical record. As a young boy of fourteen, I watched them come from the provinces outside Calcutta because there was no food. Yet it was a man-made famine. They died in the streets of Calcutta and not a single loaf of bread was stolen though they died outside shops stocked with bread. Now whether this was a crass stupidity or outright moral bravery I have never found out.

And I had to go again to mother and ask, "Mother, what is this? I hear one thing in school and I see another thing in the world. How do you explain this? — this apparent disjointedness, this lack of a relationship between values and reality? What kind of a world is this in which we live?"

And then Ghandi came. (All this is interwoven, you see. I cannot separate my life from my beliefs, and I cannot separate my life from what I see around me.) And then Ghandi came along and said, "Leave India. Just get out." And the British said, "Yes, but what happens when we get out? The Japanese are coming." Ghandi said, "Well, that's our business. We'll look after the Japanese. You get out. You mind your own business."

And at Saint Xavier's we could see it was a call for non-violence, for people rooted in truth came out in the streets of Calcutta, marchers ten abreast without any weapons whatsoever. Naturally, with all this clamor going on all around in the streets of Calcutta, classes would have to be disbanded, and we students would go out, age fourteen, age fifteen, and look at what was going on outside while they taught us such beautiful things inside. And the British tommies would come. (They had stopped trusting Indian soldiers.) Under Section 144, people in groups of more than five were illegal assemblies. So the sergeant would say "No more" to the marchers. I saw with my own eyes that the tommies fired the first shots and the first row fell; the second row moved forward, the second shots were fired, the second row fell; the third row moved forward. The third time when the order was given to fire they wouldn't fire. And I remember Ghandi said, "We won. We've changed their hearts."

Yes, but I had a problem. I had to *do* something in this context. So I did something, and it didn't seem to solve very much. Since we had to wear ties, I decided I would come to class without my tie. What a terrible, terrible decision! It was like dying the day I walked into class one day with my tie in my pocket. My teacher (he's my son's teacher, too) said, "Lal, where's your tie?" I said, "Father, my conscience doesn't permit me to wear a tie." He said, "Why?" I said, "Father, to me it's a badge of slavery." He said, "That may be, Lal, but you'd better go downstairs to the prefect and see that next time you don't do it. There are rules here in this college." So I went downstairs and I received what is called "six of the best" — that is a nice euphemism — and a warning never to come back again without a tie on.

That was a terrible struggle. I learned then what is meant by a struggle with conscience, what it means to wrestle with the angel. I decided, no, I would do it again. People were dying outside. If I couldn't do that (and after all, the Catholics had taught me about the primacy of conscience), then nothing about conscience was here. So I went to class without a tie the second time, but this time there were five other boys sitting without ties in my class, and one of them happened to be the son of the president of a large steel corporation. So ties were made optional. I've never worn a tie since then.

That still didn't solve the problem. I still went back to my mother and asked, "What kind of world is this where there's dying and there are conscience problems and people don't know what's right or what's wrong?" And she told me another parable, an old, old folk story that's told again and again in India. (It's also retold by Andre Malraux in his book, *Anti-Memoirs.*) Malraux, once the French minister of culture, learned this story from professors at the Sanskrit University in Benares, the holy city.[3] This is the story that was told him, the story that was told me by mother, the story that is floating in the folklore of India, a story that every Indian, every Hindu, in a sense, learns. It's a story of a *lota,* of the brass vessel for water. I'll give it to you. It might help you. It helped me a little bit — not very much — to make sense of the famine and to make sense of the crisis of conscience. All my questions had not been solved — just a few, just a very few and not even solved completely.

This is a story of Narada, the Brahmin who lives in Vishnu's heaven. He's a very strange character. He has long hair. He carries a one-string sitar, and he asks the wrong questions, which are really the right questions, questions that cannot be answered. So he goes to Vishnu and says, "Vishnu, I hear that

the world is *maya*." And Vishnu says, "Yes, the world is *maya*."
(*Maya* is defined in Webster's Third International as the Hindu
theory of cosmic illusion by which the phenomenal world
appears to be real. Isn't that beautiful? Webster knows everything. But is it real? Is it not? It appears to be real.) So he asks
Vishnu, the preserver of the world, "What is *maya*?"

Vishnu smiles: "I can't answer that question. *Maya* can be
experienced but it cannot be communicated."

And so Narada says, "I see your game, Vishnu. You refuse
to tell me what *maya* is. You make *maya* but you cannot explain *maya*. Very well. I have a trick up my sleeve, too. If you
cannot explain to me what *maya* is, I will withhold my worship
from you." (Now, we know what happens when human beings
withhold their worship from gods. The gods vanish. It's as
simple as that. The gods we worship are the gods we create. We
cannot worship the gods who create us. This I learned or was
told, at least, a long time ago.) So Vishnu steps down and says,
"Narada, all right. I'll tell you what *maya* is. Please worship
me."

So they walk together, not a word from Vishnu. (What can
he say? You cannot explain *maya*; it's an experience. It cannot
be communicated. It can only be felt.) So they walk together
and finally Vishnu slumps down under a tree at the edge of a
desert. And he looks up at Narada and says, "Narada, you
know I would like to tell you what *maya* is, but my throat is
parched and I need some water. Can you get me some water?
Here's the *lota*." So he produces the brass vessel and gives it to
Narada. (Now I warn you in advance that this parable has the
haunting black lucidity of a Ingmar Bergman film. Some of you
may see the lucidity and some may just see the blackness but
you won't forget the haunting.) And Narada says, "Where do I
get the water? This is a desert here." And Vishnu points to a spot
in the desert and says, "Look out there. There's an oasis." Sure
enough it is. (Don't get me wrong. It's not a mirage. It's the real
thing.) And Vishnu says, "How long do you think it will take?"
And Narada says, "That's not very far, about fifteen minutes.
I'll be back in half an hour for you. Will you be waiting here?"
"Yes." "You will tell me what *maya* is if I get you the water?"

"Yes." "You promise this, a divine promise?" "It's a divine promise." "It's a deal."

Narada sets out. Blazing heat, incandescent heat, Indian summer — I mean, *my* Indian summer. Sure enough, in about fifteen minutes he reaches the oasis. There's a hut. He shouts, "Is anyone there?" The door opens, and believe it or not he looks into the eyes of a beautiful girl. They are the eyes of Vishnu, haunting, mischievous, smiling, and enigmatic. (Not Mona Lisa eyes. I must make this distinction. The Mona Lisa smile has been described as the smile of a slightly constipated lady. This is merely the smile of Vishnu. This is the Buddha smile, the smile of serenity, the smile that cannot be compared, that has no opposites.) He says, "This is very strange. I thought I left Vishnu at the edge of the desert. How is it that Vishnu is here? It doesn't matter. There is a more important thing." He produces the *lota* and gives it to her and says, "This is very important. Life, death, right, wrong, good, evil, black, white, day, night, illusion, reality — everything depends on this. I will know at last what *maya* is. Can you get me some water?" "Sure," she says, "plenty of water here. Come in and sit down." He goes in, he sits down, she takes the *lota*, and she goes into an inner room. (Beware of Indian girls that go inside. Anyone who's been to India knows that she will never come out.) He's a stranger and it would be slightly awkward for an orthodox girl to appear before a stranger. So she doesn't come out.

Instead her parents come and they have a brass platter with food on it and a glass of water but no *lota*. They give him the platter and say, "Please, eat." And he says, "But do you know who I am? I am Narada. I live in Vishnu's heaven. I drink ambrosia, the nectar of immortality." (Incidentally, the word *ambrosia* comes from a Sanskrit word meaning immortality which the Greeks took up). "I drink nectar, the drink of the gods. I don't want this food. I haven't come here to be entertained. I've come here to get that *lota* of water. Where is your daughter?" And they look at him. "Eat." He cannot refuse Indian hospitality. "All right," he says. "I'll eat." And he takes that brass platter and he eats.

And he's so tired by this walk through the incandescent heat that he dozes off. He goes off to sleep. When he wakes up the next morning, at the back of his mind there's a voice saying, "I came here for a *lota* of water. I'm late. I'd better get back." There is another voice now cutting through that first voice and the second voice says, "That girl you saw has lovely eyes, hasn't she? You've never seen such eyes." (Now, we know what happens to young people when they speak like that. They get married.)

Sure enough, one week later he goes to her parents and asks for her hand in marriage. And sure enough, her parents agree to it. That's exactly what they've been waiting for. Now we know why parents are hanging around. (There's no real reason for parents to hang around, believe me.) At the back of his mind there's a voice saying, "But—" "All right," he says. "Later." One year passes. A son is born to them. (Isn't it strange how these things happen?) The voice grows fainter and fainter night after night. Two years pass and a daughter is born to them. Five years pass and his in-laws die. Isn't that strange? Now we know why the in-laws are hanging around. To die, of course. They leave property behind. And now we know why property is hanging around. To be left behind. So this man who came for a *lota* of water is now a big man in a small village. He has a lot to lose. He has property, he has crops, he has a wife, he has two children. He's a little lord in that village, and in the twelfth year (there's always a twelfth year. Don't ask me why. Andre Malraux says when he was told the story in Benares it was the twelfth year) the floods came. Now, you may well ask where the floods come from in that desert. I don't know. (I have no idea where floods come from. They come like the bombers of Hiroshima and Nagasaki. One fine day, on a sunny day, 80,000 people disappear because a bomb falls in Hiroshima. On another day in Nagasaki, another 80,000 people disappear. Floods come. They come to Provo. They come everywhere, the floods.)

And when the floods come, his hut is swept away, his field is swept away, his wife is swept away. When he goes to save her in the swirling waters, his children are swept away. He goes to save them and she is gone. And he blacks out, loses consciousness. When he wakes up, he is lying flat on the ground, his head cradled in the lap of Vishnu under the tree at the edge of the desert. Vishnu, looking down from Nirvana, says, "Narada, do you know what *maya* is now?" And Narada says, "Vishnu, don't tell me what I think you're going to tell me. Don't tell me that all that happened to me didn't happen. It happened." And Vishnu smiles that same slightly mischievous, slightly wise, serene, haunting smile and tells him, "But Narada, you wanted to know what *maya* was, didn't you? Do you know now or do you still have to learn?"

And then Narada realizes in a flash that it is this world in which people die, in which famines take place, in which non-violent people are shot down week after week. Then he knows that *maya* is this desert of a world into which we've come to get a *lota* of water for Vishnu who is waiting at the edge of the desert. And instead of getting that *lota* of water of Vishnu, young boys have been looking into the eyes of young girls, and young girls have been looking into the eyes of young boys, and somewhere along the line they got sidetracked.

That was the parable I was told to explain the famine and the nonviolence of India. Does it make sense? I don't know. But it made sense to me at the time. It helped.

And then we grow older. There's only one more parable that I will say. (There's not much one knows. There's so little one knows.) I grew older, and in 1947 we got freedom. I was eighteen years old and we were free. And there were problems after freedom. I had to get a job. I went to the other person who came without a tie, the son of the president of the large steel corporation. The old school tie didn't work. And then I wondered. The Jesuits taught us parables. The parable of the talents was constantly repeated (see Matt. 25:14-30). There was a servant that had five talents; and when his master went away, he doubled them and made them ten. The master came back and said, "You had five and you made them ten. Sit on my right hand." And there was another servant who had two and made them four and the master said, "Sit on my right hand." And there was a servant who had one and kept it one because he was afraid that he might lose it. And when the master came back, he was cast

out into the outer darkness where there was weeping and gnash-
ing of teeth.

It always puzzled me. What kind of a world was this again?
It didn't make sense to begin with, why one man should have
five talents. Why couldn't all have five talents to begin with? It
was not a question to which I got an answer. We were told,
"That's the way the parable is. You accept it like that." And so
in the Indian context I tried to understand it. And I thought,
yes, maybe that's their *karma*. One deserved five, another deserved two, another deserved one. You just double it — it
doesn't matter whether you make ten or four or one. You just
make it two — double it, double it, whatever you have. But I
didn't even have one. I was looking for one. There was no one
to give it to me. How does one reconcile injustice with freedom?
We had become free, and there was injustice all around. What
was the purpose of life? If we could change the sorry scheme of
things entire, would we not shatter it to bits and remold it
nearer to our heart's desire?[4]

So there was another parable I had been told to explain this
problem that faced us all the time, and this was a parable of the
wish-fulfilling tree. That is magnificent. In fact, I will have to
end with that because I'll have nothing more to say.

An uncle goes to the city and he comes back to his village
where his nephews and nieces are playing with toys and sticks
and stones and pieces of string — simple, trivial, ordinary things
— and he tells them, "Look, you fools, this is no way to play.
Don't you know that there's a wish-fulfilling tree right outside
your cottage? All you have to do is go to the tree and stand
there under the tree and start wishing and the tree will give you
exactly what you want. All you have to do is go there and ask
for it."

And these children are very smart like all kids nowadays and
know that's not true because, after all, you don't get what you
want. You have to work very hard to get what you want. And
even if you work hard, someone else is working harder and he
gets it first. And besides, some others have connections. They
really get it first. So they don't believe him and he goes away.

As soon as he goes away, guess what they do? They rush to the tree and start wishing. (This is a tree whose roots are in the sky and whose fruits are in earth. It's the tree in the *Bhagavad Gita,* chapter 15.) And they start wishing. And of course we know what kids wish for: sweets, candy. And you know what kids get — stomachaches. (What did you think they would get?) The trouble is that the tree will give you exactly what you want and with it, its opposite. Guaranteed. Nothing in this world comes single; everything comes with its built-in opposite. (Don't ask me why; I didn't make the world. I'm just suffering as much as anyone else, believe me.)

And so what else do they want? They want toys. And what do they get? Boredom. And they want bigger toys. They get bigger boredom. Bigger and better toys. Bigger and better boredom. Mattel toys. Swell boredom. There's no getting out of that. The tree will give you exactly what you want, guaranteed, with its built-in opposite. Don't forget that. That's part of the game.

So the kids grow older. They're suffering and they don't know what's happening. Now they're called what I was in 1947 — a young adult. (How nice. Fancy phrases. Overgrown kids.) They stand under the tree. (There's nowhere else to stand. That's where we all are. Where will you go? The tree is everywhere.) And now, of course, they don't want kid stuff, not toys and sweets. They want other things — the four fruits that hang from the tree: sex, fame, money, and power. These are the four fruits; there's nothing else available. Nothing else. (If there is, please let me know, because as a Hindu that's what I was told.) All you have to do is reach out, grab them, and you've got them. Reach out, grab it, you've got it — and you've had it — because the tree will give you the opposite too. Guaranteed. The tragedy of life is not that you don't get what you want. The tragedy of life is that you get exactly what you want — and with it, its opposite. You dream it, you wish it, you think it, you do it, you grab it, you've got it — and you've had it — because the tree will give you the opposite too. Guaranteed. That's the real tragedy of life—that you discover too late the curse of getting exactly what you want. You dream it, you wish it, you think it, you do it, you grab it, you've got it — and you've had it. There's no getting out of this. And here I was, looking for a job, and I was being told this parable. So the kids suffer and they agonize. They don't know why they agonize.

Now they grow old. That's all you can do under the tree. Now there's another fancy name for them. Senior citizens. They're under the tree waiting to be carried to the funeral pyre where they'll be burned to the proper Hindu crisp. And now they are terribly worried. There's not much time left. They huddle in groups and one group says, "Oh, it's a hell of a world." Fools, they've learned nothing from life. And there's a second group which says, "You know, we have the answer. We made the wrong wishes. This time we'll go and make the right wish." Bigger fools. They've learned nothing at all. And there's a third group which huddles and says, "If that's the way the world is, I want to die. What's the use living?" "All right," says the tree. "You want to die? Take it." And with death comes its opposite, rebirth. Oh my goodness, there's no escape. Or is there?

Yes, there is, because the parable doesn't end here. Parables don't end like that. There's the drop of honey and the *lota* of water. And there is a lame boy, a cripple, who also ran to the tree with his companions, but he was pushed aside. He fell down and he couldn't get up easily; so when he got up, he found his friends under the tree wishing away. He crawled back into the hut and he waited. He said, "I'll wait. There'll be some time under the tree when it will be vacant. I'll go then and make my wish." (Now I don't know what cripples want. Whatever they want is what he would wish for.) So he waited, looking out of the window. He saw his companions under the tree. Young children asking for sweets and getting stomachaches and suffering. He saw them asking for toys and getting boredom and suffering. He saw them as young adults grabbing sex, fame, money, and power. He saw them suffering, he saw them getting the opposite, he saw them agonizing and not knowing why they were agonizing, and he saw them dividing into three groups, one group saying, "It's a hell of a world," another group saying,

"We made the wrong wishes," and a third group saying, "I want to die," but getting reborn. And in one dazzling, illuminating spectacle he saw this whole thing and stood there, marveling at the spectacle of the universe — these are the words now, very carefully used when the story is told again and again by village storytellers, by mothers, by others, whoever tells it, "marveling at the spectacle of the universe" — at the cosmic swindle of life, at the divine comedy (well, tragi-comedy). There was a gush of compassion in his heart for his companions under the tree. And in that gush of compassion, he forgot to wish. He forgot to wish *and the tree couldn't touch him.* He was free. (And it wasn't the British who gave us that freedom. That was a freedom I learned from my mother.) The tree couldn't touch him.

He had not done the good act, which is very easy to do: you must make up your mind to be good, and what you'll get is heaven, and heaven is a punishment for good deeds because the Hindu heaven is temporary and you're born again. He had not done the bad act, which is also very easy to do: just be selfish all the time, and you'll get hell and then you're born again — it's a temporary hell. He had not done the absurd act. (We don't even think of it; we leave it to the French. They are very expert in that kind of thing. The Hindu mind is not so subtle.) He had done what is known as the pure act. The act — well, I won't define it. That act cuts through *karma,* cuts through *maya,* cuts through the tree at the root, and gets what? If freedom could be had by just punching a few buttons — if you knew the coordinates of freedom — would it be freedom anymore? He's free, let's put it that way.

And of course, the question always is, "But how is it possible? What kind of thing is this pure act that you talk about, this nonwishing gush-of-compassion act?" And inevitably the storyteller says, "Don't ask me. Ask any mother why she puts the baby on the dry side of the bed at night and puts herself on the wet side, joyfully. Is it because she wants the baby to look after her twenty years later? Could be a very calculated act. Is it because it's instinctive? Could be. Let's ask a psychologist. Is it because she's irrational? Could be. Is it because she gets a Freudian kick out of it? Could be. Ask *her* and she'll say,

'Would you mind not wasting my time? You go to college and find out. Meanwhile, let me look after the baby, please.' She just does it. And the others try to find out what's going on."

That's one way the storyteller explains it. The other explanation he gives is to ask the people, "Does any one of you have a rupee note?" (A rupee note is hardly ten cents.) Everyone has it and they produce it. He says, "Now you can do four things with it. One, you give it to charity, you do good to someone, you put your name to it — you do for yourself, too — you'll get heaven. Serves you right — you'll be born again. You can take the rupee note and spend it all on yourself, act as if you live in a vacuum and no one else exists in the world, you'll get hell. Serves you right — you'll be born again, and given another chance to do better. You can do the absurd act. (The French have found that out.) You can take the rupee note, tear it into little bits, and put it into the trash can. It's your life; you're free any time to take it. Or you can do the pure act, too. You can take the rupee note and give it in charity and, like the mother who puts the baby on the dry side of the bed and puts herself on the wet side at night joyfully, like the boy who stood there marveling at the cosmic spectacle of the universe, you, in a gush of compassion, give it; and though you want to add your name to it, you, in that gush of compassion, forget to add your name to it and by doing so you have done the pure act.

Ah, but don't *remember* to forget or the tree will get you.

And that's all the literature of belief that I know.

NOTES

1. Translated by Amiya Chakravarty as "The first day's sun" in *Visva-Bharati*, Calcutta, 1942, revised in *A Tagore Reader* (New York: MacMillan, 1961), p. 374: "The first day's sun/ asked/ at the new manifestation of being—/ Who are you?/ No answer came./ Year after year went by,/ the last sun of the day / the last question utters/ on the western sea-shore, / in the silent evening — / Who are you? / He gets no answer."

2. See Robert Browning, *Pippa Passes,* pt. I: "God's in his heaven—/ All's right with the world"; and William Shakespeare, *Hamlet* 1.5.187-88: "The time is out of joint; O cursed spite, / That ever I was born to set it right!"

3. See trans. Terence Kilmartin (New York: Holt, Rinehart and Winston), pp. 181-82.

4. Edward Fitzgerald, trans., *The Rubaiyat of Omar Khayyam* (1859; reprint ed., New York: Random House, 1947), p. 48. Poem 73: "Ah Love!/ Could thou and I with Fate conspire/ To grasp this sorry Scheme of Things entire,/ Would we not shatter it to bits—and then/ Re-mould it nearer to the Heart's Desire!"

6

Joseph Campbell

Masks of Oriental Gods: Symbolism of Kundalini Yoga

Professor emeritus of literature at Sarah Lawrence College in New York, Joseph Campbell enjoys a worldwide reputation as an authority in the field of comparative mythology. He has written and edited some twenty-five books on comparative religions and mythology including his influential interpretation of the hero myth, The Hero with a Thousand Faces, *and his important four-volume study of world myths,* The Masks of God. *He is currently writing and compiling a two-volume historical atlas of world mythology.*

In 1974, Professor Campbell published The Mythic Image, *a lavishly illustrated presentation of some major visual motifs in comparative mythologies. His paper on Kundalini yoga is taken from this work. Because Professor Campbell's presentation at the symposium was a slide-lecture, and hence difficult to reproduce, the Religious Studies Center secured permission from Princeton University Press to reproduce the relevant portions of*

*The Mythic Image, along with a few of its superb illustrations.
This book was the hundredth and final title in the Bollingen
Foundation's "Bollingen" series, a landmark publishing effort
with which Professor Campbell has been associated since its
inception.*

*In his keynote presentation at the symposium, Professor
Campbell laid some essential groundwork by wryly defining
mythology as "other people's religion" and then by giving a
working definition of yoga as "the intentional stopping of the
spontaneous activity of the mindstuff." On this foundation he
built a literate and visually attractive edifice which he invented
his audience to enter. What he structured was a comprehensive
and captivating introduction into one of the most ancient of
spiritual disciplines — Kundalini yoga.*

Our subject, the literature of belief, is of profound historical
importance, since in its various forms it has played the decisive
role in both the harmonization and the discord of religions. A
distinction is to be made in the first place between belief in the
literal nature of a revelation and in the experience of its symbolic reference. One of the great problems in dealing with religious imagery — in dealing with poetic imagery even — is to go
past and through the historically conditioned image to its transcendental reference without losing the image and without losing appreciation for its historically conditioned special quality
and sense.

I have a favorite definition of mythology: mythology is
other people's religion. We have a way of saying, "You worship
God in your way, I worship God in his." And my favorite definition of religion is: misunderstood mythology. The misunder-
standing consists typically in interpreting spiritual symbols as
though they referred finally to historical events and characters.
The historical character or event is but the vehicle of a spiritual
message, and if you stay with the event, you lose the message.

Anything that can be named, anything that can be envisioned, is but a reference to what is absolutely transcendent, and that which absolutely transcends all reference, all naming, and imaging, is the essence not only of the universal mystery but also of your own being; so that that which transcends all is immanent within all and is not really named in any naming.

One of the very great systems for interpreting the stages in amplification of our understanding and experience of the reference of these signs and symbols is the Indian system that I am to talk about today, the Kundalini yoga. I do not practice yoga myself. I am a scholar; therefore I can talk about it. The great Indian saint of the last century, Ramakrishna, in Calcutta, was a virtuoso in the experience of the Kundalini transformations. When his disciples would ask him, "Oh Master, how is it when the Kundalini energy is of the first center? the second center? the third center? the fourth center?" he would tell them. But when he went above the fourth, he passed out. My advantage in being a scholar is that I am not going to pass out and shall take you right up the line of the Kundalini centers.

It is my belief that this concept of the Kundalini yoga is India's greatest gift to us. I find it useful in relationship to symbolic and religious understanding and studies everywhere and anywhere; it relates to all the mythologies of the world. India's long season of inward turning and experience has given a kind of power of interpretation to the Indian religious traditions that is unmatched anywhere else.

Now yoga is defined in the standard textbook of yoga, *The Yoga Sutras of Patanjali,* in the following way: "Yoga is the intentional stopping of the spontaneous activity of the mind-stuff." The notion is that there is within the gray matter—the physical matter or gross substance of the brain—a subtle substance that changes form very rapidly. This subtle matter takes the form of what is seen, heard, or felt, and so on. That is how what is outside is translated into an inside experience. Look around very fast and you will see how quickly this subtle matter changes form. The problem is that it never stops changing. It continues to move. Try to hold in your mind for a couple of seconds one idea or one image—of someone you love, let us say. You will find within a few seconds, if you are honest with yourself, that you are having associated thoughts and have not become fixed on a still point.

The first function, then, the first goal and the ultimate goal of yoga is to make the mind stand still. Now you may ask yourself, "Why should we want to make the mind stand still?" The answer is given in the way of an analogy. The analogy is of the mind as the surface of a pond that is rippled by a wind. All the images on that pond are changing form. They are flashing, they are coming, they are going, and they are broken. We identify ourselves with one of those flashing images on the surface of our pond, namely, the image that we call ourselves. It comes, it goes. You are born, you die. "Oh my, here I come, there I go!" Make the pond stand still. Turn to the first verse in the book of Genesis which records that the spirit (the wind) of God was brooding or blowing over the waters. That is the wind that brings on the creation of the world. If you can make the wind stand still, the pond then becomes a perfect mirror. In it is then seen one fixed image, the image of images, the image that was broken and changing all over the place. Also the waters have cleared and you can see down to the bottom, into the inwardness of your own being. That is the image that is ultimately you, not the you that was born, not the you that will die, not the you that your friends all love and that you take such nice care of. This familiar you is but the you in the flashing reflection of the mind. The ultimate you is one with all the other passing images, because we are all broken images of that which is seen when the mind stands still. These are now understood to be simply flashing, momentary references to that one, which is finally no image.

Some become so entranced in the still-standing mind that they stay there; and then, as they say in India, the body drops off. But that is only half the story. The other half is to come back, to open your eyes. Let the wind blow and see and recognize and take joy in the ever-changing forms.

And that is the wonderful ambiguity that is involved in the literature of belief — not to lose the joy of participation and appreciation for the image that is your own image, your own religion's way of imaging this universal model, while at the same time pointing past it. What you will find is that you will not lose your religion in that context; it receives a new dimension of power and wonder. One can then remain in the world with the wisdom of the absolute and yet with joyful participation in the sorrows of the world. All life is sorrowful. Learn how to participate in this sorrow with joy.

And so now we come to the specifics of the Kundalini.*

It was during the centuries of the burgeoning of the various pagan, Jewish, and Christian Gnostic sects of Rome's Near Eastern provinces (the first four centuries of the Christian Era) that in Hindu and Buddhist India the first signs of what is known as Tantric practice appeared. The backgrounds of both movements, the Gnostic and the Tantric, are obscure, as are their connections with each other. Rome at the time was in direct commerce with India. Buddhist monks were teaching in Alexandria, Christian missionaries in Kerala. The halo (a Persian, Zoroastrian motif) had appeared abruptly in the Christian art of the time as well as in the Buddhist art of India and China; and in contemporary writings evidences abound of what must have been a very lively two-way traffic.

The elder Pliny (A.D. 23-79) wrote, for example:

> In no year does India drain us of less than 550,000,000 sesterces, giving back her own wares, which are sold among us at fully 100 times their first cost. . . . Our ladies glory in having pearls suspended from their fingers, or two or three of them dangling from their ears, delighted even with the rattling of the pearls as they knock against each other; and now, at the present day, even the poorer classes are affecting them, since people are in the habit of saying that "a pearl worn by a woman in public is as good as a lictor walking before her." Nay, even more than this, they put them on their feet, and that not only on the laces of their sandals but all over the shoes; it is not enough to wear pearls, but they must

---

*From this point, the material is reprinted from Joseph Campbell, *The Mythic Image*, Bollingen Series C. Copyright © 1974 by Princeton University Press, Chapter 4, part 5, "The Lotus Ladder" and figures 306, 312-314, and 332-334, reprinted by permission. The notes have been renumbered for this reprint.

tread upon them, and walk with them under foot as well."[1]

Mircea Eliade, in his masterful *Yoga: Immortality and Freedom*, has suggested something of the obscurity and complexity of the problem of the origins and development of Tantric thought:

> It is not easy to define tantrism. Among the many meanings of the word *tantra* (root *tan*, "extend," "continue," "multiply"), one concerns us particularly — that of "succession," "unfolding," "continuous process." *Tantra* would be "what extends knowledge" (*tanyate, vistaryate, jnanam anena iti tantram*). In this acceptation, the term was already applied to certain philosophical systems (*Nyaya-tantresu*, etc.). We do not know why and under what circumstances it came to designate a great philosophical and religious movement, which, appearing as early as the fourth century of our era, assumed the form of a pan-Indian vogue from the sixth century onward. For it was really a vogue; quite suddenly, tantrism becomes immensely popular, not only among the active practitioners of the religious life (ascetics, yogins, etc.), and its prestige also reaches the "popular" strata. In a comparatively short time, Indian philosophy, mysticism, ritual, ethics, iconography, and even literature are influenced by tantrism. It is a pan-Indian movement, for it is assimilated by all the great Indian religions and by all the "sectarian" schools. There is a Buddhist tantrism and a Hindu tantrism, both of considerable proportions. But Jainism too accepts certain tantric methods (never those of the "left hand"), and strong tantric influences can be seen in Kashmirian Shivaism, in the great Pancaratra movement (c. 550), in the *Bhagavata Purana* (c. 600), and in other Vishnuist devotional trends.[2]

It would be ridiculous to pretend that in a few pages, or even a considerable tome, anything more than a suggestion of the jewel tree — or rather, jewel jungle — of this truly astounding body of psychologized physiological and mythological lore might be offered. Even a glimpse will suffice to make the point, however, that there is evidence in this body of material of a highly developed *psychological* science: one, moreover, that has shaped and informed every significant development of Oriental doctrine — whether in India, Tibet, China, Korea, Japan, or Southeast Asia — from the first centuries of the Christian Era. And since there is evidence, furthermore, already in the earliest Upanishads — the *Brihadaranyaka* and *Chhandogya* — that something like an elementary foreview of the Tantric movement had been known to India long before the general vogue, we shall have to take into account the possibility that its sudden popularity, to which Professor Eliade alludes, represents not so much a novelty as a resurgence in freshly stated terms of principles long familiar to the pre-Aryan — or even, possibly, pre-Dravidian — populations of the timeless East.[3]

The essential alphabet of all Tantric lore is to be learned from the doctrine of the seven "circles" (*chakras*) or "lotuses" (*padmas*) of the *kundalini* system of yoga. (See fig. 306.) The long terminal *i* added to the Sanskrit adjective *kundalin*, meaning "circular, spiral, coiling, winding," makes a feminine noun signifying "snake," the reference in the present context being to the figure of a coiled female serpent — a serpent goddess not of "gross" but of "subtle" substance — which is to be thought of as residing in a torpid, slumbering state in a subtle center, the first of the seven, near the base of the spine: the aim of the yoga then being to rouse this serpent, lift her head, and bring her up a subtle nerve or channel of the spine to the so-called "thousand-petalled lotus" (*sahasrara*) at the crown of the head. This axial stem or channel, which is named *sushumna* ("rich in happiness, highly blessed"), is flanked and crossed by two others: a white, known as *ida* (meaning "refreshment, libation; stream or flow of praise and worship"), winding upward from the left testicle to right nostril and associated with the cool, ambrosial, "lunar" energies of the psyche; and a red, called *pingala* ("of a sunlike, tawny hue"), extending from the right testicle to left nostril, whose energy is "solar, fiery," and, like the solar heat of the tropics, desiccating and destructive.[4] The first task of the yogi is to bring the energies of these contrary powers together at the base of his sushumna and then to carry them up the central stem, along with the uncoiling serpent queen. She, rising from the lowest to the highest lotus center, will pass through and

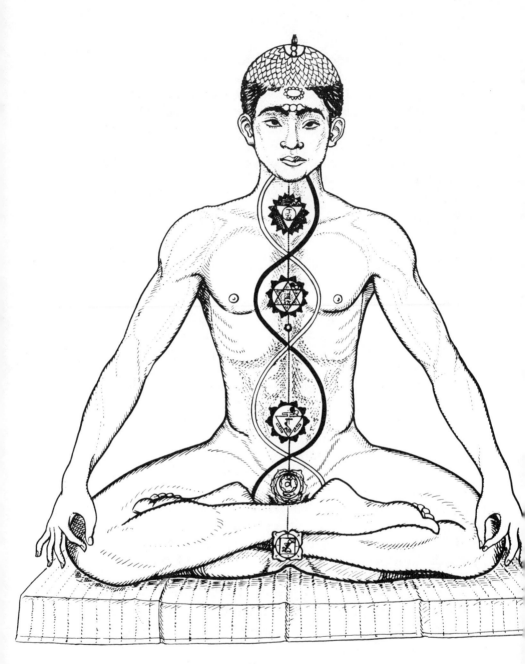

Figure 306. Seven Lotus Centers of the Kundalinī

wake the five between, and with each waking the psychology and personality of the practitioner will be altogether and fundamentally transformed.

Now there was in the last century a great Indian saint, Ramakrishna (1836-1886), who in the practices of this yoga was a veritable virtuoso. "There are," he once told his devotees, "five kinds of samadhi"; five kinds, that is to say, of spiritual rapture.

> In these samadhis one feels the sensation of the Spiritual Current to be like the movement of an ant, a fish, a monkey, a bird, or a serpent.
>
> Sometimes the Spiritual Current rises through the spine, crawling like an ant. Sometimes, in samadhi, the soul swims joyfully in the ocean of divine ecstasy, like a fish. Sometimes, when I lie down on my side, I feel the Spiritual Current pushing me like a monkey and playing with me joyfully. I remain still. That Current, like a monkey, suddenly with one jump reaches the Sahasrara. That is why you see me jump up with a start. Sometimes, again, the Spiritual Current rises like a bird hopping from one branch to another. The place where it rests feels like fire. . . . Sometimes the Spiritual Current moves up like a snake. Going in a zigzag way, at last it reaches the head and I go into samadhi. A man's spiritual consciousness is not awakened unless his Kundalini is aroused.

He goes on to describe a certain experience:

> Just before my attaining this state of mind, it had been revealed to me how the Kundalini is aroused, how the lotuses of the different centers blossom forth, and how all this culminates in samadhi. This is a very secret experience. I saw a boy twenty-two or twenty-three years old, exactly resembling me, enter the Sushumna nerve and commune with the lotuses, touching them with his tongue. He began with the first center at the anus, and passed through the centers at the sexual organ, navel, and so on. The different lotuses of those centers—four-petalled, six-petalled, ten-petalled, and so forth—had been drooping. At his touch they stood erect.
>
> When he reached the heart—I distinctly remember it —and communed with the lotus there, touching it with

his tongue, the twelve-petalled lotus, which was hanging head down, stood erect and opened its petals. Then he came to the sixteen-petalled lotus in the throat and the two-petalled lotus in the forehead. And last of all, the thousand-petalled lotus in the head blossomed. Since then I have been in this state.[5]

The earliest serious studies in English of the principles of Tantra appeared during the first quarter of this century in the publications of Sir John Woodroffe (1865-1936), Supreme Court Judge at Calcutta, three of whose imposing volumes are indispensable to any Western reader seeking more than a passing knowledge of this learning: *Principles of Tantra* (Madras, 1914), *Shakti and Shakta* (Madras, 1928), and *The Serpent Power* (Madras, 3rd rev. edn. 1931). Add to these the more recent work by Dr. Shashibhusan Dasgupta, *Obscure Religious Cults as Background of Bengali Literature* (Calcutta, 1946), and the compendious handbook of Professor Eliade, already mentioned, and the patient student will be enabled to open to himself many hidden approaches to the interpretation of symbols and their relevance to his own interior life.

At the outset, however, two warnings are generally given: first, not to attempt to engage alone in the indicated exercises, since they activate unconscious centers, and improperly undertaken may lead to a psychosis; and second, not to overinterpret whatever signs of early success one may enjoy in the course of practice. Sir John Woodroffe explains:

> There is one simple test whether the Shakti is actually aroused. When she is aroused intense heat is felt at that spot, but when she leaves a particular center the part so left becomes as cold and apparently lifeless as a corpse. The progress upwards may thus be externally verified by others. When the Shakti (Power) has reached the upper brain (Sahasrara) the whole body is cold and corpse-like; except the top of the skull, where some warmth is felt, this being the place where the static and kinetic aspects of Consciousness unite.[6]

And so, to begin, then, at the beginning:

One is to sit in a posture of perfectly balanced repose, and in this so-called "lotus posture" to begin regulating the breath. The psychological theory underlying this primary exercise is that the mind or "mind power" (*manas*) and breathing or "breath power" (*prana*) interlock and are in fact the same. When one becomes angry, the breathing changes; also, when one is moved with erotic desire. In repose, it steadies down. Accordingly, control of the breath controls feeling and emotion, and can be made to serve as a mind-regulating factor. That is why in all serious Oriental mind-transforming enterprises the fundamental discipline is *pranayama*, "control of the breath." Steadying the breath one correspondingly steadies the mind, and the resultant aeration of the blood, furthermore, sets going in the body certain chemical processes that produce predictable effects.

Now this breathing will seem a little strange. One is to inhale through the right nostril, imagining the air as pouring down the white or "lunar" spinal course, ida, cleaning it out, as it were. One is to hold the breath a certain number of counts and to breathe out, then, with the air coming up through pingala, the tawny "solar" nerve. Next: in through the left, and after a hold, out through the right; and so on, strictly according to counts, the mind in this way being steadied down, the whole nervous system clarified; until presently, one fine day, the serpent goddess will be felt to stir.

I have been told that certain yogis, on becoming aware of this movement, press their hands to the ground and, elevating themselves a little from their lotus seats, bang down, to give the coiled-up one a physical jolt to rouse her. The waking and elevation are described in the texts in terms altogether physical. The references are to that "subtle" physical matter already mentioned, however, not the gross matter to which the observations of our scientists are directed. As Alain Danièlou has remarked in his compact little volume, *Yoga: The Method of Reintegration:* "The Hindu will therefore speak indifferently of men or of subtle beings, he intermingles the geography of celestial worlds with that of terrestrial continents, and in this he sees no discontinuity but, on the contrary, a perfect coherence; for, to him, these worlds meet at many common points, and the passage from one to the other is easy for those who have the key."[7] Much the same could be said of almost any of the mythologically structured, protoscientific traditions of the ancient past.

So now we have got the serpent started: let us follow her up the spinal staff, which in this yoga is regarded as the microcosmic counterpart of the macrocosmic universal axis, its lotus stages being thus equivalent to the platforms of the many-storied ziggurats, and its summit to the lofty marriage chamber of the lunar and solar lights.

The lotus at the base of the sushumna, called the "Root Support" (Muladhara), is described as crimson in hue and having four petals, on each of which a Sanskrit syllable is inscribed (reading clockwise, from the upper right: *vam, sam, sham,* and *sam*). (See fig. 312.) These are to be understood as sound-counterparts of the aspects of spiritual energy operative on this plane. In the white center is a yellow square symbolic of the element earth, wherein a white elephant stands waving seven trunks. This animal is Airavata, the mythic vehicle of Indra, the Vedic king of the gods, here supporting on its back the sign of the syllable *lam,* "which," Woodroffe writes, "is said to be the expression in gross sound of the subtle sound made by the vibration of forces of this center."[8] The elephant, he continues, is symbolic of the strength, firmness, and solidity of earth; but it is also a cloud condemned to walk upon the earth, so that if it could be released from this condition it would rise. The supervising deity made visible in this lowest center is the world-creator Brahma, whose shakti, the goddess Savitri, is a personification of solar light. On the elephant's back is a downward-pointing triangle symbolic of the womb (*yoni*) of the goddess-mother of the universe, and within this "city of three sides," this "figure of desire," is seen the first or basal divine phallus (*lingam*) of the universal masculine principle, Shiva. The white serpent-goddess Kundalini, "fine as the fiber of a lotus-stalk," is coiled three and a half times around this lingam, asleep, and covering with her head its Brahma-door.[9]

Now to be exact, the precise locus of this center at the base of the human body is midway between the anus and the genitals, and the character of the spiritual energy at that point is of the lowest intensity. The world view is of uninspired materialism, governed by "hard facts"; the art, sentimental naturalism; and the psychology, adequately described in behavioristic terms, is reactive, not active. There is on this plane no zeal for life, no explicit impulse to expand. There is simply a lethargic avidity in hanging on to existence; and it is this grim grip that must finally be broken, so that the spirit may be quit of its dull zeal simply to be.

One may think of the Kundalini on this level as comparable to a dragon; for dragons, we are told by those who know, have a propensity to hoard and guard things; and their favorite things to hoard and guard are jewels and beautiful young girls. They are unable to make use of either, but just hang on, and so the values in their treasury are unrealized, lost to themselves and to the world. On this level, the serpent-queen Kundalini is held captive by her own dragon-lethargy. She neither knows nor can communicate to the life that she controls any joy; yet will not relax her hold and let go. Her key motto is a stubborn "Here I am, and here I stay."

The first task of the yogi, then, must be to break at this level the cold dragon grip of his own spiritual lethargy and release the jewel-maid, his own shakti, for ascent to those higher spheres where she will become his spiritual teacher and guide to the bliss of an immortal life beyond sleep.

The second lotus of the series, called Svadhisthana, "Her Special Abode," is at the level of the genitals. (See fig. 313.) It is a vermilion lotus of six petals, bearing the syllables *bam, bham, mam, yam, ram,* and *lam.* Water being the element of this center, its inner field is the shape of a crescent moon, within which a mythological water monster known as a *makara* is to be seen, supporting the sign of the water syllable *vam.* This is the seed sound of the Vedic god Varuna, lord of the rhythmic order of the universe. The presiding Hindu (as distinct from early Vedic) deity here is Vishnu in the pride of early youth, clothed

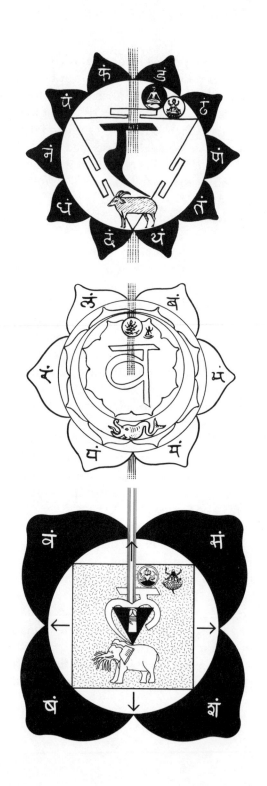

Figures 312, 313, 314. Chakra 1: Muladhara (bottom); Chakra 2: Svadisthana (center); Chakra 3: Manipura (top).

in yellow and holding a noose in his hand. Beside him sits a wrathful form of his shakti, Rakini by name, of the color of a blue lotus, bearing in her four hands a lotus, a drum, a sharp battle-ax, and a spear, her teeth showing fiercely, her three eyes blazing red, and her mind exalted from the drinking of ambrosia.[10]

When the Kundalini is active at this level, the whole aim of life is in sex. Not only is every thought and act sexually motivated, either as a means toward sexual ends or as a compensating sublimation of frustrated sexual zeal, but everything seen and heard is interpreted compulsively, both consciously and unconsciously, as symbolic of sexual themes. Psychic energy, that is to say, has the character here of the Freudian libido. Myths, deities, and religious rites are understood and experienced in sexual terms.

Now of course there are in fact a great many myths and rites directly addressed to the concerns of this important center of life — fertility rites, marriage rites, orgiastic festivals, and so on — and a Freudian approach to the reading and explanation of these may not be altogether inappropriate. However, according to Tantric learning, even though the obsession of the life-energies functioning from this psychological center is sexual, sexuality is not the primal ground, end, or even sole motivation of life. Any fixation at this level is consequently pathological. Everything then reminds the blocked and tortured victim of sex. But if it also reminds his doctor of sex, what is the likelihood of a cure? The method of the Kundalini is rather to recognize affirmatively the force and importance of this center and let the energies pass on *through* it, to become naturally transformed to other aims at the higher centers of the "rich in happiness" sushumna.

Chakra three, at the level of the navel, is called Manipura, "City of the Shining Jewel," for its fiery heat and light. (See fig. 314.) Here the energy turns to violence and its aim is to consume, to master, to turn the world into oneself and one's own. The appropriate Occidental psychology would be the Adlerian of the "will to power"; for now even sex becomes an occasion, not of erotic experience, but of achievement, conquest, self-reassurance, and frequently, also, revenge. The lotus has ten petals, dark as thunderheads heavy laden, bearing the seed syllables *dam, dham, nam, tam, tham, dam, dham, nam, pam,* and *pham*. Its central triangle, in a white field, is the sign of the element fire, shining like the rising sun, with swastika marks on its sides. The ram, its symbolic animal, is the vehicle of Agni, Vedic god of the sacrificial fire, bearing on its back the syllable *ram*, which is the seed syllable or sound form of this god and his fiery element. The presiding Hindu (as distinct from Vedic) deity is Shiva in his terrible guise as an ascetic smeared with the ashes of funeral pyres, seated on his white bull Nandi. And at his side is his goddess shakti, enthroned on a ruby lotus in her hideous character of Lakini. Lakini is blue, with three faces, three eyes to each; fierce of aspect, with protruding teeth. She is fond of meat: her breast is smeared with grease and blood that have dripped from her ravenous jaws; yet she is radiant, elegant with ornaments, and exalted from the drinking of ambrosia. She is the goddess who presides over all rites of human sacrifice and over the battlefields of mankind, terrible as death to behold, though to her devotees gracious, beautiful, and sweet as life.

Now all three of these lower chakras are of the modes of man's living in the world in his naive state, outward turned: the modes of the lovers, the fighters, the builders, the accomplishers. Joys and sorrows on these levels are functions of achievements in the world "out there": what people think of one, what has been gained, what lost. And throughout the history of our species, people functioning only on these levels (who, of course, have been in the majority) have had to be tamed and brought to heel through the inculcation of a controlling sense of social duty and shared social values, enforced not only by secular authority but also by all those grandiose myths of an unchallengeable divine authority to which every social order — each in its own way — has had to lay claim. Wherever motivations of these kinds are not checked effectively, men, as the old texts say, "become wolves unto men."

However, it is obvious that a religion operating only on these levels, having little or nothing to do with the fostering of inward, mystical realizations, would hardly merit the name of religion at all. It would be little more than an adjunct to police authority, offering in addition to ethical rules and advice intangible consolations for life's losses and a promise of future rewards for social duties fulfilled. Hence, to interpret the imagery, powers, and values of the higher chakras in terms of the values of these lower systems is to mistranslate them miserably, and to lose contact in oneself, thereby, with the whole history and heritage of mankind's life in the spirit.

And so we ascend to chakra four, at the level of the heart, where what Dante called *La Vita Nuova,* "The New Life," begins. And the name of this center is Anahata, "Not Struck"; for it is the place where the sound is heard "that is not made by any two things striking together." (See fig. 332.)

Every sound normally heard is of two things striking together; that of the voice, for example, being the sound of the breath striking our vocal cords. The only sound *not* so made is that of the creative energy of the universe, the hum, so to speak, of the void, which is antecedent to things, and of which things are precipitations. This, they say, is heard as from within, within oneself and simultaneously within space. It is the sound beyond silence, heard as OM (very deeply intoned, I am told, somewhere about *C* below low *C*). "The word OM," said Ramakrishna to his friends, "is Brahman. Following the trail of OM, one attains to Brahman."[11]

In the Sanskrit Devanagari script OM is written either as ॐ or as आँ , and in the posture of the dancing Shiva image the pose of the head, hands, and lifted foot suggests the outline of this sign — which makes the point that in the appearance of this god the sound resounds of the wonder of existence. OM is interpreted as the seed sound, the energy sound, the shakti, of all being, and in that sense analyzed in the following way by the seers and teachers of the Upanishads.

Firstly, since the vowel O in Sanskrit is regarded as a fusion of A and U, the syllable OM can be written also as AUM — आँ — and in that augmented form is called the syllable of *four* elements; namely, A, U, M, and the SILENCE that is before, after, and around it, out of which it rises and back into which it falls — as the universe, out of and back into the void.

Figures 332, 333, 334. Chakra 4: Anahata (bottom); Chakra 5: Vishuddha (center); Chakra 6: Ajna (top).

The A is announced with open throat; the U carries the sound-mass forward; and the M, then, somewhat nasalized, brings all to a close at the lips. So pronounced, the utterance will have filled the whole mouth with sound and so have contained (as they say) all the vowels. Moreover, since consonants are regarded in this thinking as interruptions of vowel sounds, the seeds of all words will have been contained in this enunciation of AUM, and in these, the seed sounds of all things. Thus words, they say, are but fragments or particles of AUM, as all forms are particles of that one Form of forms that is beheld when the rippling surface of the mind is stilled in yoga. And accordingly, AUM is the one sound spelled in all possible inflections on the petals of the Kundalini series.

Allegorically, the initial A of AUM is said to represent the field and state of Waking Consciousness, where objects are of "gross matter" (*sthula*) and are separate both from each other and from the consciousness beholding them. On this plane of experience, I am not you, nor is this that; *A* is not *not-A*; cause and effect, God and his world, are not the same, and all mystical statements are absurd. Moreover, the gross objects of this daylight sphere, to be seen, must be illuminated from without. They are not self-luminous, except, of course, in the instances of fire, lightning, stars, and the sun, which suggest gates to another order of existence. Anything perceived by the waking senses, furthermore, must already have come into being, and so is already a thing of the past. Science, the wisdom of the mind awake, and of "hard facts," can consequently be a knowledge only of what has already become, or of what in the future is to repeat and continue the past. The unpredictably creative, immediate present is inaccessible to its light.

And so we come to the letter U, which is said to represent the field and state of Dream Consciousness, where, although subject and object may *appear* to be different and separate from each other, they are actually one and the same. A dreamer is surprised, even threatened, by his dream, not knowing what it means; yet even while dreaming he is himself inventing it; so that two aspects of the one subject are here playing hide-and-seek: one in creative action, the other in half-ignorance. And the objects of this world of dream, furthermore, being of "subtle matter" (*sukshma*), shine of themselves, rapidly changing shape, and therefore are of the order of fire and the radiant nature of gods. In fact, the Indo-European verbal root *div*, from which the Latin *divus* and *deus*, Greek Ζεύς , and Old Irish *dia* as well as Sanskrit *deva* (all meaning "deity") derive, signifies "to shine"; for the gods, like the figures of dream, shine of themselves. They are the macrocosmic counterparts of the images of dream, personifications of the same powers of nature that are manifest in dreams; so that on this plane the two worlds of the microcosm and macrocosm, interior and exterior, individual and collective, particular and general, are one. The individual dream opens to the universal myth, and gods in vision descend to the dreamer as returning aspects of himself.

Mythologies are in fact the public dreams that move and shape societies; and conversely, one's own dreams are the little myths of the private gods, antigods, and guardian powers that are moving and shaping oneself: revelations of the actual fears, desires, aims, and values by which one's life is subliminally ordered. On the level, therefore, of Dream Consciousness one is at the quick, the immediate initiating creative *now*, of one's life, experiencing those activating forces that in due time will bring to pass unpredicted events on the plane of Waking Consciousness and be there observed and experienced as "facts."

So then, if A is of Waking Consciousness, gross objects, and what has become (the past), and U of Dream Consciousness, subtle objects, and what is becoming (the present), M is of Deep Dreamless Sleep, where (as we say) we have "lost" consciousness, and the mind (as described in the Indian texts) is "an undifferentiated mass or continuum of consciousness unqualified," lost in darkness. That which when awake is conscious only of what has become and in dream of what is becoming, is in Deep Dreamless Sleep dissociated from all commitments whatsoever, and so is returned to that primal, undifferentiated, and unspecified state of latency, chaos, or potentiality from which all that will ever be must in time arise. But alas! The mind that there contains all is lost in sleep. As the *Chhandogya Upanishad* describes it: "Just as those who do not know the spot might pass over a hidden treasure of gold again and again but not find it, even so do all creatures here go to that Brahma-world, day after day, in deep sleep, and not find it."[12]

So also in C. G. Jung's account: "The deeper 'layers' of the psyche lose their individual uniqueness as they retreat farther and farther into darkness. 'Lower down,' that is to say as they approach the autonomous functional systems, they become increasingly collective until they are universalized and extinguished in the body's materiality, i.e., in chemical substances. The body's carbon is simply carbon. Hence, 'at bottom' the psyche is simply 'world.' "[13]

Briefly stated, then: the goal of every yoga is to go into that zone awake; to sink to where there is no longer any resting on this object or on that, whether of the waking world or of dream, but there is met the innate light that is called, in Buddhist lore, the Mother Light. And this then, this inconceivable sphere of undifferentiated consciousness, experienced not as extinction but as light unmitigated, is the reference of the fourth element of AUM: the Silence that is before, after, within, and around the sounding syllable. It is silent because words, which do not reach it, refer only to the names, forms, and relationships of objects either of the daylight world or of dream.

The sound AUM, then, "not made by any two things striking together," and floating as it were in a setting of silence, is the seed sound of creation, heard when the rising Kundalini reaches the level of the heart. (See figure 332.) For there, as they say, the Great Self abides and portals open to the void. The lotus of twelve red petals, marked with the syllables *kam, kham, gam, gham, ngam, cham, chham, jam, jham, nyam, tam,* and *tham,* is of the element air. In its bright red center is an interlocking double triangle, the color of smoke, signifying "juncture" and containing its seed syllable *yam* displayed above an antelope, which is the beast, swift as wind, of the Vedic wind-god Vayu. The female triangle within this letter holds a lingam like shining gold, and the patron Hindu deity is Shiva in a gentle, boon-bestowing aspect. His shakti, known here as Kakini, lifts a noose and a skull in two hands, while exhibiting with her other two the "boon-bestowing" and "fear-dispelling" gestures.

Just below this lotus of the heart there is pictured a lesser, uninscribed lotus, at about the level of the solar plexus, supporting on a jeweled altar an image of the Wish-Fulfilling Tree. For it is here that the first intimations are heard of the sound OM in the Silence, and that sound itself is the Wish-Fulfilling Tree. Once heard, it can be rediscovered everywhere and no longer do we have to *seek* our good. It is here — within — and through all things, all space. We can now give up our struggle for achievement, for love and power and the good, and may rest in peace.

Or so, at first, it will seem.

However, there is a new zeal, a new frenzy, now stirring in the blood. For, as Dante states at the opening of *La Vita Nuova*, describing the moment when he first beheld Beatrice:

> At that moment, I say truly, the spirit of life, which dwells in the most secret chamber of the heart, began to tremble with such violence that it appeared fearfully in the least pulses, and, trembling, said these words: "Behold a god stronger than I, who coming shall rule over me."
>
> At that instant the spirit of the soul, which dwells in the high chamber to which all the spirits of the senses carry their perceptions, began to marvel greatly, and, speaking especially to the spirit of the sight, said these words: "Now has appeared your bliss."
>
> At that instant the natural spirit, which dwells in that part where our nourishment is supplied, began to weep, and, weeping, said these words: "Woe is me, wretched! because often from this time forth shall I be hindered."[14]

Once the great mystery-sound has been heard, the whole desire of the heart will be to learn to know it more fully, to hear it, not through things and within during certain fortunate moments only, but immediately and forever. And the attainment of this end will be the project of the next chakra, the fifth, which is at the level of the larynx and is called Vishuddha, "Purified." (See fig. 333.) "When the Kundalini reaches this plane," said Ramakrishna, "the devotee longs to talk and to hear only of God."[15]

The lotus has sixteen petals of a smoky purple hue, on each of which is engraved one of the sixteen Sanskrit vowels, namely, *am, am, im, im, um, um, rm, rm, lrm, lrm, em, aim, om, aum, am,* and *ah.* In the middle of its pure white central triangle is a white disk, the full moon, wherein the syllable *ham,* of the element space or ether, rests on the back of a pure white elephant. The patron of this center is Shiva in his hermaphroditic form known as Ardhanareshvara, "Half-Woman Lord," five-faced, clothed in a tiger's skin, and with ten radiant arms. One hand makes a "fear-dispelling" gesture and the rest are exhibiting his trident, battle-ax, sword, and thunderbolt, a fire, a snake-ring, a bell, a goad, and a noose, while beside him his goddess, here called Sakini, holds in her own four hands a bow, an arrow, a noose, and a goad. "This region," we are told in a Tantric text, "is the gateway of the Great Liberation."[16] It is the place variously represented in the myths and legends of the world as a threshold where the frightening Gate Guardians stand, the Sirens sing, the Clashing Rocks come together, and a ferry sets forth to the Land of No Return, the Land Below Waves, the Land of Eternal Youth. However, as told in the *Katha Upanishad:* "It is the sharpened edge of a razor, hard to traverse."[17]

The yogi at the purgatorial fifth chakra, striving to clear his consciousness of the turbulence of secondary things and to experience unveiled the voice and light of the Lord that is the Being and Becoming of the universe, has at his command a number of means by which to achieve this aim. There is a discipline for instance, known as the yoga of heat or fire, formerly practiced in Tibet and known there as *Dumo (gTum-Mo),* which is a term denoting "a fierce woman who can destroy all desires and passions"[18] — and I wonder whether the classical legend of the Maenads beheading Orpheus, who had been brooding on his lost Euridice, may not have been a covert reference to some esoteric mystery of this kind. What this yoga first requires is the activation of the energy at the navel chakra, Manipura (chakra three), through a special type of breath control and the visualization of an increasing fire at the intersection (just below the navel) of all three spiritual channels:

At the start the blazing tongue of Dumo should not be visualized as more than the height of a finger's breadth; then gradually it increases in height to two, three, and four fingers' breadth. The blazing tongue of Dumo is thin and long, shaped like a twisted needle or the long hair of a hog; it also possesses all four characteristics of the Four Elements — the firmness of the earth, the wetness of water, the warmth of fire, and the mobility of air; but its outstanding quality still lies in its great heat — which can evaporate the life breaths (*pranas*) and produce the bliss. [19]

What is happening here is that the powers of the lower chakras are being activated and intensified, to force them to open and to release the energies they enclose; for these are the energies that in the higher chakras are to lead to sheerly spiritual fulfillments. In this introverted exercise, the aggressive fires of chakra three are being turned inward, against enemies that are not outside but within: to burn away obstructions to the Mother Light that are lodged within oneself. Thin as a needle, the Dumo fire is to be lengthened upward from the navel chakra to the higher centers of the head, to release from these an ambrosial seminal dew (as it is called), which is to be pictured as dripping, white, into the red Dumo fire. The white nerve ida is of this seminal dew, and the red, pingala, of the Dumo fire. The imagery is obviously sexual: the fire is female and the dew that it receives and consumes is male. Moreover, as the Tantric texts advise: "If these measures still fail to produce a Great Bliss, one may apply the *Wisdom-Mother-Mudra* by visualizing the sexual act with a Dakini, while using the breathing to incite the Dumo heat." [20] Thus in this yoga the energies either of the sex instinct or of the will to power may be employed to assist in shattering and surpassing the limits of the lower instinct system itself.

A second type of exercise in this Tibetan series is known as "Illusory Body Yoga," the aim of which is to realize in experience — not simply to be told to believe — that all appearances are void. One is to regard the reflection of one's own body in a mirror and to consider (as the texts advise), "how this image is produced by a combination of various factors — the mirror, the body, light, space, etc., — under certain conditions. It is an object of 'dependent-arising' (*pratitya-samutpada*) without any self-substance — appearing, yet void. . . ." One is then to consider how one's own self, as one knows it, is equally an appearance.

Or one may practice in the same way a meditation on echoes. Go to some place where echoes abound. "Then shout loudly many pleasing and displeasing words to praise or malign yourself, and observe the reactions of pleasure and displeasure. Practicing thus, you will soon realize that all words, pleasant or unpleasant, are as illusory as the echoes themselves."[21]

In a third yoga, known as the "Dream Yoga," we immediately recognize a resemblance to certain modern psychotherapeutic techniques; for the yogi here is to cultivate and pay close attention to his dreams, analyzing them in relation to his feelings, thoughts, and other reactions. "When the yogi has a frightening dream, he should guard against unwarranted fear by saying, 'This is a dream. How can fire burn me or water drown me in a dream? How can this animal or devil, etc., harm me?' Keeping this awareness, he should trample on the fire, walk through the water, or transform himself into a great fireball and fly into the heart of the threatening devil or beast and burn it up. . . ."

Next:

> The yogi who can recognize dreams fairly well and steadily should proceed to practice the *Transformation of Dreams*. This is to say that in the Dream state, he should try to transform his body into a bird, a tiger, a lion, a Brahman, a king, a house, a rock, a forest. . . . or anything he likes. When this practice is stabilized, he should then transform himself into his Patron Buddha Body in various forms, sitting or standing, large or small, and so forth. Also, he should transform the things that he sees in dreams into different objects — for instance, an animal into a man, water into fire, earth into space, one into many, or many into one. . . . After this the yogi should practice the Journey to Buddha's Lands. . . .

Finally — and here the sense of it all becomes clear:

> The Dream Yoga should be regarded as supplementary
> to the Illusory Body Yoga. . . . for in this way, the
> clinging-to-time manifested in the dichotomy of Dream
> and Waking states can eventually be conquered.[22]

Still another yoga of this series, going past the illusory forms
of both waking and dream, is the "Light Yoga," where one is to
visualize one's entire body as dissolving into the syllable of the
heart center (in Tibet this syllable is HUM) and this syllable itself,
then, as dissolving into light. And there are four degrees of this
light: (1) the Light of Revelation, (2) the Light of Augmentation,
(3) the Light of Attainment, and (4) the Light of the Innate.
Moreover, anyone able to do so should concentrate, just before
going to sleep, on the fourth of these, the Innate Light, and
holding to it even on passing into sleep, dissolve both dreams
and darkness in that light.[23]

And with that, indeed, one will have passed into the state of
Deep Dreamless Sleep awake.

When the tasks of the fifth chakra have been accomplished,
two degrees of illumination become available to the perfected
saint, that at the sixth, known as *savikalpa samadhi,* "conditioned rapture," and finally, supremely, at the seventh chakra,
nirvikalpa samadhi, "unconditioned rapture." Ramakrishna
used to ask those approaching him for instruction: "Do you like
to speak of God with form or without?"[24] And we have the
words of the great *doctor ecstaticus* Meister Eckhart, referring
to the passage from six to seven: "Man's last and highest leave-
taking is the leaving of God for God."[25]

The center of the first of these two ecstasies, known as the
lotus of "Command," Ajna, is above and between the brows.
(See fig. 334.) The uraeus serpent in Egyptian portraits of the
pharaohs appears exactly as though from this point of the forehead. The center is described as a lotus of two pure white petals,
bearing the syllables *ham* and *ksham.* Seated on a white lotus
near its heart is the radiant six-headed goddess Hakini, holding
in four of her six hands a book, a drum, a rosary, and a skull,
while the remaining two make the "fear-dispelling" and "boon-
bestowing" signs. Within the yoni-triangle is a Shiva lingam,
shining "like a chain of lightning flashes,"[26] supporting the sign

of the syllable OM, of which the sound is here fully heard. And here, too, the form is seen of one's ultimate vision of God, which is called in Sanskrit *Saguna Brahman*, "the Qualified Absolute." As expounded by Ramakrishna:

> When the mind reaches this plane, one witnesses divine revelations day and night. Yet even then there remains a slight consciousness of "I." Having seen the unique manifestation man becomes mad with joy as it were and wishes to be one with the all-pervading Divine, but cannot do so. It is like the light of a lamp inside a glass case. One feels as if one could touch the light, but the glass intervenes and prevents it.[27]

For where there is a "Thou" there is an "I," whereas the ultimate aim of the mystic, as Eckhart has declared, is identity: "God is love, and he who is in love is in God and God in him."[28]

If we remove that glasslike barrier of which Ramakrishna spoke, both our God and ourselves will explode then into light, sheer light, one light, beyond names and forms, beyond thought and experience, beyond even the concepts "being" and "nonbeing." "The soul in God," Eckhart has said, "has naught in common with naught and is naught to aught."[29] And again: "There is something in the soul so nearly kin to God that it is one and not united."[30]

The Sanskrit term *Nirguna Brahman*, "the Unqualified Absolute," refers to the realization of this chakra. Its lotus, Sahasrara, "Thousand Petalled," hangs head downward, shedding nectarous rays more lustrous than the moon; while at its center, brilliant as a lightning flash, is the ultimate yoni-triangle, within which, well concealed and very difficult to approach, is the great shining void in secret served by all gods.[31] "Any flea as it is in God," declared Eckhart, "is nobler than the highest of the angels in himself."[32]

NOTES

1. Pliny, *Natural History* 6.26.101, 9.57.114, as quoted by Wilfred H. Schoff, *The Periplus of the Erythraean Sea: Travel and Trade in the Indian*

Ocean by a Merchant of the First Century (New York: David McKay Co., 1916, pp. 219, 240.

2. Mircea Eliade, *Yoga: Immortality and Freedom*, Bollingen Series 56, 2nd ed. (Princeton: Princeton University Press, 1969), pp. 200-1.

3. I have discussed this matter at some length in *The Masks of God: Oriental Mythology* (New York: The Viking Press, 1962), pp. 197-206. The critical texts are *Brihadaranyaka Upanishad* 2.1; *Chhandogya Upanishad* 5.3-10, 5.11-24, 7.1-25; and *Kena Upanishad* 3.1-4.2.

4. Arthur Avalon (Sir John Woodroffe), *The Serpent Power*, 3rd rev. ed. (Madras: Ganesh and Co., 1931), p. 111, note 2.

5. *The Gospel of Sri Ramakrishna*, trans. Swami Nikhilananda (New York: Ramakrishna-Vivekananda Center, 1942), pp. 829-30.

6. Avalon, *Serpent Power*, pp. 21-22.

7. Alain Danièlou, *Yoga: The Method of Reintegration* (New York: University Books, 1955), p. 11.

8. Avalon, *Serpent Power*, p. 117.

9. *Ibid.*, pp. 115-18, 330-45, and plate 2.

10. *Ibid.*, pp. 118-19, 355-63.

11. *Gospel of Sri Ramakrishna*, p. 404.

12. *Chhandogya Upanishad* 8.3.2.

13. C. G. Jung, "The Psychology of the Child Archetype," *The Archetypes and the Collective Unconscious, The Collected Works of C. G. Jung*, trans. R. F. C. Hull, Bollingen Series 20, 17 vols. (Princeton: Princeton University Press; London: Routledge and Kegan Paul, 1960), 9.1. par. 291.

14. Dante, *La Vita Nuova*, vol. 2, trans. Charles Eliot Norton, *The New Life of Dante Alighieri* (Boston and New York: Houghton Mifflin Co., 1867), p. 2.

15. *Gospel of Sri Ramakrishna*, p. 499.

16. *Shatchakra Nirupana* 30; Avalon, *Serpent Power*, p. 386.

17. *Katha Upanishad* 3.14.

18. Garma C. C. Chang, *Teachings of Tibetan Yoga* (New Hyde Park, N.Y.: University Books, 1963), p. 73.

19. "The Epitome of an Introduction to the Profound Path of the Six Yogas of Naropa," trans. Chang, *ibid.*, pp. 63-64.

20. *Ibid.*, p. 68.

21. *Ibid.*, pp. 82-83.

22. *Ibid.*, pp. 92-94.

23. *Ibid.*, pp. 96-101.

24. *Gospel of Sri Ramakrishna*, pp. 80, 148, 180, 191, 217, 370, 802, 868.

25. *Meister Eckhart*, ed. Franz Pfeiffer, trans. C. de B. Evans (London: John M. Watkins, 1924-1931), No. 96 ("Riddance"); 1:239.

26. *Shatchakra Nirupana* 33; Avalon, *Serpent Power*, p. 395.

27. Swami Yatiswarananda, "A Glimpse into Hindu Religious Symbology," in Sri Ramakrishna Centenary Committee (ed.), *Cultural Heritage of India*, 3 vols. (Calcutta: Belur Math, 1937), 2:15.

28. "The Soul Is One with God," *Meister Eckhart*, 2:89.

29. "Riddance," *ibid.*, 1:239.

30. "The Soul Is One with God," *ibid.*, 2:89.

31. *Shatchakra Nirupana* 40-41; Avalon, *Serpent Power*, pp. 417-28.

32. "The Soul Is One with God," *Meister Eckhart*, 2:89.

7

Wing-tsit Chan

Influences of Taoist Classics on Chinese Philosophy

Born in Kwangtung, China, in 1901, Professor Chan was educated at Lingnan University in Canton and Harvard University. He is currently the Anna D. R. Gillespie Professor of Philosophy at Chatham College and adjunct professor of Chinese thought at Columbia University. He has given over a thousand lectures on China throughout the United States and has taught at Dartmouth College and Lingnan university. His Source Book of Chinese Philosophy *has been a classroom classic for sixteen years. In addition to writing several books, he has contributed essays on Chinese philosophy and religion to some thirty-eight anthologies, was editor for the Chinese philosophy section of the* Encyclopedia of Philosophy *and has contributed articles on this subject to the* Encyclopedia Britannica. *The year before giving this lecture, he received the highest academic honor available to a Chinese scholar: election to the Academia Sinica.*

With charm and energy, his presentation introduced Taoism's history and philosophy with clarity, personalized it with tales of the major participants, and vivified it with examples. Evenhandedly he dealt with the points of resemblance and difference between Confucianism, Taoism, and Buddhism and between Taoism and Western philosophy, then suggested his personal reconciliation between their apparently conflicting claims. In so doing, he not only presented a model of how to make a complex and potentially confusing subject lucid and involving, but he also typified that intellectual courtesy which respects history without the distortion of dogmatism or special pleading.

I have always insisted that anyone majoring in any aspect of China should read at least one whole Chinese classic. But it is very difficult to choose from among the abundant Confucian and Taoist texts because there are so many. It has always been most difficult for me to choose between "The Classic of the Way and Virtue" or *Tao-te Ching,* and the *Chuang-Tzu.* So you had better read both.

This afternoon I am going to concentrate on the Taoist classic, the *Tao-te Ching,* a very brief work of only about five thousand characters, divided into eighty-one chapters. It has been ascribed to Lao Tzu. According to the *Historical Records,* Lao Tzu was a custodian of documents in the capital of the Chou state. When he got old, he retired. Riding a buffalo, he came to a pass, and the warder of the pass said, "Sir, you are a wise man. Why do you not write down what you have to say for the benefit of posterity?" Thereupon Lao Tzu wrote down what we call "the five-thousand-character classic."

But there are difficulties about this man because in the same historical record he was confused with another man who lived about 273 B.C. In addition to difficulties about the historicity of this man, we also have had a lot of difficulty about the text's authenticity, authorship, arrangement, terminology, literary style, and so on—so much so that in the 1920s and 1930s, Chinese scholars old and young, fired with the spirit of revolt, denounced and rejected Chinese tradition and said there was no such man as Lao Tzu or that Lao Tzu did not live in the sixth century B.C. or the third or fourth century B.C., and that the *Tao-te Ching* was a product of the third century B.C. This view became very popular in this country—so much so that if anyone still believed in the traditional account that Lao Tzu was a sage in the sixth century B.C. or that the *Tao-te Ching* was traceable, at least in part, back to Lao Tzu he was considered out of date.

But I, in my little work on *The Way of Lao Tzu*, tried to gather all the information I could from Japan, China, Europe, and this country and see what any scholar with anything serious to say about Lao Tzu and the *Tao-te Ching* believed. I calculated that the great, great majority of scholars twenty years ago disbelieved the tradition of Lao Tzu. But about ten years ago I brought out a very long article on ancient Taoism for an Academia Sinica publication and found that by then hardly any scholar still believed that Lao Tzu was a mythical person or that he had lived as late as the fourth century B.C. As to the book— of course, there was no book in the sixth century B.C., only slips. These slips contained sayings which were later collected, so perhaps we can say the *Tao-te Ching* did not assume the form of a book until the third or fourth century B.C. But certainly, the ideas in that book can be traced back to the sixth century B.C. I'm not going to go into detail; you can see a good deal of material in my little book, *The Way of Lao Tzu*; and to you who want further detail, I am afraid I can claim I have presented more material than anybody else in that Academia Sinica publication.

One thing is sure: no scholar can deny that Confucius in about 520 B.C. made a trip to see Lao Tzu to ask about ceremonies and Lao Tzu told Confucius, "Never mind about the details. Eliminate your desires. Get at fundamentals." And

Confucius returned from the visit saying, "Lao Tzu is a dragon."
Lao Tzu became the hero of Confucius, and his work, the *Tao-
te Ching* has been heroic to the Chinese ever since.

Part of the myth confused Lao Tzu with a man named Li,
which means *plum*, so it is said that Lao Tzu was born under a
plum tree — obviously borrowing from Buddhism the story that
the Buddha achieved enlightenment under the *bodhi* tree; another version gives his name as Tan, meaning *ear;* and to the
Chinese, a long ear means wisdom because wisdom can be ac-
cumulated only with age. (So, in order to impress my students,
every morning when I shave I pull my ears a little bit — with no
success!) Because his origins are shrouded in ancient times, "Lao
Tzu" has been interpreted as "old master" so the myth developed
that he was born at the age of seventy-two. (His mother must
have had quite a time!)

Nevertheless, you simply have to read this book. But I warn
you: you either like it a lot or you hate it a lot. You may hate it
a lot because it tells you not to strive for achievement, not to
own any vehicles — not a Cadillac, not even a Pinto! — to live in
a primitive community, not to travel, never to seek fame, never
to run for Congress but to shun iniquity, to withdraw, to yield,
to retreat. You may not like it. Or you'll like it a lot because it's
boldly vigorous, provocative, and stimulating. Why are people
poor? Because their officials eat up all their taxes in Washington.
Why do people commit crimes? Because there are too many
laws. (The more laws there are, the more crimes people commit.
So the Taoist classic says.) This book has the strongest condemnation of war in Chinese tradition. Victory in war is like a funeral, it says. No one wins. So to the government they say,
"Leave us alone." And yet, this book says that these peaceful
methods will make you better at the best kind of virtue, not the
secondary minor virtues; that you'll get the real kind of righteousness, not the conventional secondary versions. So it is a
very stimulating book.

This afternoon I am going to lecture on how this little book
of slightly over five thousand characters has largely determined
the direction of developments in Chinese philosophy and reli-

gion. I use the world *largely*, not *exclusively*, but I think it is true, as you shall see.

I shall begin with *tao*, which is the name of the movement. *Tao*, the Chinese character, consists of the head of a human being and a walk—a way to go, the way, the path you are on, the way of doing things, and finally the way of existence. And the Way itself. All Chinese philosophers talk about the Way. Confucius had his own way. His way is the way of the ancient sages, centered on man. Lao Tzu's way is the way of nature and there is that contrast, not an irreconcilable contrast, as I shall show, but a different approach, a different perspective. This way is the Way of Existence, with all the characters of it as absolute. It is One, indestructible, everlasting, all good, and so on. From that description, we are likely to describe *tao* as the absolute, as *noumenon*, as transcendental; and it has often been equated with the Nirvana of Buddhism, with Atman or Brahman in Hinduism, but it is not quite either. It is the Chinese Way, the way of existence, the process of being. It is not to be equated with something which bifurcates subject and object. No! It is the subject itself; the Way is the thing. In other words, this philosophy is the philosophy of process, to borrow Western philosophical terms. This is the philosophy of immanence, the way of things, the way *in* things. Sometimes we assume a dichotomy, that transcendence and immanence are two different things. That must not hold in the Chinese way of thought. We do not distinguish between the human and the nonhuman. *Tao* involves both. *Tao* is transcendental, yes; but it is also immanent. I shall come back to this point a little later.

But in the Way, as a process, one of its most outstanding features is change. In this little book, you will find change repeatedly stressed. The seasons change, life and death change, and this is what impressed Lao Tzu and the Chinese in general.

Please listen to my second point. Now, if things do change, how are they related? How are they coordinated? Lao Tzu is very firm in emphasizing that *tao* is One. *Tao* is everywhere, *tao* is universal, *tao* leaves nothing out, and so on. And there are parables and knowledge in the book about that idea. Lao

Tzu said once that in moral cultivation, do not have a divided mind. Do not let your spirit be distracted. Do not divide people up as we are doing into races, religions, and economic structure. Lao Tzu said that if the king holds on the One, his kingdom will be in order. If the sun and the moon hold on the One, their courses will be regular, and so on. The emphasis on the One cannot be stronger than in the *Lao Tzu.*

The scholar who particularly emphasized this idea of the One and carried it to the philosophical level was Wang Pi 249-226 B.C.); he lived for only twenty-four years and died a very young man. Professor Richard Mather in his masterful translation of the *Shih-Shuo Hsin-Yu* has some stories about him and has done a lot of recent research about him. Wang Pi stressed the idea of Oneness, one piece, wholeness. In the *I Ching,* "the book of changes," you have 360 different hexagrams, each dealing with its particular situation. But one principle runs throughout, and you do not need the 360 hexagrams once you hold on to this one universal principle.

Am I denying, then, all the multiplicity, variations, and differences? Here we bring in a number two Taoist who lived from 369 to 286 B.C. In the Confucian schools, the study of Lao Tzu was discouraged because, as I said, it was thought to discourage many young people's ambition. In the Confucian schools in the old days, *Chuang Tzu,* the book of Chuang Tzu, was practically prohibited, it was so feared. I cannot go into detail about him but I shall give you only one parable or story.

In his first or second chapter, Chuang Tzu talks about a natural symphony. There are holes on the hillside, some big and some small, and the winds blow on them. Here the big hole makes the sound "wuuh," and the small holes make "whoo"; and thus on the cliff there is a natural symphony. It is beautiful because it is one, but the one consists of this variety of sounds. So the One involves all the differences; in fact, it is the differences that make up the One. And so Chuang Tzu said, "Let us keep our differences. If you are like a duck and your legs are short, never mind; keep them short. If you are a goose and your neck is long, never mind; keep it long. It is foolish trying to cut them so as to equalize them. If you are born a little ball, accept it, because then you can be used to hit some targets. If you are born a rooster, accept it, because then you can wake people up in the morning." Now there is a lot of fatalism in these philosophies, yet there is both a great deal of acceptance of differences and also encouragement to weak and unfortunate people in difficult situations. Chuang Tzu said, "If you are only a hunchback, never mind; you have just as much freedom and dignity as anyone." That is why Taoism as a religion particularly championed the cause of the underdog. It gave hope to the deprived, the poor, the sick, and the weak. And here you have the strength of Taoism, particularly Taoist religion, which eventually became a hotbed of protests and rebellion in Chinese history.

The man who developed this idea of differences which contributed to—in fact, which substantiated and affirmed Oneness—was Kuo Hsiang who died in 312 B.C. Thus we have two philosophical commentators of the fourth century on these two basic Taoist classics, one emphasizing Oneness to start with, the other emphasizing the differences of many to start with, and yet they converge. In other words the One involves many, the many involves One, and this leads me to my third point, namely, the relationship between the One and the Many.

Buddhism came in from India, emphasizing that the One is real and all differences are *maya* (illusion or appearance). The Chinese faced this problem; and under the impact of the Taoist philosophy in which the One and the Many supplement each other and embrace one another, the Chinese Buddhists developed a doctrine which can be translated as substance and function.

One commentator on Lao Tzu's chapter 38, which talks about substance and function, said the great virtue is substance; all these other small virtues like kindness, liberality, generosity, wisdom, and so on are small virtues. They are functions of the substance. Substance is one, irreducible, permanent. Function is operation. Perhaps you can look upon them as two phases or two aspects of the same thing, but there can never be substance without function. To have a substance without function is meaningless, is dead; nor can there be function without substance, because it doesn't have a foundation.

That concept of substance and function develops much throughout the fifth, sixth, and seventh centuries; but in the eighth century, the Buddhists had to develop a theory that would bring Buddhism down to earth instead of always going up to Nirvana or thinking that Nirvana is always beyond this world. Under the influence of the Taoists' and Confucians' emphasis on this world, they had to develop a philosophy of substance and function. They succeeded in representing that synthesis in a beautiful analogy: There is one moon. The moon shines on the lake, the moon shines on the rock, the moon shines on the leaves. They are all different. Each one is real, characteristic, individual, solid, and yet they are different. But those differences depend on this same moonlight which is one, indivisible. In other words, the moon is substance and all these reflections and so on are functions.

That synthesis developed so thoroughly in the Buddhist philosophical scheme that by the tenth and eleventh centuries A.D., the Confucians also had to accommodate that type of philosophy to Confucian ethics and morals. Their success can be summed up in the word *jen*, which can be translated as goodness, love, or humanity, as an ideal of human nature. The Confucians had always taught that one should be filial to one's parents, respectful to brothers, reverent, and so on. But to this point, Confucianism had lacked a metaphysical foundation for their ethics. Under the impact of the Buddhists and indirectly because of the influence of the Taoists, they now developed a metaphysics for their ethics, summed up by this word *jen*. Their resolution of the problem was to define *jen* as the One — the substance — and all the moralities like honesty, obedience, generosity, freedom, liberality, and so on, as a function of how *jen* operates in particular relationships and situations. In the relationship with parents, *jen* becomes filial piety, and so on. Thus, by the tenth or eleventh century, Confucianism had laid a foundation for its whole ethical structure which bound all the moralities into one coherent system. This idea of the function and substance is one of the most important developments in the history of Chinese thought.

Now I must go on to my fourth point. I have been talking about the One and the Many and I have emphasized how Lao Tzu emphasized holding on to the *everything.* Chuang Chou affirmed that same point by emphasizing paradoxically the differences which make up the One. I think you can have a very good analogy in the American population. The American population is so strong, so good, because it is composed of so many ethnic varieties. I think it makes the strength of this country.

My fourth point is in reference to chapter 38 of the *Lao Tzu.* It's very simple. The *tao* produces one, one produces two, and two produces three. Some of my students say, "How simple, how naive! Can't the Chinese count?" And yet these simple sentences have laid the groundwork and provided a pattern for all Chinese metaphysical and cosmological developments. It's very simple. Let me explain. It all begins with one, however you describe it, in any term. Then it goes into two factors: *yin* and *yang* — *yin,* the female element, *yang,* the male element. It is only by the interplay of these two elements that you have anything. And as a minimum, you have three. Commentators — and there have been something like two thousand commentaries in Chinese, Japanese, and Korean on the *Lao Tzu* of which over seven hundred are still in existence — do not agree on what the three might be. It does not matter. It simply means multiplicity.

This brief sketch describes the natural evolution of cosmology. There is an almost logical and rational development from the simplicity of the One to the paired states of the Two. In Western terms, they may appear as the psychological states of love and hate; in modern physics, they may be negative and positive; in Christianity or Islam, good and evil. The names do not matter, but the process — two elements working to produce a multiplicity of things — does. This simple formula, developed in the eleventh century as the metaphysics of neo-Confucian philosophy, has formed the basis of Chinese philosophy ever since.

Many philosophers have viewed the Chinese *tao* as diametrically opposed to Western theology and metaphysics,

which is based on a creator — God as the origin of the universe
— while the Chinese system may be seen as a kind of natural
evolution. Despite the eloquent arguments of those who see the
two positions as irreconcilable — particularly Jesuit and Domini-
can scholarship in the seventeenth and eighteenth centuries — I
see them simply as two ways of looking at the same thing, two
perspectives. If we borrow the Indian form of analogy, we can
see the Western system as a potter who creates a pot, something
you can see, while the Eastern system can be likened to a seed
that grows into a flower — not two separate things but a process
of growth from simplicity to complexity. But even in these
analogies, I do not think the two positions are irreconcilable. A
potter who creates a pot has to have a source, a motivation, a
power to command; the seed also has to have a source, a power.
To me, the two systems are simply two ways of looking at different things.

However, the Chinese system includes another aspect we
should discuss. Because the One produces two, everything has
yin and *yang*; everything embraces *yin* and carries *yang*; their
harmony brings order and peace. But how is a harmony of
opposites achieved? Philosophers have identified and argued
over at least three ways for several hundred years. One is opposition: one element must overcome the other and dominate it.
Happiness should overcome sorrow. The philosophy in China
that the husband dominates the wife comes from the same root.

A second resolution is rotation. The seasons show warm
summer giving way to cold winter. A father is succeeded by his
son. The stock market goes up, then down. (How is it today?)
And, as Professor Mather can tell you much better, the Chinese
philosophy of history is rotation, one dynasty follows another,
up and down.

But the third resolution to this conflict of *yin* and *yang* is
found in Lao Tzu's work in chapter 42: harmony makes peace
and order. In other words, he does not see these two elements as
contrasting. Yes, sometimes they dominate one another; sometimes they rotate. But the essential thing is for the two to har-
monize. In the relationship of the husband and wife, who is
more important? Lacking one, you cannot become the family.

They are equally dignified, equally indispensable, equally important. The father may go outside to earn money and serve in the government. The mother inside not only cooks and washes but brings up the children, teaches religious observances, and many more things. The two, both in and out, are indispensable. You cannot have anything with only the inside but not the outside, nor can you have anything only with *yin* and not *yang* or *yang* without *yin*. The two must be synthesized, must be mutually identified to be harmonized. The best illustration of that principle, of course, is Chinese landscape painting where mountain and water do not contrast but merge, giving a sense of the wholeness and unity of nature without contrast, shadow, or sharp demarcations. That is also the purpose of the landscape garden; the harmony of oneness coming from a harmony of the two elements was inspired chiefly by Taoist philosophy and Taoist practice.

And finally, our discussion must bring us to the ideal of *sheng-sheng*, which means to grow and grow, to give life and give further life, to produce and reproduce, to live and have renewal of life. The word *sheng* is a very prominent one in Lao-Tzu; in fact, the word *sheng-sheng* itself comes in his chapter 52. The Confucians picked up the idea and grafted it onto their ethics; thus, the whole ethic is to give life, to promote life — in the government to promote economic and social life; in families to continue the life stream by having children. Thus, the doctrine of filial piety is explained not merely in terms of gratitude to parents or the necessity of supporting parents but of continuing this life stream. You have accepted life, which, according to Confucius, is the mandate of heaven. And once you have accepted life, your most sacred duty is to carry on and enrich this life. *Sheng-sheng.* I am not saying that the Chinese have fulfilled that ideal, but it is their conviction. And Chu Hsi (A.D. 1130-1200), the greatest of all Confucians, did not like Taoism a bit; yet he wrote a commentary on chapter 6 of the *Lao Tzu*, which says: "The spirit of the valley never dies." "The spirit of the valley" has been interpreted in mythical terms as a god, among other things, including openness or the mysteriousness of the female principle. That last interpretation is Chu Hsi's, who says it means "like a mother, a big valley with an openness to give life, the source of life, inexhaustible itself." With great critical power, Chu Hsi was willing to go so far as to assimilate the idea of *sheng-sheng* in his own Confucian philosophy — making some connection to the *Lao Tzu*. That's something that's really something.

And that brings us to the relationship between Taoism and Confucianism. I think you can characterize the relationship by a lot of conflicts. Some call Confucianism the way of man and Taoism the way of nature. Well, there is no harm in doing that. Again, the Confucian emphasizes government organization more; Taoism says the less government the better. But it is the common points between the two that have served China well and that have made every Chinese a combination Confucian-Taoist. I have often been asked, "Are you a Confucian or a Taoist?" I say, "I am a chop suey — can't help it." And, the convergent point of that mixture is the ideal of *sheng-sheng*. There can be no doubt that Confucianism has dominated Chinese society in history with Taoism as a strong support.

One of the greatest advances in scholarship came in 1973 and 1974 with the discovery in the southern central part of China — near the home of Mao Tse-tung in Hunan — of two manuscripts of the *Lao Tzu* written on silk dating back to the second century B.C., which makes them four hundred years older than the manuscripts used by Wang Pi in the third century A.D., the earliest manuscripts known until this discovery in our decade. The surprising thing is that in spite of certain variations in terms, these second century manuscripts almost totally agree with the manuscripts we already had. Thus, the preservation of the text and oral traditions in China were not as unreliable as many people had postulated. The manuscripts we already had are divided into two parts: the first thirty-seven chapters about *tao*, the way, and the remaining chapters about *te*, virtue. However, in these newly discovered classics, the part on virtue comes first. As a result, some Mainland scholars claim that Taoism originally put virtue, or method, before *tao*, or metaphysics. They further claim a second tradition in addition to Taoism as we understand it — a legalist tradition expounding a method of particular virtues which predates traditional Taoism in Chinese history. Since their main support seems to be the fact that the part on *te* (virtue) comes first, I simply do not feel that there has been enough evidence to say that there is a legalist tradition in Taoism, much less to see it as a legalist tradition in Chinese history. I honestly believe in a much simpler explanation: there are two manuscripts; and when they were put together, one had to come on top.

I mention this point because you may have read some books or articles arguing that Chinese history and tradition have not really been Confucian but legalist because of the historic proliferation of laws, use of torture, and so on. I will be the first to admit that Chinese Confucians have used torture, laws, and punishments. And I admit that China has fought just as many wars as any other country. I am not going to claim that the Chinese have been a peaceful nation or that the Confucians have been a peaceful people. There is this difference, however: when the Confucians use law — and how can they avoid using law in a government? — they are ashamed of it. They try to apologize. Look in their biographies; they never emphasize what they have accomplished with their law or how many people they have punished. Never. They are much too ashamed of it. And that goes back to Confucius and Mencius: government influences people by virtue; and if you use law, they will beat you in the end. Law is no substitute for virtue. If you are a good man, you will have good laws. If you are a bad man, you will have bad laws. That is what Confucius teaches. They apologize; they are not proud of it. The legalists, however, use law as their main instrument whether they are moral or not. That's the difference between the two, and legalism is fundamentally different from Confucianism.

Now, we must discuss how the *Tao-te Ching* has determined the direction of religious development in China, particularly in Taoism. The Taoist religion has been frequently described as an imitation of Buddhism. It is said that Taoism has no sound theological basis of its own. Instead, since Buddhism has three Buddhas, Taoism has its three Pure Ones. Buddhism has its canon; so does Taoism. Buddhism has heaven and hell — even though Buddha would have turned in his grave to see Buddhism pick up heaven and hell on its way to China. But the Taoist goes Buddhism better with eighteen hells—plenty of room. And against its eighteen hells are thirty-six heavens, so our chances of going to heaven are two to one. The Buddhists have monasteries; so do the Taoists. No doubt Taoism is imitative.

But Taoism also has certain fundamental distinctions, most of which come out of the *Lao Tzu*. The first distinction is in its views about creation. The Taoist religion wove into its fabric a lot of folklore and Buddhist stories to construct a doctrine of creation. Connected with creation is the idea of mystery. *Tao* is described as illusive, inscrutable, indescribable, vague but everywhere, all-present yet with its essence very concrete; it includes further paradoxes such as being stationary yet going everywhere, and so on. It all adds up as a mystery.

In Confucianism is also an element of mystery, but this mystery merely means vastness, beyond our ears and eyes. But in Taoism, the mystery is mystery by nature, inherent mystery, mystery inseparable from its content. Sun has its mystery to evoke in you, color has its mystery to evoke. I think it is this element of mystery that has provided the Chinese with their essential religiosity, because after everything has been described and explained in rational terms, there still remains that particular mystery — life itself.

And here is the final point I wish to make about Taoism: the Taoist will search for long life. Historically, the Chinese have been looking for long life for centuries. There are formulae: meditation, bathing, medicine, food, sacrifice, witchery, all kinds of devices to prolong life. It is said that when the Taoist religion was organized formally about A.D. 146 by Chang Tao Ling, he required everybody to read the *Tao-te Ching*, partly because the *Tao-te Ching* talked about long life and no death. In chapter 33, it says one may die but not perish. We do not know what it means; but most people agree that though we may die in the sense of terminating our physical existence, our essential personality will never perish. You can describe that as immortality or whatever you like. It is also said in chapter 59 of the *Tao-te Ching* that life goes on forever. It is said that the founder of the Taoist religion utilized the *Lao Tzu* to organize a new religion, perhaps partly for his political movement in the second century A.D. That we do not know. But the idea is inescapable that the search for long life is the essence of Taoism as a religion. In fact, the *Chuang Tzu*, the second Taoist classic, even mentions some immortals. And the Chinese have been trying all ways that might lead them to become immortal.

When I was a child in the village, once in a while I would hear that an immortal had appeared on the road last night to bring justice to a certain case which had received no real justice through social means. At other times we were told, "Do you remember that beggar in the market? He was an immortal in disguise. He came to help people." That type of belief gave a lot of confidence and comfort to a lot of people, and inspired them.

For centuries, besides bathing, food, medicine, meditation, and other techniques, the Chinese have sought immortality through alchemy, hoping to turn mercury into gold. Since gold is immutable, you will be too if you can get it into your system. They finally gave up trying in the seventh century; but in the process, they discovered other metals like copper and lead. Many scholars of Chinese civilization credit Taoist experiments in alchemy with China's great scientific accomplishments. Up to the fifteenth century, the Chinese were either ahead of or on the level of the rest of the world in technological achievements. I mention gunpowder and paper as two. (After the Renaissance, of course, the West shot ahead and China stayed behind.)

All of this is merely to underline that Lao Tzu has meant a lot to the Chinese in philosophy, in religion, and in science. Taoism is an excellent thing; and the more you read the *Lao Tzu*, the more you like it. It is very much like the best kind of tea — the more you sip, the more fragrant you find it. You ask me how much a pound? Priceless, but it is free.

8

Richard B. Mather

The Impact of the *Nirvana Sutra* in China

One could say that Professor Richard Mather's interest in China began with his birth, since he is one of the few Americans teaching Asian languages and literature to be born there. Currently professor of Chinese at the University of Minnesota and chairman of its Department of East Asian Languages, he was on leave at the University of California, Berkeley, at the time he delivered this lecture. His modest claim to leave everything past the fifth century A.D. in "more competent hands" is his own understated description of a lifetime of trailblazing work in those frustratingly puzzling centuries when the foundations of Chinese civilization were laid as they would stand during the rise of the West. Author of numerous articles, monographs, and books, he most recently published his translation of Shih-Shuo Hsin-Yu, A New Account of the Tales of the World, *by Liu I-Ching, with the commentary by Liu Chun, which set a standard of excellence in format and annotation for scholars dealing with the literature of China's third through sixth centuries.*

In his lecture on the Nirvana Sutra, *he beguiles the layman into a microcosmic study of one facet of the enormous jewel of Chinese Buddhism: the impact of a single* sutra *translated twice near the fifth century* A.D. *He orients the layman using a comparison with the differences of focus and emphasis, now obscured by time, in the Christian canon of the four Gospels, traces the general outlines of Buddhism's introduction to and impact on the basically Confucian philosophy of China, and chronicles the* Nirvana Sutra's *appeals and shocks, the attacks and the counterattacks that the "new scripture" provoked from the intellectual community of monks and laymen in southern China at a time of great political instability. With one dynasty succeeding another with bewildering rapidity and with China itself divided, it would seem a poor time for theological debates. But as Professor Mather's unsorting of that tangled argument shows us, when would men have a greater hunger to know the processes of salvation than in just such an epoch?*

I want to talk about Buddhism. In fact, this is, I guess, the only paper in the symposium directly devoted to Buddhism; however, my subject is not Indian Buddhism, but Chinese Buddhism — Buddhism as it was apprehended by Chinese intellectuals, especially during the period of its incorporation into Chinese culture from the first century A.D. until about the sixth century. That's where I stop. It gets so complicated after that that I leave it to more competent hands. I will talk about the influence of one particular Buddhist *sutra*, the *Nirvana Sutra*, which reached China about the beginning of the fifth century and is one in a series of very important events in the history of Chinese Buddhism.

Every religious tradition goes through significant shifts as it develops within the historical setting. Some are the result of the natural unfolding of ideas latent within the tradition, and some are reactions to external influences. Thus, to take a familiar example, the Gospel narratives of the life of Jesus in the New Testament, though recording essentially the same events, reveal striking differences in emphasis that reflect internal and external shifts of climate between the first and second centuries when they were written.

First of all, Mark, somewhere in the middle of the first century, aiming to preserve an oral tradition which was in danger of being forgotten, gives us a simple chronicle with a minimum of interpretation. A little later, Matthew, in a limited campaign to convert his fellow Jews in Palestine and the Hellenistic world, attempts to connect the life of Jesus with the Messianic prophecies of the Old Testament, hoping to show that he was indeed the long-expected Messiah of the Jewish people. Still later, Luke wrote an account aimed not so much at the Jews but at a wider audience, the whole Mediterranean world, showing that Jesus was not just the promised king of the Jews, but the Savior of the world whom even the gentiles could call on for forgiveness and help in a troubled world. And finally, John, probably in the second century, wrote an account which transcended even the universal appeal of Luke: Jesus was not only the Savior of mankind but the eternal Word, the Son of God himself, the Alpha and Omega of all existence. Now from our vantage point in the twentieth century, we tend to blend all of these shifts, which were certainly very conspicuous in their own time, into an image which gathers all the points of view, in spite of their contradictions, into one synoptic view. This process naturally blurs differences and minimizes change. Another example of a shift in our own religious tradition that we would all recognize as still traumatic occurred in the sixteenth century with the Protestant Reformation.

In the case of Chinese Buddhism, everyone is already aware of the major shift that had already occurred in India, when the first split of the Mahasanghika sector later developed into the Mahayana. This split is still carried on in contemporary Buddhism. The Theravada traditions of Sinhalese and Southeast Asian Buddhism are still representative of the lonely, arduous quest for enlightenment. The Mahayana tradition, the much more universal and accessible quest for personal salvation through *bodhisattvas* (saviors), is practiced in most of the communities of northeast Asia. And still further shifts in the Mahayana tradition, especially in China during the first five centuries of the Christian era, continued a logical expansion toward a more universal scope, just as the successive Gospel writers in our own tradition did for the early Church.

The first Buddhist missionaries reached China between about A.D. 50 and 200, which we may take as one era, although there were constant changes then, too. The missionaries elicited their most enthusiastic response when they demonstrated superior medical knowledge and techniques of yoga and breath control because of the parallels with practices in the Taoist tradition. It is therefore no accident that among the earliest translated Buddhist *sutras* was a treatise on breath control, the *Anpanshou-i-Ching Sutra*, a manual on meditation and the control of the breath which was translated by a Parthian missionary in the middle of the second century.

A little later, in the third century, the climate of philosophical thought in China was itself shifting, away from a preoccupation with the Confucian classics, and especially philological interpretations of them, toward a mystical reassessment of Confucius. No longer was he seen as the world-oriented teacher but as Confucius the Sage who embodied nonbeing (*t'i wu*), which was the current expression for a mystical union with the ultimate principle of the universe. The Chinese intellectuals thus began showing an interest in translations of the *Prajnaparamita Sutras* that were trickling in from India. There were several of those, and the Chinese especially liked the *Vimalakirti-nerdesa Sutras*, which represented a polemical attack on Hinayana or the Theravada type of Buddhism. These *sutras* attacked the vulgar realism of the Hinayana and proclaimed the view of the Madhyamika school of Mahayana, then dominant in India, that all the *dharmas* — all phenomena — are empty, that they lack independent existence, but instead contain emptiness or *sunyata* itself, sometimes translated as relativity. These *sutras* thus claimed that *sunyata* is the principle of all existence, and the Chinese found *sunyata* identical to what Lao Tzu and Chuang Tzu meant when they talked about nonbeing. Consequently, there was a great surge of interest, at least among the intellectuals, in the various translations of the *Prajna Sutras*. And most of the students of these *Prajna Sutras* were already heavily influenced by this revived interest in the three basic mystical texts, or San Hsuan as they are called in China, namely the *Lao Tzu*, the *Chuang Tzu*, and the *I Ching* ("Book of Changes"). Thus, *prajnaparamita* Buddhism in China was really a blend of India's Madhyamika Buddhism with philosophical Taoism.

But after Dharmaraksha had translated the *Lotus Sutra* (the *Saddharmapundarika*) in the late third century, and when its retranslation by Kumarajiva appeared later, the new trend intensified in Chinese Buddhism. This *sutra* had a tremendous effect and is still the basic *sutra* of many of the Chinese sects. The *Lotus Sutra's* contribution—beyond the *Prajnaparamita's* polemical attacks—was the idea that it is not enough just to prefer a universal and compassionate soteriology of the *bodhisattva* to the selfish and isolated enlightenment of a Sravaka or Pratyeka Buddha. Ultimately there is only one vehicle of salvation, the Buddhayana. It is the eternal Buddha who saves everybody. All the other vehicles are merely instances of what is known as soteriological expedience (*upaya*), deceptive allurements to entice beings to leave the burning house of *samsara*; once free of it they realize that their liberation has been effected by the power of the Buddha alone. The introduction of the *Lotus Sutra* was also the beginning of a more devotional kind of religion which reached its highest expression in the Pure Land sect a century or more later.

Now it is at this point, after the introduction of the *Lotus Sutra*, that I want to step in for a closer look at what was happening early in the fifth century in the Buddhist community in China, especially among the intellectuals and more especially among the literate laymen in the southern capital. (China at that time was divided into two countries; the southern capital was modern Nanking.) If it is the eternal Buddha in his cosmic aspect, the *dharmakaya*, who becomes the object of worship, and if mystical union with him becomes the goal of one's own quest for enlightenment, then the way has been prepared for an even more drastic shift since this Buddha is not localized in time or space but is eternal and omnipresent, existing within every being in embryonic form. There is a kind of seminal buddha-nature (the *buddhagotra*) inside of each person which can become the real self.

Now if you know anything about Buddhism you know that Buddhism was opposed to the very idea of a self. But this new *sutra*, the *Nirvana Sutra*, talks about the real self (the *chen-wo*), in every being. The old negative idea of *anatman*, which applied only to *samsara*—to this worldly existence—is now replaced by a positive affirmation of personal identity which is indestructible even in Nirvana. Nirvana itself is conceived of as a joyous place, like the paradise of Amitabha in the West. Now this concept of a real self was essentially the message of the *Nirvana Sutra*, Sanskrit texts of which began to trickle into China at the beginning of the fifth century. The Buddhist pilgrim Fa-hsien left China by the Silk Road across central Asia in the last year of the preceding century, in A.D. 399; and after perilous travel on foot through central Asia and India where he studied and gathered Sanskrit texts, he returned by sea in 413. His ship was driven off course and landed on the coast of North China. Since China was divided, it was extremely difficult to travel between the two, but he gradually worked his way back to the southern capital and between 417 and 418 spent his whole time in collaboration with an Indian missionary named Buddhabhadra translating the first Chinese version of the *Nirvana Sutra* in six scrolls.

Now this edition contained some teachings about the real self already referred to, the joyousness of Nirvana, and the presence of the buddha-nature in all sentient beings. The *sutra* implied that this real buddha-nature which every one of us has within us will be revealed when it is liberated from the successive layers of delusion which keep it hidden. If you do not realize that you have the buddha-nature within you, it is not that it is not there; it is just that it is hidden.

There was, however, an exception made for one class of beings, mentioned only in this early version of the *Nirvana Sutra*. They are the so-called *icchantikas*, the hopeless unbelievers who are void of the seed of enlightenment and forever beyond the reach of salvation. This last exception was challenged by one Chinese monk by the name of Tao-sheng, who lived between 360 and 434. He intuitively felt that making exceptions of this sort was contrary to the whole spirit of the *Nirvana Sutra* and said so publicly; but because the *sutra* had mentioned the *icchantika* specifically, he was thought to be quite heretical and was driven out of the capital.

Quite a few years later, about 430, another version of the *Nirvana Sutra* was brought to China and translated in the northwest; that northern version, translated by Dharmakshema, stated clearly that even the *icchantikas* have the buddhanature. So Tao-sheng was finally vindicated. But between 418 when the first translation was made and 430 when the second one appeared, this controversy raged.

It wasn't the only issue, though, that got people excited in those times. Implied in the buddha-nature principle is the corollary that buddhahood is within the reach of everybody. Once the coverings of delusion have been removed, a process which may take many lifetimes, enlightenment would then occur spontaneously, completely, and permanently. Long periods of study, meditation, and good works might prepare for the moment; but in the last analysis, they could not serve as a substitute for it or even provide gradual degrees of entry into it. Since enlightenment, by the definition that was accepted, is to see the truth whole, you cannot achieve it piecemeal. And if you see it whole you do not just gradually work your way into it. It is a transcendent experience. It is beyond ordinary experience. Therefore, it is beyond the realm of study and practice.

You can see why a large number of the monks and even the devout laymen wouldn't like this idea. All the effort that they had put into pursuing the goal, all the hours of study, all the money which they had contributed to the monastic establishment was being wiped out by this new doctrine. They were not at all enthusiastic about it, and it caused great controversy, especially in the area of Nanking.

You can get a feeling for the exasperation of some of these

devout laymen by reading a letter that one of them wrote to Tao-sheng himself. The man's name is Fan T'ai and his letter, I am sure, represents the views of many people:

> The customs of foreign countries differ among themselves. When Sanghadeva first came to Chien-k'ang [that was in the year 398], the monks Hui-i and Tao-kuan and their followers all flocked to do him honor. But what he taught [it was the Abhidharma of the *Sarvastivada* school, a Hinayana school] was nothing but Hinayana doctrine. But they insisted it was the ultimate of all truth and that the Mahayana *sutras* which taught the doctrine of the nonorigination of the *dharmas* [in other words, the *Prajnaparamita Sutras*] were the writings of devils. After Sanghadeva's death, the Abhidharma was no longer in the highest seat. People stopped talking about it. And then later, Fa-hsien [the pilgrim whom I've just mentioned] arrived from India with the *Nirvana Sutra*, and that began to be touted as the last word. And this *sutra*, in its turn, insists that the doctrine of permanence, the permanence of the self and of Nirvana, was the greatest of all truth. *Prajna* [that is, transcendental insight, which was the highest goal in the *Prajnaparamita Sutras*] as the ultimate goal has to take second place.[1]

Then Fan T'ai, a great scientist, concludes, "Making inference from all this, I have to conclude that there are no governing principles among us. We hear some rumor and immediately we rush off to change our habits."

Into the white heat of this controversy in the southern capital, which took place around 418, came Hsieh Ling-yun. He lived between 385 and 433. Hsieh Ling-yun was an unexpected champion of a new doctrine of sudden enlightenment, (*tun-wu*) as it was advocated by the monk Tao-sheng. This year 418 was two years before the fall of the eastern Chin dynasty and was, as you can imagine, a rather unstable political period. Hsieh Ling-yun himself was also undergoing a series of personal traumas. On learning that one of his retainers had been carrying on an affair with his favorite concubine, he had murdered the man with his own hands and thrown his body into the Yangtze River. The incident had eventually been reported. Of course,

being a member of the aristocracy he could get away with murder, quite literally, but he was dismissed from his post as cap-
tain of the guard for the heir of Liu Yu, the future founder of the
Sung dynasty, the next dynasty in line.

Later, barely after the new dynasty had become established,
Hsieh, who was valiant in its service, was reinstated in his
former post. You see, the policy of the founder of the new dynasty was to conquer his enemies by loading them with kindness. In a sense, he was very much afraid of Hsieh Ling-yun, but
he forgave him all of his past misdemeanors and put him back in
his old post. The heir that he was now guarding, though, was
actually the crown prince since the new dynasty had been
founded. And the crown prince's younger brother became Hsieh
Ling-yun's best friend, a fatal friendship since this younger
prince plotted in the year 422 to replace his brother as crown
prince. This conspiracy of course got Hsieh Ling-yun in trouble;
this time they shipped him off to a hardship post on the southeast coast, a town called Yung-chia in what is now Chekiang
Province. He remained there between 422 and 423, in what he
described as poor health. But it was not too poor to let him
spend most of his time climbing mountains, writing poetry, and
discussing Buddhist doctrines with the local monks.

The main subjects, as you might guess, were the *Nirvana
Sutra* and sudden enlightenment. Fortunately we have his complete correspondence on this subject with three monks and the
layman Wang Hung, the man, ironically enough, who four
years earlier had reported his crime of murder. This correspondence, which ultimately involved some monks from the capital
and from the area of modern Soochow, was finally edited by
Hsieh himself and put into a treatise called, "A Discussion on
Discerning the Goal" (*Pien-tsung lun*); it is preserved in the Buddhist anthology *Kuanghung-ming chi*, which was compiled in
the seventh century. That's why we have a marvelous set of
documents relating to this problem.

My purpose here is not to lay out all the arguments of this
discussion; they are very subtle and very hard to read, too,
though worth a separate study in themselves. But it is interesting to observe in broad outlines what was troubling the oppo-

nents of this new theory of sudden illumination, or sudden enlightenment, and what arguments its defenders used in parrying
their objections. But layman Fan T'ai, whose letter we have just
read, was mostly upset by the irresponsibility, the whimsical-
ness of the people in the capital who made it their only business,
as Luke once complained about the citizens of Athens, either to
hear or report some new thing (see Acts 17:21). Hsieh Ling-yun
himself was attempting to reach some kind of compromise between the best of Confucianism and the best of Buddhism. He
rejected the Confucian emphasis on the inaccessibility of sage-
hood. (According to then-current Confucian ideas, one must be
born a sage.) He liked the Buddhist teaching that everybody can
become enlightened even if it seemingly takes forever. On the
other hand, he liked the presumed Confucian mystical embodi-
ment of nonbeing, which would lead to the experience of the
one ultimate, *i-chi.*

Now this is mystical language and I am not sure I understand
it, but he seems to be saying that the Confucians believed in a
mystical union with the ultimate, an interpretation of Confucius
that the Master himself would never have recognized. But it was
the one that was current in Hsieh Ling-yun's time, and he thus
gives himself away as a child of his time. However, in the case
of Buddhism, what he had rejected was its insistence on gradual
enlightenment — what the Chinese call *chien-wu* — through ac-
cumulated study; instead he opted for their emphasis on the universal possibility of reaching enlightenment even though it takes
many years and many incarnations.

The arguments of the monks who opposed Hsieh Ling-yun
are all recorded in this treatise in dialogue form. The disputants
included Fa-hsu, Seng-wei, and two called Hui-lin but written
with different characters. Later the discussion expanded to
include people from outside their immediate constituency in
Yung-chia, people from the capital like Fa-kang, someone from
Soochow, and Wang Hung himself. This "round robin" of ar-
gumentation shows that all of them lined up to a man against
Hsieh Ling-yun's defense of the ideas of Tao-sheng. Their objections were quite simple. They said that if truth is not reached
gradually, then all the sacrifices and efforts made by the monks

and the laymen to reach that goal are in vain. To this Hsieh countered, "On the contrary, such efforts are soteriological expedients. Though fragmentary and therefore false, they would ultimately lead to a point where the truth could be suddenly grasped."

His opponents made other but similar objections. If by study one's clarity of understanding increases, is not this gradual enlightenment? Hsieh Ling-yun countered that study increases faith (*hsin*), not clarity of understanding — an interesting point. Faith in turn propels one toward goodness and motivates one to subdue all of the passions, all of which may prepare one to become enlightened. But enlightenment is not part of this process. It is beyond it. Then one of the monks, Seng-wei, asked, "What about temporary flashes of insight? Everybody has temporary moments when they see the truth for just a moment or just a corner of it. Isn't that a form of enlightenment?" Hsieh answered, "Enlightenment is either once and for all" — *i-wu* was the term he used — "complete, permanent, or it isn't the real thing."

Now there were still other objections brought forth, some of which had ethnic and class overtones. For example, the monks faulted Hsieh for being really pro-Confucian and anti-Buddhist because he claimed that the Chinese are better at perceiving the truth (*chien-li*) generally, and hence are ready for sudden enlightenment, while the Indians are better at accepting instruction (*shou-chiao*), and hence are only ready for gradual progress. The monks thus accused him of social elitism because he seemed to imply that gradual and indirect approaches are soteriological expedients employed to accommodate ignorant people while direct appropriation of the truth is suitable only for those who are ready for it, namely the intellectuals like Hsieh Ling-yun. Hsieh insisted he was not trying to make odious comparisons. "There is no superiority or inferiority," he said, "in the transcendent experience of enlightenment." (In other words, there are no good and bad sages. Once you've made it, it's all there.) Hsieh was not claiming, you notice, that he had found enlightenment himself, a very interesting point.

Finally Wang Hung, the one layman besides Hsieh involved

in this argument, pointed out that Hsieh's technique of preparing for enlightenment by first subduing the passions was really no different from any other mental technique and thus not really different from that of his opponents. Hsieh had to admit at the very end of his discussion that what is gained by such preparations is a sort of anticipation of final enlightenment. It's like the *yin* of a winter day. Winter is the *yin* season and the *yin* of a winter day is complete *yin*. But it is anticipated to a lesser degree in the *yin* of a summer night, which is also dark and cool.

There is a somewhat tragic epilogue to this debate. Hsieh Ling-yun's last recorded poem was written in 433 just before he was executed. (He was accused of trying to start a revolution and was executed in the public marketplace in what is now Canton.) He ruefully contrasted his lot with that of the hardy evergreens which survive the cold of winter:

> Still green, the cyprus after frost.
> Dew-soaked, the fungus blasted in the wind.
> Of happiness, how much is there, after all?
> Long life or short is not what troubles me.
> I grieve that my gentleman's resolve
> Has not found surcease on the mountaintops.
> To yield my heart before enlightenment,
> This torment long I have endured.
> I only pray that in my next birth
> Hate and love be leveled in my heart.[2]

If enlightenment is indeed once for all, complete and permanent, and all approximations and temporary insights are just counterfeit, then never to have found it to the very end of his life could only be one more torment added to a career already tormented by strong loves and hates. We can only hope with Hsieh that in his next rebirth he found what he was so desperately seeking.

Now I want to move to a slightly later period but one in which we are still talking about the impact of this same *sutra*, the *Nirvana Sutra*, and show how in advocating the doctrine of *ahimsa*, the debate shifted from theoretical to more practical affairs. About two generations later, we come upon another Buddhist layman who was also a poet. The controversy precipitated by the original appearance of the *Nirvana Sutra* continued well into the T'ang period and culminated in the well-known distinction between the southern Ch'an school, known in Japan as Zen Buddhism, founded by Hui Neng in the early eighth century, and the northern school of Shen-hsiu. I do not propose here to follow the subsequent turns of the argument but only to take brief notice of how the *Nirvana Sutra* itself was viewed two generations later by this second Buddhist poet and outspoken admirer of Hsieh Ling-yun, namely his biographer, Shen Yueh.

Shen Yueh was a historian, and in his history of the Liu-Sung dynasty, one of the most famous sections is the biography of Hsieh Ling-yun. He admired Hsieh Ling-yun very much and felt spiritually akin to him. Interestingly enough, Shen Yueh, while accepting the axiomatic existence of the buddha-nature in every being, did not himself believe in sudden enlightenment. On the contrary, for him the buddha-nature can only be reached by delving through layer after layer of encrusted habits and misconceptions, a long and arduous process of trimming and paring. For the final denouement, Shen was prepared to wait even until a later rebirth.

In his vow of self-dedication, written in 509 near the end of his life, he wrote: "Creeping and crawling, those teeming beings [that includes insects, you know, as well as human beings] all possess the buddha-nature. Yet except by trimming and paring, the road to enlightenment is not followed." Another document, a sort of announcement of a public Buddhist lecture written twenty-seven years earlier, shows that Shen Yueh was really consistent all his life on this point: "If by a tiny word one might enter the Way [that is, become enlightened], the matter would become difficult by reason of haste. Or if by an enlightenment once for all one might mount up to emptiness, its effectiveness would be blocked because of suddenness. Unless one heaps up the gossamers one by one to reach a fathom's depth or combines many torches to make a single light, there is no way to ride two chariots abreast through the *prajna* gate or to cross to the *dharma* shore on lashed boats."

In still another document, Shen Yueh elaborates the basic premise of gradualism, which he apparently held himself. "If in this life the merit of molding and smelting gradually accumulates, then the truth which will be recognized in future rebirths will become more and more refined, and that understanding which has become more and more refined in its future responses will eventually reach Buddhahood where it will never be cut off nor ended." Now that seems to be a pretty clear indication that he embraced the idea of gradual enlightenment and rejected that of sudden enlightenment.

Furthermore, there is a rather humorous little poem that he wrote on this subject, a poem on the eight prohibitions that Buddhist laymen follow.

> Gaining the truth
> Is not easily hoped for.
> Only after losing the way
> Does one realize its hazards.
> After missing the path
> Again and again,
> One is suddenly enlightened
> To the fact that
> Enlightenment is not sudden.[3]

To his dying day, Shen Yueh carried his conviction that full enlightenment still lay ahead of him. On his deathbed in 513 he wrote a last will and testament which ended with these words: "I humbly pray that the sage heart [by which I'm sure he meant the buddha-nature] may be repeatedly advanced and enlarged. Then as your lowly servant faces the road ahead, he will leave behind no regrets. Though his progress be gradual, yet it is well."

Why did Shen Yueh reject sudden enlightenment? Was it his own troublesome backsliding that convinced him, as Hsieh Ling-yun had also been forced to admit at his own death, that he had not yet found it, and hence he settled for gradually finding it in future rebirths? Or was he merely reflecting the general climate of opinion among lay Buddhists of his generation, who under the sobering influence of the scholastic *abidharma* of the then dominant school of Buddhism — the Ch'eng-shih school — were returning to the more practical but admittedly less intoxicating view that the *dharmas* can only be emptied one by one after all?

The answer to both questions is probably yes. Shen was certainly not unaware of the various theories of sudden enlightenment. He may even have cherished the fond hope that he might become suddenly enlightened. But mostly he seems to have been content to record this interpretation as just one of several possibilities.

There is an interesting passage — one that I had trouble with because it seems to contradict what I have just said but which as a matter of honesty I have to record — in a preface to an edition of the Buddhist canon which was being published in Shen Yueh's time. It was commissioned by one of the imperial princes, since Buddhism at that time was being accepted and even encouraged by the imperial family. Shen had been asked to write the preface since he was famous both as an author and also as a Buddhist layman. In this preface, written between 483 and 494, he explains why certain Buddhist teachings were welcomed in China, especially the idea that the buddha-nature, which is in harmony with the true principle of the universe, can be inwardly realized without study. This was an idea that you could find in the Confucianism of the time. The preface states: "The unique perceptiveness of the spirit nature [that is, the buddha-nature], can be carried within one's own bosom and the wondrous power of the divine accomplishment [that is, enlightenment] does not depend on study to be realized." Here's another passage you won't understand but I'll read it anyway. "With solitary goad [or whip] one may be riding alone, not knowing where the limits are when the whole confused welter of bounds and old habits in one stroke becomes enlightened by the truth. [Something's wrong in the translation, I'm sure.] Hearing a tiny explanation, one may stride directly to the place of enlightenment, and receiving a single word, one may mount up to the other shore. Even before the long night of nescience has ended, the barriers of the mind open by themselves like dawn." Now this seems to be describing sudden enlightenment, but he was not describing his own experience.

Further, in the same document, he talks about another practice that was becoming popular among Chinese Buddhists — that of sitting before the Buddhist image and concentrating one's attention on it. This probably is some sort of antecedent to later Tantric practices. "If one avails oneself of this 'direct mind,' that is, if through the contemplation of an image one extends his sincerity and proceeds by intuition, then in half a breath one may pursue the truth and in a single moment arrive there. All the ups and downs of the feelings disperse like clouds and mist." At first, this appears to directly contradict what Hsieh had written in the documents quoted earlier, but I think no one is more aware than Shen Yueh of different shifts and changes in the Buddhist doctrine that had occurred in his own lifetime; I think he's merely recording these different points of view. He was looking, though, for some point of coherence because like many other Buddhist laymen he was confused by these shifts. And for him, that point of coherence was found in the same *sutra*, in the *Nirvana Sutra*. For Hsieh Ling-yun, the unique teaching of the *sutra* was not the buddha-nature, nor enlightenment, nor the real self, nor the joyousness of Nirvana; instead it was ultimate compassion, what he called *chiu-ching tz'u-pei*. That means carrying the buddha-self, or ideal of saving living beings, to its ultimate conclusion, applying it even to insects.

We think that the Buddhists have always had this doctrine of *ahimsa*; they inherited it from a long tradition in India. Interestingly enough, it never caught on very well in China. The doctrine of harmlessness in India was, in a large measure, responsible for the Indian monks begging for their food rather than farming, because tilling the soil would have inevitably harmed the insects and rodents that lived in the ground. But in China, from the beginning the monks grew their own food; and although the Chinese Buddhists recognized *ahimsa* as a principle —that is, not harming life, not killing—in practice, only a handful of very devout people ever did more than observe certain specified fast days, *chai* as they're called, every month.

It seems to have taken the *Nirvana Sutra's* translation in the fifth century to make it explicit to the Chinese Buddhists that the command not to kill applied continuously and consistently to all living beings. The culmination of this realization came in the year 517 when the Emperor Liang Wu-ti, a very famous pro-Buddhist emperor, made a national prohibition against the use

of animal sacrifices. The Chinese had previously excused themselves on the grounds that the Buddhist *sutras* list three varieties
of meat consumption that were considered pure: if you have not
seen the living thing, if you have not heard its cries, and if you
do not suspect that it was killed just for you, then you can go
ahead and eat it.

There is a passage, however, in the *Nirvana Sutra* which addresses this problem directly: "At that time the bodhisattva
Kasyapa said to the Buddha, 'World-honored one, meat eaters
ought not to donate meat to the *Sangha* [in other words, to the
monks]. Why? Because in my view one who does not eat meat
has great merit.' The Buddha praised Kasyapa's words and then
went on to say, 'From this day onward I do not permit disciples
to eat meat. If they receive faithful donations from alms-givers,
they should look on this food as if it were the flesh of their own
children. The one who eats meat has cut off the seeds of compassion.' " The three pure varieties of meat consumption which
I have just mentioned were only gradually evolved according to
particular circumstances, and they were not meant to be permanent. So in Shen Yueh's essay on ultimate compassion, he said:
"The meaning of the Buddhist religion is rooted in compassion.
And among the essential ingredients of compassion, the preservation of life is the most important. Because of the difficulty
of reforming deeply ingrained habits, the Buddha at first established the three pure varieties of meat eating as an extension
of the Way of Expedience. But when it came to his later years
and his teaching just before his Nirvana [contained in the *Nirvana Sutra*, which is when he was supposed to have preached
it], he greatly clarified the meaning of compassion, bequeathing
it to later generations. Earlier, before the *Nirvana Sutra* had
appeared in China, for a space of ten or more years, [that is,
from about 400-415], among the eminent monks on Mount Lu
[this includes Hui-yuan and the Lu-shan community], there
were already some vegetarians, but they were considered freaks
somehow. Was it not a case of intuitively following their hearts'
understanding which was spontaneously in agreement with the
truth? But after the *Nirvana Sutra* came, the three pure varieties
of meat consumption came to an end. People now have taken to

heart its ultimate teaching and seized upon its models on an ever-increasing scale."

Now this is fairly straightforward documentation for the relatively late acceptance of the ultimate implications of compassion in China. Yet Shen Yueh makes clear that this involved not boiling the pupae of silk worms in the cocoon, one necessary step in the process of silk manufacturing, as well as not killing animals, fish, or fowl for sacrifices. Instead he advocates wearing linen and hemp and eating fruits and vegetables. "For the meat eater and the silk wearer share exactly the same *karma* as the hunter, the fisherman, the butcher, the silk-worm raiser, and the silk thread reeler." His statement of confession and remorse is a very moving document, full of real sincerity and candor, though it is placed in the midst of a lot of very perfunctory confessions. But he devotes fully one-fourth of the text to expressions of remorse over hunting and fishing exploits, mindless acts of cruelty to defenseless animals, sumptuous banquets on various kinds of meat, and even killing mosquitoes which had disturbed his sleep on a summer night.

At first sight the importance given to this particular aspect of compassion seems disproportionate until we realize that once more a revolutionary idea, which by now seems trite or even trivial, had suddenly gripped the imagination of the literate members of the Chinese Buddhist community.

To summarize what has been said concerning the impact of the *Nirvana Sutra* in the early fifth century and at the turn of the sixth, I would stress that the earlier excitement centered around theoretical considerations, such as the doctrine of the universal buddha-nature, the identity and permanence of the real self even in Nirvana, whereas the later interest of Shen Yueh was of the far more practical sort involving the consistent practice of vegetarianism. It would be simpleminded to conclude that there was a shift during the fifth century from ideas to action, since there is plenty of evidence that both practical and ideological concerns were felt throughout the whole Six Dynasty period. But it is an interesting example of how perceptions of the same philosophy gradually change, even in the space of two generations.

NOTES

1. *Hung-ming chi* 12 (Taisho 52.224c-228a). Unless otherwise noted, translations are by the author.

2. *Kuang hung-ming chi* 18 (Taisho 52.356a).

3. Ting Fu-pao, *Ch'uan Han San-kuo Chin nan-pei-ch'ao shih* (Taipei reprint, I-wen Book Co., 1962), p. 1230.

LATTER-DAY
SAINT
SCRIPTURE

9

Adele Brannon McCollum

The First Vision: Re-Visioning Historical Experience

Associate professor of philosophy and religions at Montclair State College in New Jersey, Adele McCollum's first degree was in psychiatric nursing, a health interest that later surfaced in a broader form when she developed a course for Montclair on religious aspects and traditions of death and dying. She continued her education at Syracuse University and Colgate Rochester Divinity School; her doctorate was awarded in 1972 from Syracuse with concentrations in the history of religions, religion and culture, myth and history, and religion and psychology. Her publications range widely: the philosophy of time, philosophy of history, polytheism, Jung, mythohistory, women and religion, and various aspects of Mormon studies.

In this paper Professor McCollum invites the reader to turn, even if temporarily, to possible Greek parallels with Mormonism. She emphasizes the audacity of Joseph Smith's claim to have seen God the Father and Jesus Christ in vision, a claim reiterated by every believing member of The Church of Jesus Christ of Latter-day Saints ever since. Her double-pronged investigation probes first what it means to claim that such a vision occurred, and second, the content of that vision — the nature of God. To Latter-day Saints, comfortable with several generations of believing in perfection in human form that occupies definite time and space, she emphasizes the audacity of claiming a multiplicity of gods and ties it to a current theological development called "the new polytheism" that offers a way to make religion meaningful in a pluralistic age.

In a recent article, Jacob Neusner remarks that some of us have performed "a negative miracle." We have, he says, taken a subject, namely religion, which is "rich in life, and made it dull," have "turned the humanistic study of religion into a technology."

We have established religious studies as a respectable academic discipline, but perhaps we have done so at the expense of burying the *experience* of religions as they are practiced. Neusner continues:

> The [dead] subject we propose to describe and interpret in our classroom remains alive outside. Yet for many of us, particularly in history of religions (perhaps also in the philosophical side of things), that is an unpleasant fact, one we ignore. I think this is so because among our colleagues are some who do not really like religion in its living forms, but find terribly interesting religion in its dead ones. That is why an old Christian text, one from the first century for example, is deemed a worthy subject of scholarship. But a fresh Christian expression (I think in this connection of the *Book of Mormon*) is available principally for ridicule, but never for study. Religious experience in the third century is fascinating. Religious experience in the twentieth century is frightening or absurd. [1]

Neusner goes on to explain that we have taken on the jargon of a pseudo-science, that we have lost sight of the central issues of human experience which both religious studies and humanities should address:

> [The disciplines of philosophy, literature, history, and religion] explore the great works of imagination and passion, not alone of intellect, and allow us to experience, in the deeds and vision of other men and women, hitherto unimagined thoughts, unseen visions, unheard sounds, unplumbed depths of mature emotion, by which we measure and shape our own capacity and so transcend our small and limited selves.
>
> If we study religion, how can we insist that it is illegitimate to pay heed to the deeds and visions of those we study, but only proper to reduce them to textual variants on the one side, or to examples of a sociological sport, on the other. If we admit to learning the unimagined thoughts and unseen visions not only of poets but also of religious geniuses, as I think we must do, then is our understanding of our scholarly and educational work not subject to a measure of revision?[2]

The need for Neusner's having to write this particular article may be invisible here at Brigham Young University because we are in a place where the religion of the classroom is, for the most part, the religion of experience outside the classroom. But there are other places. Places in which students, colleagues, and administrators still remain unconvinced that religion addresses the great questions of lived reality, questions of love and dying, of self-transcendence, of sacrifice and resignation, of what it means to be human, to wait, to hope, to expect, to interrogate the cosmos expecting an answer. "Some men and women have known how passionately to care and dream for what is sacred. These we teach: the creations of their caring, their passion, and their sacrifice."[3]

All of which is to say that I am delighted to be included in a program which, while dealing with the literature of belief, extends to the expression of the religious *experience* in sacred texts. I take this to mean that we expect a certain transparency of text which allows the experience of the *numinous* to show through.

We might, I suppose, get entangled in the "expression" or linguistic part of this title; but I have chosen to dwell on the experiential aspect: on the idea that, as Stanley Hopper might have said, text can in some way be seen to be the "ambush of the Marvelous,"[4] that which has laid hold of the great and glorious theophany.

I have taken the liberty of subjecting a Mormon text to the same sort of comparative study which we are willing to apply to other texts, believing that this can be an illuminating venture, rather than a reducing exercise. In so doing, I have allowed myself to be caught between a rock and a hard place. I have agreed to take seriously the Mormon vision, which leaves me open to the ridicule of my colleagues in the East. For this essay, I have agreed to allow the Mormon text to speak its own experience alongside the texts of other religions, distinguishing none as more true than another. That leaves me open to criticism from those within who might wish the Mormon text could in some way be raised aloft or set apart from other texts before it is subjected to scholarly scrutiny rather than after.

For this paper I have selected a very small portion of a Mormon text, Joseph Smith's account of his first vision. In fact, it is one of the more obscure Mormon texts, being tucked away in the Pearl of Great Price, perhaps the least-known, outside the Church, of all Christian texts. It is referred to in the "Explanatory Introduction" to the Doctrine and Covenants but only gradually received the attention which accompanied the Joseph Smith visions of Moroni, possibly because the later visions led directly to the unearthing of the Book of Mormon, which gained immediate attention. Certainly, outside the Church the First Vision is frequently overlooked. I cannot here discuss the reasons for this lack of attention since it is my intention to deal with the experience related to the text rather than with the historiographical development of the text. Other scholars have documented the First Vision in its historical setting.[5]

A testimony of the truth of Mormonism consists not only in the affirmation of the *content* of the revelations made to Joseph

Smith, but also in the belief *that* there is a modern-day revelation which began with his First Vision. That is to say, Mormons believe first *that* there was a vision and second believe *what* that vision included. Consequently, it is necessary to engage in a two-pronged investigation. The first inquiry will be directed toward the questions, "Did Joseph Smith have a vision?" "What is the visionary experience?" "Is a vision necessarily a religious experience; and if so, how, as religious experience, is it different from ordinary profane experience?"

Second, I will try to direct attention toward the *content* of that vision, most particularly the plurality of personages which appeared to Joseph Smith.

When we concern ourselves simply with the account of the First Vision, we have no more to commend it to us than we have in the visions of George Fox or Theresa of Avila. We have what Joseph Smith says: "I saw a vision." (JS—H 1:25.) He is insistent upon it as is every person who believes he or she had a vision. William James has said that "the genuineness of religion is . . . indissolubly bound up with the question whether the prayerful consciousness be or be not deceitful. The conviction that something is genuinely transacted in this consciousness is the very core of living religion."[6]

Joseph Fielding Smith alludes to another kind of awareness when he says: "Great was his [Joseph Smith's] faith—so great that he was able . . . to penetrate the veil. . . . It was not, therefore, with the power of the natural eye that this great Vision was beheld, but by the aid of the eye of the spirit. The natural man without the saving grace of the power of the Lord, could not behold his presence in this manner, for he would be consumed."[7]

Here we have the testimonies of a philosopher / psychologist and of a believer / historian attesting to the same thing: we must judge religious experience by criteria different from those applied to other phenomena. And in some way both James and Joseph Fielding Smith direct us to faith as a useful instrument in this evaluative process. James is further helpful in pointing out that theories which discredit religious experience because of its origins are not only unsuccessful but unintelligent as well. No one, he claims, would attack the findings of a genius in the natural sciences by discoursing upon his medical history, family financial status, moral conduct, or otherwise. Neither, says James, can we discredit religious genius by referring to epilepsy, syphilis, disreputable occupations, etc. "By their fruits ye shall know them, not by their roots." It is, then, what issues from a religious experience that counts, not the past life of the visionary. Were that not the case we could not listen at all to Paul or to Siddhartha Gautama or to Mahavira the Jain, all of whom seemed given to excess at one time in their lives. As James says, let "the bugaboo of morbid origin . . . scandalize your piety no more."[8]

Despite the best efforts of James and others, I am still plagued by those who ask, "How can anyone as smart as you are believe such junk?" The only appropriate answer seems to be Chesterton's remark that he is constantly amazed that people will believe that chickens come from eggs but not that princes come from frogs when he has seen many more princes that looked like frogs than chickens that looked like eggs.[9]

As for Joseph Smith's vision, he is certain that it occurred. He was first seized by some dark power of destruction which departed with the coming of the light. When a Methodist minister attacked him for reporting the vision, he was astonished; neither did he understand the prejudice directed toward him by those who could not see the truth of his vision. It was, as far as he was concerned, a fact that he had beheld a vision. He had actually seen the light and neither hatred, ridicule, nor persecution could convince him otherwise. It was true, and he could better withstand the attacks of his fellow human beings than he could withstand God. He *knew* he'd had the vision and he was convinced that God knew it. So convinced was he of this experience that he had full confidence that other divine manifestations could occur.

Our point, as scholars of religion, is not to argue whether or not the vision occurred. It is, instead, to learn what we are able from Smith's visionary experience. Jacob Neusner would no doubt remind us that few question Arjuna's vision of Krishna or the visions of Black Elk in quite the same way we question the visions of Joseph Smith.

We question the validity only of that which can immediately impinge upon our current experience. While we never question ancient revelation, we question modern revelation because it is threatening. It threatens our experience of our world, the world that is stale and dull but nevertheless reliable precisely because it is not affected by revelations popping up at us just when we have things all sorted out. To risk believing in modern revelation is to risk changing a way of life. And that is a terrifying risk. (This fact we ought not to forget when we preach about modern-day prophets.) The human experience of the divine is awesome and it is just this awesomeness that confronts anyone who must deal with the real possibility of experiencing revelation. Undoubtedly it was part of the experience of Joseph Smith.

This is the awesomeness that Rudolph Otto has called the *Numinous*, the *Mysterium Tremendum et Fascinans* — that which terrifies and yet at the same time entices, fascinates, draws us into it in such a way that we experience the reality of another kind of thinking. We experience the eruption of the divine and that experience is too much for us.[10] How many times people have been frozen in fear at the presentation of divinity: the Philistines who steal the Ark are given a plague; Moses is warned not to let his people ascend Mount Sinai; Jesus warns Peter, James, and John as they return from the Mount of Transfiguration, "Tell no man what ye have seen"; the fear and trembling of Arjuna at the presentation of the divine form of Krishna in the *Bhagavad Gita*.[11] It is claimed that no man looks on God and lives. And to believe in the vision of Joseph Smith is to believe that one may have to look on God and yet live. And that risk is great because one will never again live in the same way. To look upon God is to die to the old and to become the new. And we are too comfortable with the old. The hierophany, the eruption of the Holy — that is indeed, as Joseph Fielding Smith reminds us, something to be viewed only with the eyes of faith lest we be consumed.

The experience of the *numinosum*! That is the visionary experience. Sadly, I find it is missing in the lives of most of my students. Nothing grasps them, least of all anything categorized as "religious." They are bereft of a whole range of experience because they have neither the eye of faith nor the four-fold vision of William Blake.

It is this experience of the *numinous* which both draws and repels that makes the difference between *Geschichte* and *Heilsgeschichte* (history and sacred history). Faith in this first vision of Joseph Smith as the manifestation of God in human history, as the first theophany of the new dispensation, is what makes the linear daily existence of the Mormon different from the daily existence of the nonbeliever. Events are not seen by the believer simply as strings of incidents to be "gotten through" in order to get on to the next event. In sacred history each event, each encounter, is endowed with meaning because it is done in the recognition that human history is of vital importance because it is through the dailiness of living that God draws near to man, confronts and challenges human life, and finally makes demands on human thinking and behavior. This, by the way, is also recognized by rabbinic Judaism, hence the seemingly nitpicking detail of parts of the Talmud. In fact, both rabbinic Judaism and Mormonism agree that God is concerned about the small things of daily life: eating, traveling ("take us home in safety"), health, sex. History becomes a series of hierophanies.

One who has been taken hold of by a vision such as the first vision of Joseph Smith no longer lives in quite the same historical frame as one who has not experienced the eruption of the *numinous* in human affairs. Mormons say that Joseph Smith had that first vision in the Sacred Grove. In fact, he had it in a clump of trees which then became the Sacred Grove. We testify to the First Vision when we say that we have a testimony that Joseph Smith was a prophet. If we say that in honesty, what we mean is that we too are aware that the divine is indeed at work in the midst of us.

One of the most important things about Joseph Smith's account of his first vision is his certainty that some divine manifestation would come once again. This absolute surety that the finite and infinite, the transcendent and immanent meet grows, for Joseph Smith and the Latter-day Saints, out of the conviction *that* the First Vision occurred. It also becomes certain as we look at the accounts of *what* was revealed in that First Vision.

Here I will speak only of one aspect of the content of the vision. Nevertheless, it is the *thatness* of the First Vision which urges the discussion I wish to begin. I am speaking of the nature of God.

It seems to me that there is a logical inconsistency in experiencing a theophany such as a vision and thereafter making the assertion that God is abstract, cannot be known, is purely invisible spirit. Quite obviously, if one has experienced a vision of the divine, the divine can be known, at least to some degree. This is not to imply that visionary experience provides exhaustive knowledge of God. Nor is it to suggest that every paradox ought to be resolved. It is to suggest, however, that every appearance of the divine in the realm of the finite ought to give at least the intimation that there is a finite aspect to the divine and/or a divine aspect to the finite. In other words, God and man are in some way sufficiently similar that they can know and understand each other. It is on this issue that most of the accusations of heresy against Mormonism depend.

Of the several accounts of Joseph Smith's first vision and of the testimonies of others of Joseph's account of the vision, only the 1832 account fails to mention the fact that there were involved and present two distinct personages.

It was the matter of the two personages that caused the Methodist minister to whom Joseph first spoke of the vision to brand him a heretic. While I have, until now, been speaking of the experience of the vision in and of itself, I wish now to turn to the experience of the *content* of the vision insofar as it can be related to the matter of the two personages of the Father and the Son appearing separate and distinct from each other.

Once more we can turn to Joseph Fielding Smith: "The doctrine was taught that the Father, Son and Holy Ghost were incomprehensible, without body, parts, and passions. A revelation of the Father and the Son as separate persons, each with a body tangible and in the form of the body of man, was destructive of this doctrine, as revelation [the vision] was [destructive] of the doctrine of the closed heavens.[12]

If we are still to deal with experience, the question now becomes, "What is the difference between God experienced as One and God experienced as Many?"

It seems to me that before all else, the experience of Many allows room for univocal experience. Zeus alone, Shiva alone, Wakan Tanka alone, or at least one at a time. Joseph Smith appears to think similarly, for while insisting on the plurality of Gods, he also affirms that there is one *for us*. It is less clear how the experience of One and only One allows for the experience of Multiplicity.

Joseph Smith spoke frequently of there being not God, but Gods. Perhaps his two strongest statements on that matter are found just a year apart in sermons delivered on Sunday mornings in June of 1843 and 1844. The statement of 1844 is the most emphatic. In it he speaks of the persecution received from those who say that his preaching a plurality of Gods shows he has fallen; and he says that the thought has been with him for some time that he ought to clarify his ideas for the people. He then commences to preach on the plurality of Gods. He repeats that he has never preached otherwise and that the elders have been preaching the same doctrine for fifteen years. (That would date back to 1829, before the organization of the Church, so the belief has been there from the beginning and this does not represent a change in his thinking):

> I have always declared God to be a distinct personage, Jesus Christ a separate and distinct personage from God the Father, and that the Holy Ghost was a distinct personage and a Spirit: and these three constitute three distinct personages and three Gods. If this is in accordance with the New Testament, lo and behold! we have three gods anyhow, and they are plural: and who can contradict it?
> . . . The doctrine of a plurity [sic] of Gods is as prominent in the Bible as any other doctrine. It is all over the face of the Bible. It stands beyond the power of controversy. A wayfaring man, though a fool, need not err therein.

Paul says there are Gods many and Lords many. I want to set it forth in a plain and simple manner; but to us there is but one God — that is *pertaining to us;* and he is in all and through all. But if Joseph Smith says there are Gods many and Lords many, they cry, "Away with him! Crucify him!"[13]

The Prophet then continues that no one has seen the eternal world to offer proof that there is only one God. He answers the arguments of those who accuse him of worshipping heathen Gods: "Paul says there are Gods many and Lords many; and that makes a plurality of Gods, in spite of the whims of all men. Without a revelation, I am not going to give them the knowledge of the God of heaven. You know and I testify that Paul had no allusion to the heathen gods. I have it from God, and get over it if you can."[14]

Joseph then makes his argument from linguistic evidence, concluding that "the word *Eloheim* ought to be in the plural all the way through — Gods: The heads of the Gods appointed one God for us; and when you take [that] view of the subject, *it sets one free to see all the beauty, holiness and perfection of the Gods.*[15]"

We must here add "and the beauty, holiness and perfection of man" since the Prophet continues his sermon to include the teaching that men shall also be gods.

There is no question that Joseph believed and expected others to believe that there were many gods and would yet be many more and that they would all be gods which were in some sense finite in that they occupied time and space.

What is remarkable here is the fact that the gods are experienced as nonabsolutistic characters. The experience of the gods as in some sense finite and near, it seems to me, is quite different from the orthodox Christian view of God as wholly Other, transcendent only, definitely not finite in any way, shape, or form. The problem of the "infinite qualitative distinction" which makes it impossible to "experience" God directly or only as an abstract Other, simply does not apply in Mormonism. God is not "supernatural" in the way the word is generally used and consequently is felt, not as distant or discontinuous with human experience, but as an integral part of the human experience. In fact, the experiencing of God is so much a part of human experience that man is endowed not only with the capacity to experience god *qua* God, but also with the capacity to experience himself as god, that is, to experience God-ness.

Because man participates in the same necessity of being that God does, traditional problems with which the sincere orthodox Christian is buffeted — problems of contingency, meaninglessness, and alienation — are not a necessary part of Mormon experience. This is not to say that Mormons don't experience these things or that if they do they need only pray more, do more church work, and visit the temple more often, and it will all go away; but it is to say that if Mormon experience includes any of the above problems, the person is not fully experiencing the possibilities available and accorded to him in LDS theology. (This is a descriptive statement and is not to be construed as assigning blame or responsibility.)

In Mormonism, man, though finite, is not completely separated from God, a concept which, along with those just mentioned, rests in some sense upon the details of the First Vision. Joseph Smith had a vision in which two godly personages appeared to him in space and time, and they were recognizably constructed in the same image in which man is constructed. We have in this small portion of Mormon thought almost all of the "heresies" of the nineteenth century. The canon is not closed, God has a body, there is more than one God, man can be godly (no original sin), God occupies space and time, not in the complex manner of the *homoousia / homoiousia* controversy but in the same manner in which man occupies space and time.

Human action in history takes on importance because God and man intersect. No wonder Joseph Smith was told to join none of the existing churches. Had they understood him, they would not have admitted him anyway.

I want now to deal with only one branch of this extraordinary theology: that of the multiplicity of gods. What is the experience of one who perceives the gods as multiple? How is it different from the experience of one who perceives God as only One?

Let me refer to a very small book which was published first in 1974 and was reissued in French in February 1979, David L. Miller's *The New Polytheism*. We can call Joseph Smith's idea the "plurality of gods," "multiplicity of gods," or whatever, but there may be reasons why it *ought* to be called polytheism or at least "the new polytheism."

Miller makes some insightful prefatory remarks: "The multiple patterns of polytheism allow room to move meaningfully through a pluralistic universe. They free one to affirm the radical plurality of the self, an affirmation that one has seldom been able to manage because of the guilt surrounding monotheism's insidious implication that we have to 'get it all together.' "[16]

Miller cites the multifaceted richness of Greek structures of consciousness, long forgotten, sneered at, or pronounced heretical, but which, nevertheless, are a major part of the Western intellectual inheritance. One can wonder with Miller what the polytheistic experience has to do with the general cultural situation of the age, and also *how* (or even *if*) the modern experience of polytheism is related to ancient polytheism and/or to traditional Christian experience.

Miller's book is not germane to this paper because he suddenly discovers that Mormonism was right all along. In fact, he concerns himself only with the Greek gods and goddesses, ignoring entirely the Hindu pantheon because, he says, "we are willynilly Greeks because we are Western." At the time his book was written, Miller had no knowledge of the pluralistic impulses of Mormonism. Rather, his book is important because it raises the issue of the experience of multiplicity in Western thought. What does it mean to experience gods rather than God? And why is the issue so pertinent to the contemporary life of religion?

First, it is of import because our experience is manifold. We speak of polyphonic meaning in psychology, "polymorphous reality as a key to . . . history" (Brown), "plurisignificative knowing" (Wheelwright), "polysemous functioning of imaginal discourse" (Hart), "pluralistic ethnic communities" (Novak), and polyarchic government (Robert Dahl).

Nietzsche, says Miller, says it "straight out:" Polytheism! He refuses to hide behind "academic verbiage." And polytheistic to Miller means concrete, real, taking place in the lived reality of people, rather than in the false unity of the abstractions of Greek philosophy. It means being saved, as Mormonism is, from absolutism, since absolutism does not mix well with a finitistic god.

However, along with naming our experience polytheistic, Nietzsche (and Miller) also announce the death of God. Of this Miller says, "The announcement of the death of God was the obituary of a useless single-minded, and one-dimensional norm." A God who never existed in the form which was pronounced dead.

I find it most interesting that Miller sees "an incipient polytheism lurking always in democracy," because, he believes, social monotheism ends in fascism, imperialism, feudalism, and monarchy. "In calling our time polytheist, we are saying something about the state of democracy of our time."

We know from 2 Nephi that there must needs be "an opposition in all things" (2:11). Miller would call that statement a kind of philosophical polytheism since philosophical monotheism would attempt to raise Truth, Goodness, and Beauty to such heights that opposition would be eliminated.

Psychologically, Miller continues, "polytheism is a matter of the radical experience of equally real, but mutually exclusive aspects of the self. Personal identity cannot seem to be fixed. Normalcy cannot be defined." In polytheism, this experiencing of the self in many facets is not seen as pathological: "One gets along quite well in reality; in fact the very disparateness of the multifaceted self seems to have survival power. It seems to carry with it a certain advantage in the face of the times."

Miller uses the word "polytheistic" to apply to the social, philosophical, and psychological realms because he believes that behind all these lies a *religious* situation. Miller further points out that religious polytheism leaves room for a monotheism of sorts. Greece, India, Egypt, and Mesopotamia in fact were in some ways "consecutive monotheisms" or henotheisms. So with Joseph Smith. The gods are plural, but *there is one for us here and now.* Other places, other worlds? Joseph Smith fully expected they would have their own gods.

Miller makes a further point in regard to the early polytheistic cultures in commenting that religious practice and theology are or can be quite separate from one another. One might, and most did, worship one god — Vishnu, Wakan Tanka, Baal — but it required a polytheistic system to explain religious behavior, which is to say that the real practice of monotheistic religion may require a polytheistic theology to account for multiple experiences of faith. This, I want to suggest, is what we have in Mormonism. While one God is worshipped there is yet a polytheistic theology to account for multiple faith experiences. Individual revelation and free agency are the final appeal because Mormonism recognizes multiple faith experiences.

What fails a people in a time when life is experienced polytheistically is not their God but their monoprincipled thinking and theologizing. "Monotheistic thinking" cannot handle "pluralistic understanding" and we are left with incomprehensible explanations of the Trinity which finally cause those trying to explain it to give up and say, "Well, it's all a mystery anyway."

It is this steadfast refusal to admit to polytheism which contorts even the most lucid theologian's explanation of the Godhead. No such problem exists for Mormonism. If orthodox Christianity is working with a symbol system which is inadequate to the task of disclosing experience, Mormonism is not.

Polytheism is not merely an academic matter. It is a feeling for the reality of polyvalent experience and the discovery that revelation has not occurred once and for all, that neither God nor vision are dead, but instead were confined by a theological understanding which disallowed process because it focused on the being of God instead of on the becoming of the Gods.

I would like to suggest that the experience of Joseph Smith, our experience, and the experience which David Miller is trying to describe and locate in the traditions of the Greeks, is one of becoming rather than of being. Not only are men becoming gods, but God is becoming more godly. The process theology of Whitehead and Hartshorn attempted to finitize the divine in something called just that — process; but process theology never became the backbone theology of any practicing body of believers.

Process, eternal progression, continuing revelation—all of these ideas have indeed become the backbone of a large body of believers. For some reason, the polytheistic theology of Mormonism has become a way of articulating our diversity, our pluralistic situation. A becoming God rather than a being God is the central figure of the monotheistic worship and practice of Mormonism, and that becoming God of practice is buttressed by a polytheistic theology. It is this very fact which allows LDS religious thought to be congruent with its religious experience.

Once again I must quote David Miller: "The explanation systems of Western monotheism failed us—by putting it all together abstractly, rationalistically, pseudomystically, and artificially. Such strategy is essentially contrary to the new polytheism, which simply does not lend itself naturally to theologizing and philosophizing in the monotheistic manner. It is lived in one's deepest feelings."[17]

But to return to the Greeks. Ancient Greek religion was blatantly polytheistic and anthropomorphic, but at some point in history that polytheistic religion mutated to a mono-principled abstract philosophy which sought the One beyond the Many in which all things were grounded and from which all meaning derived.

Eric Voegelin in *Order and History*[18] traces this demise to Xenophanes, who became tired of the anthropomorphisms of the Greeks and desired to find and recognize the "One who is greatest." Xenophanes moves to a concept of universal divinity (one God). But there is a problem in Xenophanes which Christian theologians have overlooked. It is that while trying to establish one God he also often speaks of the gods. The Greeks, who had a word for everything, had no word for religion. Neither did they have words for polytheism or for theology until late in their history. Plato invented theology (*theologia*); the science of divine things is first mentioned in *The Republic*. (One might want to interpret that as "what is said about the gods.") Aristotle in the *Metaphysics* includes Hesiod and Homer as examples of theologs.[19] The word meant simply talk (*logoi*) about the gods (*theoi*). No theoretical abstraction is implied. Miller cites Gerardus van der Leeuw: "Theology was not yet composed of doctrines, theories, and formal structures of logical argument; myth had not yet intellectualized itself into dogma." Then Miller comments: "There is a sort of fascism about rationalism and intellectualism — a sort of rigid one-party dictatorship of the mind which forcibly suppresses feelings and intuitions expressed in concrete images and symbolized in the telling of stories. . . . The mind simply cannot account for all of life. By itself it is finally impotent. Thinking monotheistically about the deepest matters of the heart and spirit cannot put man in touch with life as can another sort of *theologia*: the telling of the tales of the Gods and Goddesses in personified concreteness."[20] I must here refer to James B. Wiggins, *Religion as Story,* a collection of essays, each of which is a different way of "restorying" history and theology.[21]

I have been known to say that Mormonism uses its history as its theology. It becomes clear to me now why I have thought this is so. I have even been known to complain that Mormonism has no theology. What I have meant, of course, is that it had no theoretical theology. I have been guilty of attempting to force a monotheistic theoretical theology on the polytheistic thought of Mormonism instead of realizing that while Mormon religious practice is monotheistic, the supporting structure of any religion which will survive in today's pluralistic culture must be polytheistic, and polytheistic theology means telling the stories of the gods and goddesses — including potential gods and goddesses. It means telling the story of Joseph Smith's first vision and of his subsequent visions as well. It means telling the stories of the Saints, the pioneers, of the potential gods and goddesses. It also means telling the story of the God of religious practice and of his Son.

I have perused my bookshelves: *Classic Stories from the Lives of Our Prophets, Outstanding Stories by General Authorities, Stories from Mormon History, Utah: The Story of Her People, Book of Mormon Stories, The Mormon Story, The Story of the Pearl of Great Price, Provo: A Story of People in Motion, The Story of the Latter-day Saints.*

Mormons are the world's best raconteurs. And rightly so it would seem. According to Miller:

> Narrative theology may be the only way in our time to revivify an irrelevant doctrinal theology which has abstracted itself out of life by managing to kill God. Concrete images make for a theology of the imagination and an imaginative theology [dare one say vision and visionary?], as opposed to formal theologizing of a conceptual sort. Placing the concrete images in a narrative adds the dimension of time and temporality to a theology which otherwise offers only spatial constructs of meaning, ruled over by a logic which may be able to tell true from false, but cannot account for what is real, a reality in which truth and falsity, life and death, beauty and ugliness, good and evil are forever and inextricably mixed together. . . . Religion means being gripped by a story.[22]

Mormonism, unlike monotheistic (one-centered) abstract theology, is gripped by a story; and instead of stale theoretical formulations, its theologians and historians tell the tales (*Story of the Latter-day Saints*), its Orpheuses sing the epic songs ("Come, Come Ye Saints," "Oh, How Lovely Was the Morning"), its dramatists write the plays (*Promised Valley, America's Witness for Christ, Because of Elizabeth*).

Wiggins and Miller both argue convincingly that polytheistic theology is best done by the people, not by the monotheistic, university-trained theologians. Wiggins insists that all the people tell their stories, hence testimony meeting. We gather to hear each other's stories. We gather to hear people tell of concrete experiences like the first vision of the Prophet Joseph. We gather to share our visions. And after the manner of Homer and Hesiod, Mormon historians tell the tales of the visions of the Gods and of the becoming of the potential gods and goddesses.

It is now time to refer to the subtitle of this paper, "Revisioning Historical Experience." What one may make out of all this is that to accept the first vision of Joseph Smith is to accept a way, not only of believing but also of becoming, of envisioning (putting the vision in), of returning (a way of turning back) toward the time when the gods were finite and inhabited time and space, a way of turning toward the time when history was the story of the divine moving through time and space. It is to turn toward a time when religion speaks to what is real and concrete and to turn away from a time when it is dominated by the monotheistic thinking of logical positivism and of abstraction. It is to return to sacred history. And it is, most importantly, to experience the meaning of vision in the historical dimension of time and space.

NOTES

1. "Religious Studies: The Next Vocation," *Council on the Study of Religion Bulletin* 8 (December 1977): 118.

2. *Ibid.,* p. 119.

3. *Ibid.,* p. 120.

4. Stanley Romaine Hopper delivered an address entitled "The Ambush of the Marvelous" at Syracuse University in 1970. The phrase itself is, I believe, taken from a poem of Delmore Schwartz.

5. Milton V. Backman, Jr., *Joseph Smith's First Vision: The First Vision in Its Historical Context* (Salt Lake City: Bookcraft, 1971). Perhaps it will soon find its way back into print. James B. Allen, "Eight Contemporary Accounts of Joseph Smith's First Vision: What Do We Learn from Them?" *Improvement Era* 73 (April 1970): 4-13, and "The Significance of Joseph Smith's First Vision in Mormon Thought," *Dialogue: A Journal of Mormon Thought* 1 (Autumn 1966): 28-45. See also Dean C. Jessee, "The Early Accounts of Joseph Smith's First Vision," and Richard L. Anderson, "Circumstantial Confirmation of the First Vision through Reminiscences," *Brigham Young University Studies* 9 (Spring 1969): 275-94, 373-404.

6. William James, *The Varieties of Religious Experience* (New York: Collier Books, 1961), p. 362.

7. Joseph Fielding Smith, *Essentials in Church History* (Salt Lake City: Deseret Book, 1953), p. 41.

8. James, *Varieties,* pp. 34-35.

9. See G. K. Chesterton, "The Ethics of Elfland," in *G. K. Chesterton: A Selection From His Non-Fictional Prose,* ed. W. H. Auden (London: Faber and Faber, 1970), p. 179.

10. See Rudolf Otto, *The Idea of the Holy,* trans. John W. Harvey (1931; reprint ed., London: Oxford, 1968).

11. See 1 Sam. 5:6-9; Exod. 19:12-13; Matt. 17:9; *Bhagavad Gita*, ch. 11. Many good translations exist. I would recommend the Penguin edition, trans. Juan Mascaro.

12. Joseph Fielding Smith, *Essentials*, p. 42.

13. Joseph Smith, *History of The Church of Jesus Christ of Latter-day Saints*, ed., B. H. Roberts, 7 vols. (Salt Lake City: Deseret Book Co., 1932-1951), 6:474. Hereafter cited as *History of the Church*.

14. *Ibid.*, p. 475.

15. *Ibid.*, p. 476; italics added.

16. David L. Miller, *The New Polytheism: Rebirth of the Gods and Goddesses* (New York: Harper and Row, 1974), p. ix. Next several quotations from pp. ix, 3, 5-7.

17. *Ibid.*, p. 65.

18. Eric Voegelin, *Order and History*, 4 vols. *The World of the Polis* (Baton Rouge: Louisiana State University Press, 1957), 2:179-80.

19. Aristotle, *The Metaphysics*, B4, 1000 ᵃ9; A3 983 ᵇ 28.

20. Gerardus van der Leeuw, *Religion in Essence and Manifestation*, trans., J. E. Turner (New York: Harper and Row, Torchbook, 1963), p. 560, cited in Miller, *New Polytheism*, p. 26; *ibid.*, pp. 26-27.

21. James B. Wiggins, ed., *Religion as Story* (New York: Harper and Row, 1975).

22. Miller, *New Polytheism*, pp. 29-30.

10

Steven P. Sondrup

On Confessing Belief: Thoughts on the Language of the Articles of Faith

A professor of comparative literature at BYU, Steven Sondrup graduated magna cum laude from the University of Utah with an honors B.A. in German in 1968 and later earned his A.M. and PhD from Harvard University with emphasis in modern German and Scandinavian literature. With speaking or reading ability in nine languages, he has published two books on Hugo von Hofmannsthal, numerous reviews and articles examining various aspects of nineteenth- and twentieth-century literature, and a number of translations. As executive secretary of the Association for Mormon Letters since its founding, he has broadened his interests to include Mormon literary documents and was awarded the 1979 AML prize for critical writing for his article, "The Literary Dimensions of Mormon Autobiography," Dialogue, 11 (Summer 1978): 75-80.

In this paper, Professor Sondrup points out some of the ways that the Articles of Faith, though not formally a creed of

The Church of Jesus Christ of Latter-day Saints, still perform some of the actions of a creed without binding members to a fixed set of doctrinal tenets, an impossibility in a church that asserts the primacy of continued revelation. Designed primarily for use in explaining gospel doctrines simply and briefly to non-members, these statements still show a surprising depth and richness of nuance suggested by the different meanings of "I believe," the phrase that opens twelve of the thirteen articles. Professor Sondrup points out that this phrase expresses meanings of agreement, trust, and confidence—ranging from the believer's giving assent to a proposition to his exercising faith that a given statement is, in fact, representative of verity. Another element of that phrase's supple richness shows when compared to the assertion that usually precedes a member's public affirmed testimony: "I know . . . ." Belief is not simply a weak form of knowledge, argues Professor Sondrup, but "is a mode of being and a course of action." And the communal feeling expressed by "we believe" stands in fruitful tension with the individualistic proposition, "I know," making "the dichotomy between them . . . a source of energy and enlightenment."

Man kann den eigenen Sinnen
mißtrauen, aber nicht dem
eigenen Glauben.
(One can mistrust one's own
senses, but not one's own belief.)
Ludwig Wittgenstein
Philosophische Untersuchungen

I n The Church of Jesus Christ of Latter-day Saints, the Articles of Faith are surely among the best-known scriptures. They are memorized and recited by thousands of Primary children each year, they are the basis of countless talks, and they are used by missionaries in a variety of ways ranging from door approaches to visiting cards. They are in fact so familiar, such an integral part of the fabric of Mormon religious life, that it is often forgotten that they belong to that exalted class of statements called scripture. Although the Articles of Faith are not formally regarded as a creed, as similar statements in other churches are, they, in their cogent and succinct summary of Mormon doctrine and experience, come as close as anything to a creedal statement. It is, moreover, in the context of creed-like statements that the language of the Articles of Faith can be profitably investigated in terms of three major considerations:

1. In contrast of form and function to other Christian creedal statements.
2. In terms of making explicit some of the implicit assumptions of the "language game" of confessing one's faith.
3. In the framework of particularly Mormon insights, beliefs, and practices.[1]

A creed or a creedal statement is, in general, a public pronouncement or a formal avowal in which the essential doctrinal content of religious belief is set forth. A creed may be simple and straightforward or relatively complex; it may be very brief or comparatively lengthy. The earliest Christian creeds are found in the Bible: "Thou art the Christ" (Mark 8:29), for example, or "Thou art the Christ the Son of the living God" (Matt. 16:16), or the more extended "There is but one God, the Father, of whom are all things, and we in him; and one Lord Jesus Christ, by whom are all things, and we by him" (1 Cor. 8:6).

From these and other similar New Testament models, many different creeds developed to meet widely varying needs. One of the earliest of these was the baptismal creed by means of which the newly converted Christian could profess his faith as he entered into the fold. Alongside the baptismal formulae, creeds developed with declaratory, instructive, and informative intents. Some of these assumed their most eloquent and soul-searing form, tradition holds, when uttered by martyrs in the moment they faced a violent death at the hands of their enemies. By the beginning of the fourth century, though, the nature of these creeds had changed and evolved into something quite new. Formerly, creeds had been relatively simple expressions of heart-felt conviction; they had been spoken by the believer in order to profess his faith or to align himself with the Christian cause; they had often been conceived in order to declare the nature of the Christian message to the hostile and antagonistic pagan on the one hand and to the indignant and offended Jew on the other. The earliest Christians understood that the profession of faith was fraught with danger and that the possibility of death was always imminent.

By the fourth century, though, matters had changed. Creedal statements were no longer motivated primarily by the need to confess the faith before a belligerent and inimical world but rather by theologic controversies within the church itself. Creeds often became pointed and aggressive polemics against heretics and were used as norms for assessing the orthodoxy of any individual or any position. The Nicean Creed was conceived, for example, as a definition of orthodoxy for the bishops and bristles with anti-Arian dogma and rhetoric. Gradually Roman Catholic creeds became less personal in emphasis and more doctrinal in orientation; the individual act of confessing the faith receded into the background while the institutionalized definitions of the faith advanced. The decrees of the First Vatican Council (1870), for example, began, "*Sancta catholica apostolica Romana Ecclesia credit et confitetur, unum esse Deum verum et vivum . . . .*"[2] Although it may be argued that Protestant creeds have tended to preserve some of the personal quality lost in the Catholic tradition, some institutionalization may be observed.

The Articles of Faith certainly have some similarities with the great Catholic and Protestant creeds but many differences can also be observed. Like the great creeds, they are public pronouncements in which the essential doctrinal content of the Mormon faith is set forth. James Talmage, though, notes an important and central difference: "Beliefs and prescribed practises of most religious sects are usually set forth in formulated creeds. The Latter-day Saints announce no such creed as a complete code of faith; for they accept the principle of continuous revelation as an essential feature of their belief." Against the background of this caveat, Talmage, nonetheless, concludes that the Articles of Faith are "an epitome of the tenets of the Church"; that "they include fundamental and characteristic doctrines of the Gospel as taught by the Church;" and that they are an "authoritative exposition" of Church doctrine as formally accepted by the Church on 6 October 1890.[3]

As was the case with many early Christian creeds, the Articles of Faith emerged out of the interaction between believers and nonbelievers. They appear in a letter dated 1 March 1842 from Joseph Smith to a certain John Wentworth, editor and proprietor of the *Chicago Democrat,* in response to his request for a "sketch of the rise, progress, persecution, and faith of the Latter-day Saints."[4] Desiring, perhaps, to distinguish the Articles of Faith from other creedal statements, B. H. Roberts makes a telling observation concerning their composition: "[The Articles of Faith] were not produced by the labored efforts and the harmonized contentions of scholastics, but were struck off by one inspired mind at a single effort to make a declaration of that which is most assuredly believed by the church, for one making earnest inquiry about her history and her fundamental doctrines."[5] B. H. Roberts thus situates the Articles of Faith much nearer the spontaneous confessions of faith of the earliest followers of Christ than the doctrinally polemic statements of the later Church fathers.

Like the immediate and direct confessions of belief of the first Christians and differing from the subsequent more formal creeds, the Articles of Faith have no official liturgical function and play no particular role in Church ceremonies or observations. They do not have any function that is even remotely equivalent to the use of creeds as baptismal formulae during the first and second centuries, that even faintly resembles the role of the creed in the Catholic mass, or that generally parallels the recitation of the creed in many Protestant services. Beyond serving as an authorized summary of beliefs, the Articles of Faith function most notably in a missionary context.[6] B. H. Roberts stresses that they were written for anyone "making earnest inquiry" about Mormonism.[7] The context in which they appear in the letter from Joseph Smith to Mr. Wentworth is indicative of this fact:

> Our missionaries are going forth to different nations, and in Germany, Palestine, New Holland, Australia, the East Indies, and other places, the Standard of Truth has been erected; no unhallowed hand can stop the work. from progressing; persecutions may rage, mobs may combine, armies may assemble, calumny may defame, but the truth of God will go forth boldly, nobly, and independent, till it has penetrated every continent, visited every clime, swept every country, and sounded in every ear, till the purposes of God shall be accomplished, and the Great Jehovah shall say the work is done.[8]

What is obvious from the individual articles following is that Joseph Smith intended to summarize succinctly and cogently the particular tenets at the heart of the Mormon religious experience. All but one of the articles begin, accordingly, with the pronouncement "we believe"; and while the substance of each article is relatively easily grasped, the full force and significance of the almost introductory "we believe" can be, and in point of fact is, often overlooked. The verb "to believe" is, moreover, arrestingly complex and disarmingly rich in its communicative range. In general, it is used in three relatively distinct and different ways:[9]

1. "To believe" can be used in the sense of "believe that," meaning "accept that," "have the opinion that," or "agree that." In this sense, it corresponds to the Greek πιστεύω ὅτι or the Latin *credo quia*. For example:
   a. I believe that it is snowing.
   b. "We believe that we shall also live with him" (Rom. 6:8).
      Πιστεύομεν ὅτι καὶ συζήσομεν αὐτῷ.
      Credimus quia simul etiam vivemus cum Christo.
   c. "I believe that it shall be according as thou hast said" (Alma 19:9).
2. "To believe" can be used in the sense of "to trust" corresponding to the Greek πιστεύω or the Latin *credo*.

    a.   It can be used in this context with reference to a person or to God:

        i.   "I believe him," meaning "I believe that he is telling the truth."

        ii.   "Be of good cheer: for I believe God" (Acts 27: 25).

           Εὐθυμεῖτε, ἄνδρες· πιστεύω γὰρ τῷ θεῷ.

           Propter quod bono animo estote viri: credo enim Deo.

    b.   It can also be said of a statement:

        i.   I believe what you told me.

        ii.   "They believed the scripture, and the word which Jesus said" (John 2:22).

           Ἐπίστευσαν τῇ γραφῇ καὶ τῷ λόγῳ ὃν εἶπεν ὁ Ἰησοῦς.

           Crediderunt scripturae, et sermoni, quem dixit Iesus.

        iii.   "I believe all the words of my father" (1 Ne. 11:5).

3.   "To believe," finally, can be used in the sense of "believe in" or "believe on." In this sense, it corresponds to the Greek πιστεύω εἰς or ἐν and the Latin *credo quia* and means "to have faith in," or "to have confidence in."

    a.   It can be said of a person:

        i.   Son, I believe in you.

        ii.   "Whosoever believeth in him should not perish, but have everlasting life" (John 3:16).

           Πᾶς ὁ πιστεύων εἰς αὐτὸν μὴ ἀπόληται ἀλλ' ἔχῃ ζωὴν αἰώνιον.

           Omnis, qui credit in eum, non pereat, sed habeat vitam aeternam.

        iii.   "We believe in Christ" (2 Ne. 25:24).

    b.   It can be said of a statement, a pronouncement, or a doctrine. For example: I believe in what you tell me.

    c.   It may be said in a general sense of an institution, practice, or concept.

        i.   I believe in democracy.

ii.   I believe in free enterprise.
iii. "Thousands were brought to believe in the
      traditions of the Nephites" (Alma 23:5).

This list, reflecting both modern parlance and scriptural usage, is by no means exhaustive, yet it suggests at least some of the subtle variations in meaning that the verb "to believe" can communicate. It would, moreover, be an unnecessary and misleading restriction to argue that any particular attestation of "to believe" cannot function in more than one of these categories at once. Some of the richness and depth of the Articles of Faith can, in fact, be inferred directly from the realization that all three major senses of the verb "we believe" are represented in the twelve times it is used.

1. "Believe that" in the sense of "agree" or "accept that."
   a. No. 2: "We believe that men will be punished for
       their own sins and not for Adam's transgression."
   b. No. 3: "We believe that through the Atonement of
       Christ, all mankind may be saved, by obedience to
       the laws and ordinances of the Gospel."
   c. No. 4: "We believe that the first principles and ordi-
       nances of the Gospel are: first, Faith in the Lord
       Jesus Christ; second, Repentance; third, Baptism by
       immersion for the remission of sins; fourth, Laying
       on of hands for the gift of the Holy Ghost."
   d. No. 5: "We believe that a man must be called of
       God, by prophecy, and by the laying on of hands,
       by those who are in authority to preach the Gospel
       and administer in the ordinances thereof."
2. *Believe* in the sense of *trust*.
   a. No. 8: "We believe the Bible to be the word of God
       as far as it is translated correctly; we also believe
       the Book of Mormon to be the word of God."
   b. No. 9: "We believe all that God has revealed, all
       that He does now reveal, and we believe that He
       will yet reveal many great and important things
       pertaining to the Kingdom of God."

3. "Believe in" in the sense of "trust," "have faith in," or "have confidence in."

    a. No. 1: "We believe in God, the Eternal Father, and in His Son, Jesus Christ, and in the Holy Ghost."

    b. No. 6: "We believe in the same organization that existed in the Primitive Church, viz., apostles, prophets, pastors, teachers, evangelists, etc."

    c. No. 7: "We believe in the gift of tongues, prophecy, revelation, visions, healings, interpretation of tongues, etc."

    d. No. 10: "We believe in the literal gathering of Israel and in the restoration of the Ten Tribes; that Zion will be built upon this [the American] continent; that Christ will reign personally upon the earth; and, that the earth will be renewed and receive its paradisiacal glory."

    e. No. 12: "We believe in being subject to kings, presidents, rulers, and magistrates, in obeying, honoring, and sustaining the law."

    f. No. 13: "We believe in being honest, true, chaste, benevolent, virtuous, and in doing good to all men; indeed, we may say that we follow the admonition of Paul—We believe all things, we hope all things, we have endured many things, and hope to be able to endure all things. If there is anything virtuous, lovely, or of good report or praiseworthy, we seek after these things."

The sense of the first group—those beginning "We believe that . . ."—is, perhaps, most directly accessible. Each article in this group expresses agreement with or assent to a proposition —agreement that, for example, "men will be punished for their own sins" and that "through the Atonement of Christ, all mankind may be saved." This is an acknowledgement that what we publicly declare as eternal principle is privately and inwardly so received and accepted. The emphasis is on rational assent or agreement, which stresses the cognitive and propositional while minimizing any element of profound self-involvement.

In the case of the next group — "We believe the Bible to be
the word of God . . ." and "We believe all that God has revealed . . ." — the emphasis is somewhat different: here it is not
principally a question of assent but rather of placing trust and
confidence in a proposition. To believe all that God has revealed
is to value, to trust in, to have confidence in his revelations, just
as Nephi's assertion that he believed all of the words of his
father implied a trust upon which action could be based, a confidence that opened new spiritual vistas. Etymologically, the
verb "to believe" suggests precisely this underlying notion of
valuing or esteeming and is related, moreover, to the verb "to
love." The *Oxford English Dictionary* traces the word back to a
common Germanic root meaning "to hold estimable, valuable,
pleasing or satisfactory, to be satisfied with" and gives as its first
definition "to have confidence or faith in (a person), and consequently to rely upon, trust to." Similarly, the Latin *credo*,
usually translated "I believe," etymologically implies "I trust,"
"I place confidence in," or "I rely upon," just as the Greek
πιστεύω , "I believe," is closely associated with πίστις ,
"trust."[10]

This sense of the word is even more marked and generally
more central in the last group of articles, those expressing belief
in something. The first Article of Faith, "We believe in God, the
Eternal Father, and in His Son, Jesus Christ, and in the Holy
Ghost," is not primarily asserting, for example, the existence of
God, Jesus Christ, and the Holy Ghost: their existence is taken
as a given, an implicit assumption behind the statement. Just as
in nonreligious discourse the statement "I believe in my son" is
not primarily cognitive and propositional but rather bespeaks a
personal involvement and a special relationship, so the similar
utterance "I believe in God, the Eternal Father" also centers on a
relationship of involvement and confidence. This Article of
Faith is, thus, primarily an assertion of trust, reliance, and perhaps even love. Its assumption is the existence of God; its message is one of confidence and hope. The same is true of the
assertion of belief in "the same organization that existed in the
Primitive Church" and of belief "in the gift of tongues, prophecy, revelation, visions, healings, interpretation of tongues."

All of the articles expressing belief in something — in God, in the organization of the primitive church — posit self-involvement, commitment, and indeed a deeply personal relationship.

The Articles of Faith, though, are not just accounts of inward spiritual attitudes. They are assertions, they are statements. They present in concentrated and distilled form the doctrinal substance of Mormon theology and of the Mormon theological tradition. They instruct those seeking information about Mormon beliefs and often, perhaps, remind believers privately and inwardly of the most important tenets of the religious community.

The Articles of Faith in both their public as well as their private use, though, have a dimension or function beyond that of simple assertion. Just as the statements "I covenant" or "I promise" both state the substance of the covenant or promise and perform an action — that of promising or covenanting — the Articles of Faith also have a performative element. The performative function does not derive simply from uttering the words "I believe." It necessarily presupposes that this expression is used in good faith and represents not only an inward attitude but also a specific mode of relating to reality. Paul seems to be making a similar point when, in addressing the Romans, he taught that "if thou shalt confess with thy mouth the Lord Jesus, and shalt believe in thine heart that God hath raised him from the dead, thou shalt be saved. For with the heart man believeth unto righteousness; and with the mouth confession is made unto salvation" (Rom. 10:9-10). In this context, the statement of belief is not just a report on a mental state but an action which, like covenanting, contributes to salvation. To be sure, confession of belief is not performative in precisely the same way as promising, vowing, or covenanting, yet it is more than simply saying, contending, or asserting.[11]

Since the oral confession of faith has this performative function that plays a role in the economy of salvation, it is not surprising that many churches provide a formal framework within which the belief in Christ can be confessed. Although the Mormon church does not use the Articles of Faith for this or for any similar function, ample opportunity is, nonetheless, provided for confessing the faith. The monthly testimony meetings along with many less formal occasions for testimony-bearing offer abundant possibilities for the expression of one's belief. Although the form for the expression of testimony is not rigidly prescribed, it has in the course of years become highly formulaic. A comparison of some aspects of the well-established formulae with the more formal and canonized Articles of Faith is revealing. Testimonies typically bear witness of the existence of the Father, the Son, and the Holy Ghost, of the divinity of Jesus Christ, of the divine calling of Joseph Smith and the current prophet, seer, and revelator, and of the divine mission and eternal efficacy of the various activities of the Church. Although these statements do not have exact parallels among the Articles of Faith, they correspond in a general sense to the assertion of belief in God the Eternal Father (number 1), of belief that a man must be called of God by prophecy (number 5), and of belief in the same organization that existed in the primitive church (number 6). In any particular testimony additional points may be made which may or may not correspond to other Articles of Faith. One of the most arresting differences between testimony bearing and the Articles of Faith, though, is in the use of verbs. Whereas the Articles of Faith assert "we believe," testimonies typically proclaim "I know."

Even without considering some of the most difficult aspects of religious epistomology, it appears that the major intent of the testimonial "I know" is one of propositional surety and confidence. The expression "I know" in this context stands at the end of a continuum containing such elements as "I assume," "I guess," "I think," "I feel certain," and "I am positive" along with many other expressions denoting various degrees of cognitive certainty. Just as the assertion "I know it is raining" is taken to be a significantly more substantial claim than "I believe it is raining," so the testimony, "I know that God lives," it might be argued, maintains far more than the simple "I believe in God." This line of thinking, though, represents an unnecessary over-simplification of a somewhat more complex issue. The difference between "I know" and "I believe in" is not just a question of the degree of certainty in the speaker's mind: "I believe in" asserts confidence and trust and implies existence, but the testimonial "I know" cannot simply be construed as intensification. Even while being used in a thoroughly religious context, the verb "to know" carries some of the force it has in a secular — indeed in scientific — usage for many Mormons. It typically suggests knowledge that is taken to be roughly equivalent to knowledge obtained by means of ordinary sensory experience. Ultimately the assertion "I know that God lives" is understood within the uniquely Mormon interpretive matrix to be based on experience with the Divine that can be framed in language — though admittedly, at times, metaphorical language — that is cognitive rather than impressionistic, that is repeatable, and that is, at least in principle, universally accessible. The assertion "I know that God lives" thus directly avers the existence of God and indirectly implies — at least in many cases — experience or personal involvement with God.

The expressions "I know" and "I believe," therefore, are complementary rather than antithetical. Taken in a broad context, they fulfill and extend one another rather than simply suggesting more or less subtle variations in the strength of a claim. The first — "I know" — asserts the existence of God and implies, within the framework of Mormon parlance, experience with God; the second — "I believe in" — asserts, on the other hand, involvement with God and implies his existence. While it is entirely understandable how the testimonial formula "I know that God lives" describes a certainty that goes beyond "I assume," "I guess," "I think," "I feel certain," or even "I am positive," the scriptural declaration "we *believe in* God the Eternal Father" with its implied assertion of trust, confidence, and perhaps even love should not be forgotten or deemed an inappropriately modest claim.

On the contrary, in terms of traditional religious values, the assertion of "belief in" may be more significant than the assertion of "knowledge that." For example, the statement "I believe in Jimmy Carter" with its endorsement and indication of support bespeaks more than the observation "I know that Jimmy Carter exists" which in comparison is relatively detached and noncommittal. Whereas the difference in personal involvement and commitment is obvious when the statements are used with reference to a living person, the distinction seems to be at least partially obscured or even reversed when applied to deity. This fact could, perhaps, be explained by arguing that the words have different grammars when referring to human beings as opposed to divinity. A simpler explanation, though, may be seen in the divergent contexts in which the two terms are used. Since the existence of Jimmy Carter is not seriously questioned by anyone, the assertion of his existence adds nothing to the prevailing climate of opinion. But his policies and actions are hotly debated — as would be those of any politician — and the endorsement communicated by the phrase "I believe in" may contribute in substantial measure to one side of the debate. In the case of God, the situation is reversed: the existence of God is frequently questioned, and thus the assertion of his existence may well challenge prevailing attitudes. If, however, the existence of God, of Jesus Christ, and of the Holy Ghost is accepted, a belief in them in terms of all that "believe in" suggests, though by no means a foregone conclusion, is relatively easily understood.[12]

Nonetheless, even when the existence of God is fully accepted, to believe in him is still a significant spiritual endeavor and by no means a trivial assertion in the confession of the faith. The Book of Mormon provides some telling examples of the dynamics of "belief in." At the conclusion of his farewell address, King Benjamin leaves his people with a challenge: he quite simply says, "Believe in God." He then describes in detail what this means:

"believe that he is, and
              that he created all things, both in heaven and in
              earth;
believe that he has all wisdom, and all power, both in hea-
              ven and in earth;
believe that man doth not comprehend all the things which
              the Lord can comprehend.
"And again,
believe that ye must repent of your sins and forsake them,
              and humble yourselves before God; and ask

in sincerity of heart that he would forgive
you" (Mosiah 4:9-10).

For King Benjamin, believing in God consists of giving credence
to the notion that God exists, that he created all things, that he
is omniscient and omnipotent, and that man must humble himself before God. In this context, "believing in" is an encompas-
sing and broad spiritual program, yet what follows is even more
significant. King Benjamin, still elaborating on what it means to
believe in God, adds, "and now, if you believe all these things
see that ye do them" (Mosiah 4:10). Far from being just a
passive inward attitude, "believing in" is a mode of being and a
course of action. "Belief that," indeed, "knowledge that" becomes "belief in" when translated into action and being. When
Ether maintains, that "whoso *believeth in* God might hope for a
better world, yea, even a place at the right hand of God"
(Mosiah 12:4; italics added), he surely understands "believing
in" to denote a mode of existence as King Benjamin described it
rather than the facile and often vacuous "Yea, Lord, I believe."
Similarly, 3 Nephi reports that the unbelievers set aside a day
for the execution of "all those who *believed in* those traditions"
(the traditions concerning the birth of Christ), unless the
prophesied sign of Christ's birth were given (1:9). If the belief in
the traditions had only been an inwardly held state of mind,
would they have aroused such anger and hostility on the part of
the unbelievers? The necessary conclusion is that this belief in
the traditions involved a way of living and relating to exter-
nality that was offensive to those not holding the belief. "Belief
in" is, thus, once again not only an attitude but a mode of being.

   Joseph Smith's explanation that we—meaning the mem-
bership of the Church—believe in God the Eternal Father, in the
same organization that existed in the primitive church, or in the
gift of tongues, prophecy, revelations, visions, healing, and the
interpretation of tongues is in the broadest sense a description of
a spiritual program leading to a mode of existence that justifies
—indeed invites—a sure hope in a better world and a place at
the right hand of God.

   One final observation remains to be made about the difference between the testimonial formula, "I know," and the

creedal, "we believe." The difference between the first person singular and the first person plural is symptomatic of a much larger issue centering on the relationship of the individual as individual to the group. In the Church, it has become almost a cliché, for example, to point out that one cannot live — usually meaning live eternally — on borrowed light. Each individual must eventually gain a testimony for himself, must come to a knowledge of the gospel for himself. Each individual must, perforce, establish his own relationship with Christ and must come to know Christ individually. Indeed, knowledge can only be held on an individual basis. Common knowledge in this context is knowledge held by each individual member of a group on an individual and particular basis. It is, thus, significant that the assertion "*I* know" can be and, in point of fact, is made. The testimonial "I know" emphasizes that the speaker has this knowledge on the all-important individual basis, that he is not acting according to the testimonies of others, that he is not living on borrowed light.

In contrast to the emphasis often given to the need for individual testimony, one is also frequently reminded that man cannot be saved alone. This warning is made most typically with regard to the import of family unity in an immediate as well as a historical sense but certainly applies with reference to the religious community at large. Mormon theology has always stressed that salvation and exaltation come, at least in part, as a result of promises made to groups — the seed of Abraham or the house of Israel, for example — and are contingent upon the realization of social, group-oriented goals which are strongly reminiscent of many aspects of Old Testament theology. The concepts of the house of Israel, the city of Zion, or the kingdom of God all emphasize the communitarian and social dimensions of Mormon soteriological thinking. Given the unique prominence of such thought in Mormon theology, it is hardly surprising that the Articles of Faith should all begin with the pronoun *we*. The fact that Joseph Smith was responding to an invitation to represent the beliefs of the Church as a whole when he wrote the Articles of Faith certainly is an immediate explanation for the use of *we*, yet his understanding of the importance of a holy community in the eyes of God must have played a subsidiary though noteworthy role. It is significant, moreover, to observe that the pronoun *we*, emphasizing communitarian and social goals, is linked with the verb "to believe in" which transcends uniquely inward and private attitudes in its reach toward informing an entire mode of being.

The contrast between the private and perhaps existential "I know" and the communitarian and social "we believe" represents a source of vivifying dynamic tension within Mormon theology. The viability and vigor of both of the formulations as they exist side by side in ordinary parlance suggest that the dichotomy between them is not to be overcome but rather used as a source of energy and enlightenment. The private "I know" must be so ordered that it ultimately contributes to the common "we believe"; and conversely, the communitarian "we believe" must be so structured that it leads every member of the community to a personal "I know." The dichotomy of knowledge and politics (ἡ πολιτικἡ) is, thus, not overcome but transformed into a vitalizing syzygy, into an energizing *conjunctio oppistorum*.

The Articles of Faith, thus, confess the faith—the faith of the individual Mormon and the faith of the Mormon religious community—on many different and varied levels. Their formulation, indeed, their language, is simple and direct yet implicitly evokes insights lying far beneath the conceptual surface. The Articles of Faith have elements in common with other Christian creedal statements but are uniquely Mormon, not only in their discursive description of Mormon belief, but also in their tacit and often subtle assumptions. Along with and often in contrast to the ordinary testimonial formulae, the language of the Articles of Faith—indeed the "language game" of confessing the faith—evinces a broad and panoramic view of many of the most important aspects of the Mormon religious experience which are more extensive and inclusive than their all too frequently automatized and tradition-laden perception suggests.

NOTES

1. Within the Mormon community in general, the concept of a creed has fallen into disrepute. On the occasion of the First Vision, Joseph Smith was

told that the *creeds* of all the churches were an abomination in the sight of the Lord (see JS—H 1:19). The purpose of considering the Articles of Faith in the context of the long tradition of creedal statements is specifically and emphatically not to contrast their contents but rather to examine some of the most fundamental aspects associated with the profession of belief: it is, thus, not the substance of belief that is at question but the implications of the confession of belief. For an introduction to the tradition of creedal statements see Paul T. Fuhrmann, *An Introduction to the Great Creeds of the Church* (Philadelphia: Westminster Press, 1960) and John H. Leith, ed., *Creeds of the Churches: A Reader in Christian Doctrine from the Bible to the Present* (Richmond: John Knox Press, 1973). See also the bibliography provided in Sr. Mary-John Mananzan, OSB, *The "Language Game" of Confessing One's Belief: A Wittgensteinian-Austinian Approach to the Linguistic Analysis of Creedal Statements* (Tübingen: Max Niemeyer Verlag, 1974), pp. 156-70. It should be noted that the expression "language game" is used throughout in the sense suggested by Wittgenstein.

2. "The Holy Catholic Apostolic Roman Church believes and confesses that there is one true and living God . . ." *Enchiridion Symbolorum Definitionum et Declarationum de Rebus Fidei et Morum,* eds. Henricus Denzinger and Adolfus Schönmetzer S.I., 33rd rev., 12th ed. (Freiburg i.Br.: Herder, 1965) p. 587 (No. 3001).

3. *A Study of the Articles of Faith* (Salt Lake City: The Church of Jesus Christ of Latter-day Saints, 1924), p. 6. See Milton R. Hunter, *Pearl of Great Price Commentary* (Salt Lake City: Bookcraft, 1951) pp. 246-47, for a description of the canonization of the Articles of Faith in both 1880 and 1890.

4. Joseph Smith, *History of The Church of Jesus Christ of Latter-day Saints,* ed. B. H. Roberts, 2nd ed. rev., 7 vols. (Salt Lake City: The Church of Jesus Christ of Latter-day Saints, 1932-1951), 4:535.

5. *A Comprehensive History of The Church of Jesus Christ of Latter-day Saints,* 6 vols. (Salt Lake City: The Church of Jesus Christ of Latter-day Saints, 1930), 2:131. Recent research suggests that Joseph Smith's formulation of the Articles of Faith may not have been as spontaneous and immediate as B. H. Roberts' description might lead one to believe: Oliver Cowdery, Joseph Young—a brother of Brigham Young—Orson Pratt, and Orson Hyde each wrote a series of Articles of Faith before those written by Joseph Smith. Although Joseph Smith's bear a marked similarity to earlier versions and may have been based on them in certain respects, his are more precise, more penetrating, and considerably broader than any of the earlier versions. Even in light of these facts, B. H. Roberts is surely correct in his assertion that they "were not produced by the labored efforts and the harmonized contentions of scholastics" (p. 131). See John W. Welch and David J. Whittaker, " 'We Believe . . .' Development of the Articles of Faith," *Ensign,* Sept. 1979, pp. 51-55. See also T. Edgar Lyon, "Joseph Smith: The Wentworth Letter and Reli-

gious America of 1842," 5 December 1954, in vol. 2, *Annual Joseph Smith Memorial Sermons* (Logan, Utah: LDS Institute of Religion, 1966), pp. 116-19. Here the point is made, among others, that Joseph Smith did not intend the Articles of Faith to be a creed in the normative and prescriptive sense in which some creeds function. This fact tends to emphasize their personal, confessional quality.

6. For an example of the importance of the Articles of Faith in a missionary context, see Spencer W. Kimball, "Priesthood Session Address," *Official Report of the One Hundred Forty-fifth Annual General Conference of The Church of Jesus Christ of Latter-day Saints* [October 3, 4, 5, 1975] (Salt Lake City: The Church of Jesus Christ of Latter-day Saints, 1975), pp. 117-19.

7. *Comprehensive History,* 2:131.

8. *History of the Church,* 4:540.

9. It is, thus, only the implications and dynamics of the expression of belief that are to be considered, not the substance of belief. See Dallas M. High, *Language, Persons, and Belief: Studies in Wittgenstein's "Philosophical Investigations" and Religious Use of Language* (New York: Oxford University Press, 1967), pp. 147-48. Many aspects of the following analysis were suggested by this study. The Greek and Latin citations were taken from *Novum Testamentum Graece et Latine,* ed. Eberhard Nestle; 21st edition, eds. Erwin Nestle and Kurt Aland [which includes the 24th Greek edition] (Stuttgart: Württembergische Bibelanstalt, 1962).

10. Notably, Noah Webster in both the 1829 and 1844 editions of his *An American Dictionary of the English Language* indicates that "to believe" as a transitive verb can mean "to trust"; this definition, though, is the last rather than the first as in the case of the *OED*. He further explains that as an intransitive verb, it sometimes implies "a yielding of the will and affection."

11. See J. L. Austin, *How to Do Things with Words,* 2nd ed. (Cambridge, Mass.: Harvard University Press, 1975). Although many of his arguments do not apply in this context, his definition of a performative utterance is succinct and useful: "It indicates that the issuing of the utterance is the performing of an action — it is not normally thought of as just saying something" (p. 6).

12. Statements like "I believe in Santa Claus," "I believe in ghosts," "I believe in monsters," and, perhaps, "I believe in the devil" all seem to assert the existence of the particular being in question and have little to do with trust or confidence. Since the existence of each of them is often questioned, the assertion of belief in any one of them is basically an ontological question. When Jesus, though, said, "he that believeth in me" shall live (John 11:25), he was clearly not addressing a question of his own existence but was inviting trust, confidence, and love. In this context, belief in Christ follows — rather than precedes — conviction of his experience and is a particularly significant spiritual achievement.

11

Bruce W. Jorgensen

The Dark Way to the Tree: Typological Unity in the Book of Mormon

A graduate of Brigham Young University with a master's and doctorate from Cornell University, Bruce W. Jorgensen has taught at Brigham Young University's English Department since 1975 where he has been assistant professor since 1978. Among his academic honors are a Danforth Graduate Fellowship and a Woodrow Wilson Fellowship. His academic emphasis on American literature and prose fiction has not narrowed his interests; he has published more than twenty stories, poems, reviews, and literary essays in Mormon periodicals.

In this paper, Professor Jorgensen suggests a method for understanding the variously interpreted Book of Mormon as "a structurally unified verbal whole." From Lehi's opening vision

This paper was originally delivered at the meeting of the Utah Academy of Sciences, Arts, and Letters in December 1977, and published in the Academy's journal, *Encyclia*, 54, pt. 2 (1977): 16-24.

with its linked elements of wilderness and fulfillment, to the ul-
timate fulfillment of the risen Lord's appearance to Lehi's de-
scendants, to their final degeneration into barbarism and sui-
cidal destruction, he sees the Book of Mormon in the pattern of
a transformation "by means of the Word." The implications of
that pattern — not only for Nephite society but for ultimate
theories of history and language — are suggested in a compact
and richly allusive manner that entices the reader into studies of
his own. His "Postscript — 1980," which follows the paper,
gives a historical overview of the state of the typological art as it
relates to the Book of Mormon since then; it also suggests some
directions for further exploration that might have been taken
had the limitations for this paper been different.

T he Book of Mormon has yet to be carefully read as a literary text. Almost twelve years ago, Douglas Wilson, a non-
Mormon, summarized this situation which Thomas O'Dea had
remarked over twenty years ago and which still has not visibly
changed. To Bernard DeVoto's charge, "formless," Fawn Brodie
had countered with "elaborate design" and "unity of purpose,"
yet she did not provide analysis. Wilson predicted that critical
scrutiny from a "mythic" or "archetypal" perspective would
confirm Brodie's judgment; such an approach, he held, "would
be concerned with . . . [the book's] dramatic configurations and
structure, not with its historical validity."[1]

But Wilson's claim, too, has yet to be visibly substantiated.
Non-Mormons seem content with O'Dea's enumeration of the
book's apparent reflections of Joseph Smith's nineteenth-century
American milieu — concerned with historical validity, not literary structure. Mormons continue to publish testimonials, or
expositions for missionary uses, or compendious aids to reading
for maxims, proof texts, prophetic warnings, and exempla, or
apologetics for historical validity.[2] Of these, Hugh Nibley's trac-
ings of pattern resemblances with ancient Old World culture
might help the literary analyst, but that has not been Nibley's

concern.[3] One recent essay by Richard L. Bushman, challenging historians who find American revolutionary patterns in the book, traces instead a "divine deliverance" pattern that has importance to its literary structure.[4]

Among more specifically literary articles on the book, Robert E. Nichols limits his "close reading" to 1 and 2 Nephi and concerns himself primarily with Lehi and Nephi as heroic or epic characters.[5] John W. Welch's studies argue that a Hebraic rhetorical pattern of chiasmus also controls larger structural relations in the book.[6] Robert K. Thomas's essay, "A Literary Critic Looks at the Book of Mormon," is largely a moralistic reading of the "small plates of Nephi" and does not attempt to grasp the book's imaginative wholeness.[7] A redaction by Clinton F. Larson, the Church's finest poet, has not been seriously reviewed either in the Church press or in Mormon scholarly journals, probably because, appearing in the guise of sixteen volumes of "illustrated stories" for children, it has not invited that kind of reading.[8] BYU student Courtney J. Lassetter's short essay on "Lehi's Dream and Nephi's Vision" shows an important insight but does not develop it very far.[9]

It is surprising that since Wilson's article no one has come along with some tools from Mircea Eliade, Joseph Campbell, or Northrop Frye to unfold the archetypal structure of the book. In particular, Frye's still unpublished work on the Bible might suggest the methods and their rich potential for insight.[10] Literary description of the book in our decade might call itself structuralist rather than mythic, but surely it is possible, without either pleading for or impugning it as an historical document of whatever century, to describe the Book of Mormon as a literary text, as a structured verbal whole with an "elaborate design."

Some of the book's own internal declarations of purpose invite a kind of response that even a practicing Mormon, if he has some literary training, can call literary without compromising the book's prophetic, theological, or moral values for Mormons and without urging those values on non-Mormons. All of the Book of Mormon narrators who say anything of their "intent" use words like "persuade" or "convince" (see title page; 1 Ne. 6:4; 2 Ne. 33:4). The second narrator, Jacob, says that he and his brother Nephi desired "that all men would believe in Christ, and view his death, and suffer his cross" (Jac. 1:8). With the verbs "view" and "suffer," Jacob suggests more strongly than any of the narrators that the book's unity of purpose is ultimately kinetic and experiential, that like Bunyan's *Pilgrim's Progress* it would "make a traveller of thee," or that like Rilke's "Torso of an Archaic Apollo" it says to the reader, "Du mußt dein Leben ändern" ("You must change your life").[11] And this does not mean that the book's inclusive intention will reduce to the merely hortatory, for like many literary works and like all scriptural books, Judeo-Christian or otherwise, the Book of Mormon means its reader to have a new vision of the world and experience. What Erich Auerbach says of the Bible may equally be said of the Book of Mormon: "Far from seeking . . . merely to make us forget our own reality for a few hours, it seeks to overcome our reality: we are to fit our own life into its world, feel ourselves to be elements in its structure of universal history."[12] And Northrop Frye's remarks that the Bible is a "systematically constructed sacred book," a "typological unity," and "a single archetypal structure" or "gigantic cycle from creation to apocalypse" can apply, on a small scale, to the Book of Mormon as well.[13]

In this narrow space, if I attempt to describe the Book of Mormon as a structurally unified verbal whole, I must be severely abstract, but I hope also for a persuasive clarity. I prefer at the outset to call my approach neither mythic nor archetypal but, deriving from a term and concept used by the narrators Nephi, Jacob, Alma, and the editor-narrator Mormon, typological. After all, as Frye's work suggests, the critical activity of patristic and medieval typological exegetes, like that of Renaissance mythographers, resembles that of modern mythic or archetypal critics. Further, typological interpretation of scriptural books has, at least in the Judeo-Christian tradition, the sanction of its prophetic and messianic use in the Bible.

Auerbach defines the concept of typology under the alternative term *figure* or, in Latin, *figura*, which affords *figural*, a useful and briefer alternative to *typological*. "Figural interpretation," he says, "establishes a connection between two events or persons, the first of which signifies not only itself but also the second, while the second encompasses or fulfills the first. The two poles of the figure are separate in time, but both, being real events or figures, are within time, within the stream of historical life."[14] This last point deserves reiteration: figural interpretation is not figurative, not merely allegorical, for both figure and fulfillment, both type and antitype, or in Auerbach's words, both "sign and what it signifies" are regarded as fully historical. When Jesus cites Jonah or Moses' brazen serpent as figures of himself, when Paul cites Adam as a type of Christ, when Jacob in the Book of Mormon cites Abraham's sacrifice as "a similitude of God and his Only Begotten Son" — none of them denies the historicity of the event or person thus given the added dimension of figural meaning (see Matt. 12:40; John 3:14; Rom. 5:14; Jac. 4:5).

Turning then to the Book of Mormon, we find that the key to understanding its typological or figural unity is, as Lassetter recognized without using the concept, Lehi's dream of the Tree of Life (see 1 Ne. 8). The dream itself, not being an external event, is not properly a type or figure; rather it is an interpretive vision that reveals the figural significance of Lehi's present experience and, through a further interpretive vision given his son Nephi (1 Ne. 11-14), the figural significance of the entire Nephite history.

Nephi's vision, in fact, should impel any reader of the book toward figural interpretation, for it acts out the method: Nephi asks for and receives a vision of what Lehi saw; then, when he asks "to know the interpretation" of the brilliantly white and beautiful tree, the Spirit of the Lord responds not with explanation but with a series of visions — first, the "fair and white" virgin of Nazareth, then "the virgin again, bearing a child in her arms," then "the Son of God going forth among the children of men," his baptism and ministry, and climactically his being "lifted up upon the cross and slain for the sins of the world," so that, as in patristic Christian typology, the tree of the cross fulfills the figure of the tree in Eden (1 Ne. 11:8-9, 11, 13-15, 20, 24, 27-31, 33).

To be sure, Nephi and the Spirit (or "angel" as he is called later) do discuss abstractly "the meaning of the tree": Nephi says, "It is the love of God . . . the most desirable above all things," and the angel responds, "Yea, and the most joyous to the soul" (1 Ne. 11:21-23). But the point is that the love of God is concretely present with men in history in actions like his "condescension" to Mary and, most fully, in the personal, actual presence of the Son (1 Ne. 11:16). Further, Nephi's vision goes on for three more chapters, with the angel reiterating "Look" or "Behold" and Nephi recording "I looked and beheld," until Nephi has seen all of Nephite history and all of world history down to the last day, which he is forbidden to write because that task is reserved for the apostle John (1 Ne. 14:18-28). Like the Bible, then, the Book of Mormon has folded into it, in figure, the "gigantic cycle from creation to apocalypse"; certainly its inclusive narrative runs from the creation to the apocalypse of the Nephites.

Consider now the way Lehi's dream figurally orders that narrative. Structurally, the important features of Lehi's dream are simple: Lehi finds himself in "a dark and dreary wilderness"; then he encounters a white-robed man who bids him follow; then, after praying, he sees "a large and spacious field" and "a tree, whose fruit was desirable to make one happy"; finally he partakes of the fruit and is "filled . . . with exceeding great joy" (1 Ne. 8:4-12). The dream has obvious congruence with Lehi's present experience: living in a Jerusalem under divine condemnation, he has prayerfully responded to God's word and is now midway on the road from that spiritual waste toward a promised land of peace and abundance (1 Ne. 1-2); ultimately, as in all Judeo-Christian figures of pilgrimage, he goes through the wilderness of a fallen world toward a redeemed world abounding in the joy of God's loving presence.

Call it quest or conversion, at bottom the pattern is a simple transformation: from dark and barren waste by means of the Word to a world fruitful and filled with light. And the transformation is enacted again and again in the Book of Mormon, at both the individual and communal levels. I can cite and summarize only the most obvious instances. The book's third narrator, Enos, tells the same story: in the wilderness hunting for food, his soul hungers for a remission of his sins; remembering his father Jacob's "words . . . concerning eternal life, and the joy of the saints," he prays all day and into the night, receives forgiveness, and to the end of his days rejoices in Christ the Word and in the expectation of "see[ing] his face with pleasure" (Enos 2-5, 26-27). A much later character, Alma the elder, similarly lives in spiritual waste as a priest of the corrupt king Noah. Hearing and believing the word of the prophet Abinadi, he first tries to defend him, then, when that fails, flees into hiding, writes down that word, and begins privately to teach it; finally he gathers his followers in the wilderness near "a fountain of pure water" where he institutes the covenant ritual of baptism, beginning with himself and coming "forth out of the water rejoicing, being filled with the Spirit" or "with the grace of God" (Mosiah 17:2-4; 18:1-5, 8-16).

Perhaps the richest individual instance of this transformation occurs with the younger Alma, who rejects the world of grace and becomes a sort of wild beast ravening at the church his father has established. Like Saul of Tarsus, he is confronted by an angel with a word of warning, then stricken into a death-like coma, which lasts three days and nights while his father and other priests fast and pray for him (see Mosiah 27:8-23; Alma 36:10, 16). During this dark night of bodily insensibility and immobility, Alma later recounts, he was spiritually "racked with eternal torment" for his sins, and wished to "become extinct both soul and body"; then, remembering his father's words concerning the atonement of Jesus Christ, he cried mercy from the Son and was instantly released from pain into "light" and "joy" (Alma 36:12, 15-20). As he wakes, he announces, "I am born of the Spirit"; "I was in the darkest abyss; but now I behold the marvelous light of God" (Mosiah 27:24, 29).

Alma's experience not only follows the typology of Lehi's dream, but he deliberately uses typological language and elaborately alludes to Lehi's dream, suggesting he fully understood its figural relation to his own and his people's experience, in a missionary sermon on faith, which compares "the word unto a seed" and traces the growth of that seed, nourished by faith, to its full flourishing as "a tree springing up unto everlasting life" within the soul, upon whose fruit the faithful may "feast . . . even until [they] are filled" (Alma 32:28, 41-42). At one point Alma uses the striking synaesthetic metaphor of "tast[ing] the light" (Alma 32:35). When such a minute stylistic detail resonates with the broadest and deepest structural patterns of the whole book, critics easily chloroformed by its dully repeated "and it came to pass" and other infelicities might wake up and read on.

The narratives of the two Almas replicate a second movement of Lehi's dream that prefigures a large proportion of the Book of Mormon narrative. Having eaten the fruit and rejoiced, Lehi immediately "began to be desirous that [his] family should partake of it also" (1 Ne. 8:12); similarly, the forgiven Enos immediately "began to feel a desire for the welfare of [his] brethren, the Nephites," and then, when somewhat reassured about them, he "prayed . . . with many long strugglings for [his estranged] brethren, the Lamanites" (Enos 9-11). As later with the two Almas, the converted man is moved centrifugally outward from private partaking of grace to communal sharing— from conversion to covenant or, if you will, from the sacrament of baptism to the sacrament of the Lord's Supper. What drives the larger and more inclusive narrative of the Book of Mormon is a hunger for sanctified community: God's action in the world, of which each converted man's action becomes a component vector,[15] must culminate in the city of God which, as Ezekiel and John envision it in the Bible, is simultaneously a restoration of the betrayed, bewildered garden of the first creation (see Ezek. 40; 47:1-12; Rev. 21:2, 10; 22:1-5).

In the Book of Mormon this motive of divine action is implied by the book's second large interpretive image, Jacob's story of the olive vineyard, the figural obverse or complement of Lehi's dream (see Jac. 5). (In some Jewish legends, the tree of life is an olive.[16]) For our purposes, just a few features of this elaborate figure matter: (1) though it proceeds in a zigzag that recalls the Book of Mormon (and biblical) vision of history as a sine wave—the tedious entropic pulse of fallen time—its overall movement is from wildness to tameness, decay to fruitfulness, and it ends, like Nephi's expansion of Lehi's dream, in the expectation of apocalypse, the burning of the vineyard that will consume and refine fallen time into the grace of eternity (see Jac. 5:3-4, 18, 25, 30-37, 74-75, 77); (2) the separate trees may all be offshoots of one primal stock planted by the Lord of the vineyard, whose intention is to make them "one" (Jac. 5:68, 74); (3) finally, like Lehi desiring the fruit of the tree of life, the vineyard's Lord also looks toward "most precious" fruit in which he will rejoice, a fruit that Jacob suggests represents the perfected love of man toward God (Jac. 5:54, 60-61, 71, 74-75; 6:5-7).

Very briefly, the drive toward sanctified community—oneness among men who have each become inwardly at one with themselves and God—can most clearly be seen in the conversions and covenants of King Benjamin's people in Zarahemla and of the nomadic bands of Limhi and Alma the elder in the wilderness, in the joyous conjunction of these three groups, and in the subsequent missionary campaigns of the younger Alma and the sons of Mosiah among both Nephites and Lamanites (see Mosiah 4-5; 17-21; 22:13-14; 24:25; 27:32-37; 28:1-9; Alma 4:19-20; 5-15; 17-26.) Because the creation of godly community must proceed in a world of "opposition" that is at once fallen into the barren disorder of wrath and graced by the possibility of human participation in divine love, this narrative movement follows the wearying sine curve of demonization and sanctification as men in their agency divide themselves over pride, envy, and reciprocal anger or unite in humility, gratitude, and reciprocal love: hence the wars, contentions, and conspiracies that occupy the middle action of the book and utterly dominate its falling action, that last helpless despairing slide into the apocalypse of wrath that leaves in the dust and "dung" of a self-destroyed nation only scattered seeds of charity—Mormon, Moroni, the precious plates bearing the word (see 2 Ne. 2:11-19; Mormon 2:13-15; 5:2; 6:6, 15-22; 8:1-5; Moro. 1:3; 7; 9; 10:2.)

But before that ending, bleak as any Germanic *Götterdämmerung,* the drive toward sanctification climaxes in the merid-

ian advent of the Redeeming Son, the brief noon of Nephite
history. When Jesus, Alpha and Omega, descends to the temple
in the wasted Land Bountiful, he fulfills and renews the figures
that have shadowed his coming in an apocalyptic gesture that
both reenacts Genesis and prefigures the last destruction and
transfiguration of the world (see 3 Ne. 11:1-8). His death at
Jerusalem is typified to the Nephites by storm, earthquake, and
a "thick darkness" such that "there could be no light"—as if
creation were unraveled back to chaos (3 Ne. 8:5-22).

After three "days" of this dark, as the dawn marking the
resurrection approaches, the first note of change is "a voice"
enumerating the destruction of the wicked, pleading with the
"more righteous" survivors to turn and be made whole, and announcing, "I am Jesus Christ the Son of God," creator of "the
heavens and the earth" and "the light and the life of the world"
(3 Ne. 9:1-11, 13-15, 18). After this comes a silence for "many
hours," then another call to turn and be "gathered"; then it is
morning "and the earth did cleave together again, that it stood"
and "mourning was turned into joy, and . . . lamentations into
praise and thanksgiving" (3 Ne. 10:1, 4-5, 10). Creation has
been renewed in a perfect figure of the Son's ultimate descent in
justice and mercy at the end of time.

As his quiet voice pierces the Nephites and ignites their
hearts (see 3 Ne. 11:3), so Christ's climactic advent lays open the
core of the figural structure of the Book of Mormon, revealing
the single archetype that fires the whole: all of God's actions in
his world—creation, conversion, covenant, redemption—are
one act of transformation from dark, barren chaos, by the
Word, to a world abounding in light and joy. The Book of
Mormon, then, is a "true" myth in precisely Eliade's sense,[17] a
story of how God makes the world—and, in a Christian sense,
makes it his. It is also, despite its infelicity of style, a work
whose complexity and unity of design and whose tragic and
comic seriousness of experiential and historical vision warrant
for it at least some consideration alongside its neighbors in
nineteenth-century American literature and alongside the Bible
with which it claims kin. It is the nearest thing to a literary
classic that the Mormon culture has produced; or better, like a

classic, it created a culture. It sings love like Lucretius and wrath like Homer[18] and beatitude and redemption like Jesus and John his beloved son of thunder, and it deserves ears that will at least listen if not hear.

POSTSCRIPT — **1980**

Since I first wrote this paper in 1977, several more papers have pursued literary analysis of the Book of Mormon in illuminating ways under the auspices of the Association for Mormon Letters. Richard Dilworth Rust's " 'All Things Which Have Been Given of God . . . Are the Typifying of Him': Typology in the Book of Mormon" which follows and Steven Sondrup's "The Psalm of Nephi: A Lyric Reading" appear in the *Proceedings of the Symposia of the Association for Mormon Letters 1978-79.* From the AML's fall 1979 symposium at BYU come papers by Mark Thomas on Lehi's dream as apocalypse, by Steven Walker on the stylistic density of the text, now published as "More Than Meets the Eye: Contraction in the Book of Mormon," *BYU Studies,* 20 (1980): 199-205; and by Clifton Holt Jolley on Moroni as a tragic figure. From the AML section meeting at the RMMLA Convention in Albuquerque, October 1979, we see George Tate's analysis of Exodus typology in the book, also in this volume, At the University of North Carolina, Richard Dilworth Rust and a non-Mormon colleague, John Seelye, have begun collaboration on a handbook to the Book of Mormon as literature. And at the 1980 meetings of the Mormon History Association in Canandiagua, New York, Mark Thomas and I presented papers.

This paper is, in fact, the core of a longer projected work; yet even as a paper, its narrow limits forced omissions that I regretted in 1977. Here I'd like briefly to suggest some larger changes and additional reflections.

First, the essay tends to treat typology as having only one mode, the horizontal or historical prefiguration of either Christ's ministry or the apocalypse. In fact, various uses of typological language in the Book of Mormon ("type," "shadow," "similitude," "liken") suggest contextually that its figures foreshadow not only Christ and the End, but also the Church, its sacraments or ordinances, and the inner moral and spiritual lives of believers. At one point, when Nephi insists to his skeptically evasive brothers that his and Lehi's visions represent "things both temporal and spiritual" (1 Ne. 15:32), we might suspect that all these modes are expressions of a single interpretive effort: that for Nephi, Alma, Mormon, and Moroni, typing or figuring or likening, guided by revelation, is simply the one way to make sense of the universe, time, and all the dimensions of individual and communal human experience.

Aside from illustratively expanding my discussions of the communal narrative, the Nephite self-destruction, and the survivals of charity, I would also want to acknowledge explicitly that I have not stayed quite within the bounds of typology as traditionally construed when I have tried, as the text itself seemed to urge, to go behind the multiple typological patterns to what I have called "a simple transformation" or "single archetype," which I summarize with formulae like "from dark, barren chaos, by the Word, to a world abounding in light and joy." In using the term *archetype*, I did not wish to invoke its Jungian connotations so much as its root sense of "primal type," the one type behind all types.

My formula may suggest a theology of the Word, which in turn might suggest a philosophy of history and of language. Here I grope near the borders of my own understanding. History, as sheer chronicity endured, may well be (as we are often told these days) without teleology or plot, a sequence without story. Yet to write history is to compose it, verbally, as discourse or story — that is, to *figure* it, to order it by concept and metaphor. The minds that made the Book of Mormon clearly believed that this was not only possible but essential, even crucial, if humanity were to continue. Further, those minds believed that the master-figures were both transcendent and immanent: that God could and would reveal them to human minds, and that once received, these figures would be seen (and could be used) to order all human experience.

This is perhaps to approach the matter from the angle of "sacred" or "dogmatic theology." But from something like the angle of "natural theology" we might reach almost the same point. Consider what it means to use a word, say *man*. To use a word at all presupposes (at least by logical priority) an act of likening one object to another, since to identify two objects by the same noun is to subsume them under a concept whose definition is their shared likeness. Likening, then, on which both the typologies of sacred texts and the coherence of even the most skeptical secular histories must finally depend, not to mention the coherences of both science and poetry, might be seen as the root-act of language itself, logically prior to the utterance of any word even if temporally simultaneous with it.

Pondering the centrality of the Word — both the verbal sign and the person of Christ — in the complex system of types that shapes the Book of Mormon, I come to such guesses. Last of all, I suspect that the dynamics of the Word in the Book of Mormon entail a view of language deeply at variance with the postmodernist view that we dwell amid infinitely self-referential and nontranscendent signs. With the Bible, with Augustine and Dante (as I've lately begun to learn), indeed with Judeo-Christian tradition generally, the Book of Mormon seems to me to say that signs point beyond themselves not finally to other signs but ultimately toward God. Our trouble (and Lehi's, Nephi's, Alma's, Mormon's, and Moroni's) is to read them. Here the real work begins, and all I have said or might yet say about typology may be only preliminary to that work.

NOTES

1. "Prospects for the Study of the Book of Mormon as a Work of American Literature," *Dialogue* 3 (Spring 1968): 29-41. Wilson cites O'Dea's *The Mormons* (Chicago, 1957) and Brodie's *No Man Knows My History* (New York, 1945) on pp. 30, 31-32 and makes his own proposal on pp. 37-38.

2. A sampling of these would include a two-year series of articles in the adult Church magazine, *The Ensign*, beginning in September 1976; Glenn L. Pearson and Reid E. Bankhead, *A Doctrinal Approach to the Book of Mormon* (Salt Lake City: Bookcraft, 1962); Sidney B. Sperry, *Book of Mormon Compendium* (Salt Lake City: Bookcraft, 1968); George Reynolds and J. M. Sjodahl, *A Commentary on the Book of Mormon*, 7 vols. (Salt Lake City:

Deseret Book, 1955-1961); Daniel H. Ludlow, *A Companion to Your Study of the Book of Mormon* (Salt Lake City: Deseret Book, 1976). Of course, all these are useful in their own ways, but they will not much help a reader who seeks to understand the book's structural and thematic unity.

3. Hugh Nibley, *Lehi in the Desert and The World of the Jaredites* (Salt Lake City: Bookcraft, 1952); *An Approach to the Book of Mormon*, 2nd ed. (Salt Lake City: Deseret Book, 1964); *Since Cumorah: The Book of Mormon in the Modern World* (Salt Lake City: Deseret Book, 1967).

4. "The Book of Mormon and the American Revolution," *BYU Studies* 17 (Autumn 1976): 3-20. Bushman's "deliverance" pattern resembles both the Exodus typology discussed by George Tate, pp. 245-62, of this volume, and the pattern I will discuss here.

5. "Beowulf and Nephi: A Literary View of the Book of Mormon," *Dialogue* 4 (Autumn 1969): 40-47.

6. "Chiasmus in the Book of Mormon," *BYU Studies* 10 (Autumn 1969): 69-84. In a similar vein, John A. Tvedtnes, "Hebraisms in the Book of Mormon: A Preliminary Survey," *BYU Studies* 11 (Autumn 1970): 50-60, might afford some help to a stylistic critic but little to a critic interested in structure.

7. In Truman G. Madsen and Charles D. Tate, Jr., eds., *To the Glory of God: Mormon Essays on Great Issues* (Salt Lake City: Deseret Book, 1972), pp. 149-61.

8. *Illustrated Stories from the Book of Mormon*, 16 vols. (Salt Lake City: Promised Land Publications, 1967-1972); in all sixteen volumes, Larson is credited with "narrative and editing" while in vols. 1-11, Joseph N. Revill is listed as "correlator and writer"; Paul R. Cheesman replaces him (and additionally is called "director of research") in vols. 12-16. A rich source of literary inspiration for Larson, the Book of Mormon lies behind his plays *Coriantumr and Moroni: Two Plays* (Provo: BYU Press, 1961) and "The Brother of Jared" and "Third Nephi" in *The Mantle of the Prophet and Other Plays* (Salt Lake City: Deseret Book, 1966). Though Larson's choice of protagonists in these two pairs of Book of Mormon plays suggests deliberate thematic paralleling, no one, so far as I know, has pursued the question of Larson's implicit insights into the symbolic and thematic unity of the Book of Mormon.

Incidentally, 3 Nephi has also inspired a story by Truman Madsen, "Ye Are My Witnesses," included in his *Christ and the Inner Life*, 2nd ed. (Salt Lake City: Bookcraft, 1978), pp. 43-54, though here again no one has pursued the story's possible interpretive insights.

9. "Lehi's Dream and Nephi's Vision: A Look at Structure and Theme in the Book of Mormon," *Perspective: A Journal of Critical Inquiry* [published by the BYU College of Humanities], (Winter 1976), pp. 50-54. Lassetter and I arrived independently at similar lines of analysis; his essay appeared just after I had completed an essay requested by *The Ensign* (later rejected), " 'Most Desirable Above All Things': The Tree of Life in the Book of Mormon," the first organized result of nine years' intermittent study.

10. Frye's comments on the Bible in his *Anatomy of Criticism* (cited below, note 14) forecast the direction of his work, which he presented as a four-lecture series, "The Faces of the Bible," at Cornell from 27 March to 7 April 1972 and later expanded in a course on the Bible as literature at Harvard. As of December 1979, his projected book "The Great Code," had yet to appear.

11. John Bunyan, *The Pilgrim's Progress*, ed. Roger Sharrock (Baltimore: Penguin Books, 1965), p. 36. Rainer Maria Rilke, "Archaïscher Torso Apollos," *Gesammelte Werke*, 6 vols. (Leipzig: Insel-Verlag, 1930), 3:117.

12. *Mimesis: The Representation of Reality in Western Literature*, trans. Willard R. Trask (Princeton: Princeton University Press, 1953), p. 15.

13. *The Anatomy of Criticism* (1954; reprint ed., Princeton: Princeton University Press, 1971), pp. 315-16.

14. "Figura," trans. Ralph Manheim, in *Scenes from the Drama of European Literature: Six Essays* (New York: Meridian, 1959), p. 53.

15. John Macmurray's "The World as One Action" in *The Self as Agent* (1957; reprint ed., London: Faber, 1969) and Teilhard de Chardin's "The Divinization of Our Activities" in *The Divine Milieu*, revised Torchbook ed., (New York: Harper & Row, 1968), pp. 49-73, esp. 65-67, have helped me to formulate this conception of history, which I believe is implicit in the narrative structure of the Book of Mormon. My discussion in this and the following two paragraphs has also profited from remarks by my colleague James Faulconer (BYU Philosophy Dept.) on religious community in history.

16. Louis Ginzberg, *The Legends of the Jews*, trans. Henrietta Szold, 7 vols. (Philadelphia: Jewish Publication Society of America, 1909), 1:93; 5:119.

17. Mircea Eliade, *Myth and Reality*, trans. Willard R. Trask (New York: Harper & Row, 1963), pp. 1, 5-6, 18-19.

18. My allusion to Lucretius' *De Rerum Natura* is not meant to be as wildly out of control as it may seem. I have in mind, of course, his invocation of Venus as "sole mistress of the nature of things" at the beginning of his dogmatically materialistic and antireligious book. The Book of Mormon, it could be argued, is materialistic (certainly Mormon metaphysics is), though it goes beyond that; and it implicitly makes "love" one of the names for the Word that brings order and peace out of chaos. And it deals as much with "ruinous wrath" as does the *Iliad*.

12

Richard Dilworth Rust

"All Things Which Have Been Given of God...Are The Typifying of Him": Typology in the Book of Mormon

Professor of English at the University of North Carolina, Richard Dilworth Rust has studied at Brigham Young University, the University of Utah, and the University of Wisconsin. In addition to teaching at the University of Wisconsin and the University of North Carolina, he has been a visiting professor at Indiana University, the University of Heidelberg, and Brigham Young University. His publications include editions of Washington Irving's Astoria *and James Fenimore Cooper's* The Pathfinder, *a study of nineteenth-century literary responses to the Civil War entitled* Glory *and* Pathos, *and numerous articles on Hawthorne, Melville, Mark Twain, Longfellow, Eugene*

This paper was originally delivered at the Association for Mormon Letters meeting in Charlottesville, Virginia, 28 April 1979, and printed in *Proceedings of the Symposia of the Association for Mormon Letters 1978-79* (Salt Lake City: Association for Mormon Letters, 1979).

O'Neill, and Washington Irving; in addition he is general editor of Irving's complete works.

In this paper, he holds that the Book of Mormon fulfills its basic mission of testifying of Christ through a "pervasive typology" as well as by its direct statements, prophecies, and quotations. He defines typology, discusses Book of Mormon teachings regarding it, and then shows its application to Book of Mormon individuals, groups, and objects—with the golden book itself a type of Christ, the ultimate treasure.

———————

From its title page to the last chapter, the Book of Mormon has Jesus Christ as its central theme and character. While he is presented mainly by direct statements and quotations, much is implied about Christ by a pervasive typology which is both aesthetically pleasing and religiously enlightening.

According to the Puritan minister Samuel Mather, "A Type is some outward or sensible thing ordained of God under the Old Testament, to represent and hold forth something of Christ in the New."[1] This common definition applies well enough to New Testament typology.[2] But typology as found in the Book of Mormon would certainly include postfigurings as well as prefigurings of Christ. Whether occurring B.C. or A.D., to be types the persons, events, or things must be real in themselves and at the same time point to qualities of Christ or his kingdom.

To see how a type works in the Book of Mormon, let us look at Alma's enlightenment of his son Helaman and then at Moroni's review of the prophecies of Ether. In the first instance, Alma talks about the Liahona or compass prepared by the Lord, reviews how the "fathers" forgot to exercise their faith and therefore "tarried in the wilderness or did not travel a direct course, and were afflicted with hunger and thirst, because of their transgressions."

Alma continues:

> And now, my son, I would that ye should understand
> that these things are not without a shadow; for as our
> fathers were slothful to give heed to this compass (now
> these things were temporal) they did not prosper; even
> so it is with things which are spiritual. For behold, it is as
> easy to give heed to the word of Christ, which will point
> to you a straight course to eternal bliss, as it was for our
> fathers to give heed to this compass, which would point
> unto them a straight course to the promised land. And
> now I say, is there not a type in this thing? For just as
> surely as this director did bring our fathers, by following
> its course, to the promised land, shall the words of
> Christ, if we follow their course, carry us beyond this
> vale of sorrow into a far better land of promise (Alma
> 37:42-45).

This is a textbook example of a type: It "exists in history and
its meaning is factual";[3] it is "a prophetic symbol . . . fixed at
both of its poles of reference";[4] it shows "evidence of the Divine
intention in the correspondence between it and the Antitype
[the person or thing which is figured]";[5] and it "was instituted to
perform a specific function in God's grand design."[6] Further, it is
beautifully clear and meaningful, and satisfies the belief of Jonathan Edwards that "the principles of human nature render
TYPES a fit method of instruction. It tends to enlighten and
illustrate, and to convey instruction with impression, conviction, and pleasure, and to help the memory. These things are
confirmed by man's natural delight in the imitative arts, in
painting, poetry, fables, metaphorical language and dramatic
performances."[7]

In the second example of how a type works, Moroni in Ether
13:4-9 hearkens back to Nephite origins through the prophecies
of Ether. In what Moroni initially thought was his last word (see
Moro. 1:1), he gives in a few verses a sweeping view of the role
of his people in divine history. In verse three he quotes Ether as
declaring that the promised land is "the place of the New Jerusalem, which should come down out of heaven, and the holy

sanctuary of the Lord." In the next verse he cites Ether's reference to the type — the Jerusalem from whence Lehi should come
and which would be built up again — and subsequently quotes
Ether's declaration that

> . . . a New Jersualem should be built upon this land,
> unto the remnant of the seed of Joseph, for which things
> there has been a type. For as Joseph brought his father
> down into the land of Egypt, even so he died there;
> wherefore, the Lord brought a remnant of the seed of
> Joseph out of the land of Jerusalem, that he might be
> merciful unto the seed of Joseph that they should perish
> not, even as he was merciful unto the father of Joseph
> that he should perish not. Wherefore, the remnant of the
> house of Joseph shall be built upon this land. . . and they
> shall build up a holy city unto the Lord. . . . And there
> shall be a new heaven and a new earth; and they shall
> be like unto the old save the old have passed away, and
> all things have become new (Eth. 13:6-9).

Not only likes can be the paired type-antitype, but opposites
as well: "We speak concerning the law," Nephi said, "that our
children may know the deadness of the law; and they, by knowing the *deadness* of the law, may look forward unto that *life*
which is in Christ, and know for what end the law was given" (2
Ne. 25:27; italics added).

While we today pay little attention to Book of Mormon
typology,[8] Book of Mormon prophets accepted it naturally and
almost took it for granted. For them, types were significant, instructive, and persuasive. Indeed, Nephi affirms, "My soul de-
lighteth in proving unto my people the truth of the coming of
Christ; for, for this end hath the law of Moses been given; and
all things which have been given of God from the beginning of
the world, unto man, are the typifying of him" (2 Ne. 11:4;
italics added.)[9] In one way or another, all the major Book of
Mormon prophets refer to types in focusing on Christ's earthly
advent, his visit to the Nephites, and his second coming and
heavenly kingdom. Nephi, for example, gives in 2 Nephi 25 a
direct prophecy of Christ ("spoken plainly that ye cannot err"),
and concludes by affirming that "as the Lord God liveth that
brought Israel up out of the land of Egypt, . . . there is none

other name given under heaven save it be this Jesus Christ . . .
whereby man can be saved" (2 Ne. 25:20). In other words, the
temporal salvation of Israel from Egypt is a type of Christ's
spiritual salvation and thereby gives credence to the latter. King
Benjamin instructs his son in the typological meaning of the Liahona (see Mosiah 1:16-17); and while he preaches Christ directly, at the same time he says: "And many signs, and wonders,
and types, and shadows showed he unto them [the Israelites
under Moses], concerning his coming" (Mosiah 3:15). Abinadi
recalls for King Noah's court that "all these things [in the Mosaic
law] were types of things to come" (Mosiah 13:31), and insists,
"If ye teach the law of Moses, also teach that it is a shadow of
those things which are to come" (Mosiah 16:14). Amulek taught
that "this is the whole meaning of the law, every whit pointing
to that great and last sacrifice" (Alma 34:14). And Mormon says
that the Anti-Nephi-Lehis "did look forward to the coming of
Christ, considering that the law of Moses was a type of his
coming . . . . Now they did not suppose that salvation came by
the law of Moses; but the law of Moses did serve to strengthen
their faith in Christ" (Alma 25:15-16).

"*All* things . . . given of God" is not confined, however, to
the perpetual system of Mosaic ceremonies, sacrifices, and festivals. As Samuel Mather shows, types can be found as well in
occasional persons, things, and events. In the Old Testament,
Joseph and Moses were notable types of Christ. The beloved
son of his father, Joseph was stripped of his robe, thrown in a
cistern for three days, betrayed and rejected by his brethren,
and unjustly imprisoned. In addition to meaning "may God
add," Joseph's name may also mean "sorrowing or suffering
servant," and in that capacity he came out of "burial" in prison
to preserve for his brethren "a posterity in the earth, and to save
your lives by a great deliverance" (Gen. 45:7). Both Joseph the
man and Joseph the people are considered types repeatedly in
the Book of Mormon (see 2 Ne. 3; Alma 46:24; Eth. 13:7). For
his part, Moses was told by God that he was a type of Christ
(see Moses 1:6, 16, 41; 1 Ne. 22:20-21; Hel. 8:15; 3 Ne. 20:23).
As just several of the many ways in which he thus served,
Moses taught the word of God, brought water out of the rock

(both of which figure Christ), delivered the captive Israelites, and was a savior to his people, including lifting up the brazen serpent (see John 3:14-16; 2 Ne. 25:20; Alma 33:19).

In the Book of Mormon, Nephi combines many of the traits of Old Testament prophets in his typifying Christ. Desiring to "be strong like unto Moses," he several times likened his situation to Moses; his brothers dared not touch him because of the power of God within him; and like Moses he guided his people towards the promised land (see 1 Ne. 4:2, 3; 17:23-33; 18:22). A suffering servant like Joseph, Nephi was resisted by brothers who did not want him to be a ruler over them, yet in the end he was instrumental in saving them. Stilling the storm like Christ, Nephi was also directly like him in being an obedient son, a forgiving brother, a skillful carpenter, and a pilot.

Mosiah is like Moses and Lehi, both of whom figure Christ's leadership, in leading his people into the wilderness (see Omni 12). His son Benjamin also typifies Christ in shadowing the heavenly King (see Mosiah 2:19). This relationship is implied in Mormon's earlier editorial comment contrasting false Christs and holy prophets including King Benjamin (see Words of Mormon 15-17).

Abinadi figures Christ indirectly and directly: "His face shone with exceeding luster, even as Moses' did while in the mount of Sinai"; he was cast into prison for three days; his persecutors shed innocent blood; and at death, Abinadi cried, "O God, receive my soul" (Mosiah 13:5; 17:6; 18:19).

Alma the Elder led his flock into and then out of the wilderness like Moses, Lehi, and Mosiah. The conversion story of Alma the Younger in Mosiah 27 and in Alma 36 and 38 almost repeats that of Jonah — of whom Christ said: "For as Jonas was three days and three nights in the whale's belly; so shall the Son of man be three days and three nights in the heart of the earth" (Matt. 12:40). Alma says: "I was three days and three nights in the most bitter pain and anguish of soul; and never, until I did cry out unto the Lord Jesus Christ for mercy, did I receive a remission of my sins"; "I was in the darkest abyss; but now I behold the marvelous light of God" (Alma 38:8; see Jonah 1:17; 2; Mosiah 27:29). (To be technical, Christ was dead two nights and less than two full days — but apparently Alma was "dead" for a shorter period as well, see Mosiah 27:23. Three days-three nights seems to be a formula.) Likewise, Lamoni "lay as if he were dead for the space of two days and two nights" and is followed in his trance by his queen who, upon recovery, declares she is "saved . . . from an awful hell" (Alma 18:43; 19:29).

Ammon is a type of Christ in saving many Lamanites who were "in darkness, yea, even in the darkest abyss, but behold, how many of them are brought to behold the marvelous light of God" (Alma 26:3); and like Moses, he leads his people through the wilderness to a promised land, giving the glory to Christ. In turn, General Moroni, who with his standard of liberty demonstrated a type of the remnant of Joseph, "was a man like unto Ammon, the son of Mosiah, yea, and even the other sons of Mosiah, yea, and also Alma and his sons" (Alma 46:24; 48:18).

Nephi and Lehi repeat the imprisonment-deliverance prefigurement (see Hel. 5), with the pillar of fire related both to the Israelites' pillar of fire and to the encirclement of fire in 3 Nephi 17:24. Light overcomes the cloud of darkness when the people call on Christ after having heard an admonitory voice three times, an anticipation of 3 Nephi 9. Nephi prepares the people for the coming of Christ, compares his power to that of Moses, and sorrowfully points out that, like Moses, his prophecies of Christ are also denied by his people (see Hel. 8:11, 13).

Since *all* things given of God are types of Christ, we could expect to find figural elements in the account of each prophet in the Book of Mormon: Third Nephi is the spiritual leader, Mormon and Moroni through the Book of Mormon lead future generations of their kindred to the heavenly Jerusalem, etc. We also find groups of persons serving as types. Book of Mormon judges shadow forth Christ, the heavenly judge, whose role is affirmed by both Nephi and Moroni in their parting testimonies. High priests such as Alma and his posterity prefigure Christ, the great high priest. Alma clarifies this in his discourse on the Melchizedek Priesthood which was given that "the people might look forward on the Son of God, it being a type of his order, or it being his order" (Alma 13:16).

Of typological objects, we have already discussed the

Liahona. Like the Liahona are the brother of Jared's sixteen stones which "shine forth in darkness" and remind us of the Lord's affirmation to Nephi, "I will also be your light in the wilderness," or of his later declaration, "I am the light of the world" (Eth. 3:4; 1 Ne. 17:13; John 8:12). With such a light, the travelers would never be in darkness.

Related to everlasting light is the pillar of fire seen by Lehi in an experience reminiscent of Moses and the burning bush (see 1 Ne. 1:6). This memorable and dramatic type is linked with the previously mentioned pillars of fire in Helaman 5:24 and 3 Nephi 17:24, all figuring the God who "is a consuming fire" (Heb. 12:29). Of course this fire can be either purifying or destroying. The righteous are baptized with fire and with the Holy Ghost, receive a remission of sins by fire, are visited by a divine person "like a refiner's fire," and as part of that experience are "encircled about as if it were by fire" (3 Ne. 9:20; 2 Ne. 31:17; 3 Ne. 24:2; 19:14). But if the righteous shall be saved, "even if it so be as by fire," Mormon testifies that at the last judgment the "holiness of Jesus Christ . . . will kindle a flame of unquenchable fire" upon the unbelievers (1 Ne. 22:17; Morm. 9:5). Fire and brimstone are frequently presented as figurative torments; literal fire destroys Zarahemla, Jacobugath, and Kishkumen — described as extremely "wicked" (3 Ne. 9:9-10) — figuring in turn the end of time when "the world shall be burned with fire" (Jac. 6:3).

Directed or lit by objects requiring faith for their operation, Nephi's ship and the Jaredite barges are connected with Noah's ark in being types of baptism (see 1 Pet. 3:20-21; notice also that the Jaredite vessels "were tight like unto the ark of Noah," Eth. 6:7). They all bring the occupants *through* the water into a new life, representing in the process the death, burial, and resurrection of Christ (see Col. 2:12). Or like Jonah, the Jaredites in their vessels, like "a whale in the midst of the sea," are "buried in the depths of the sea" (Eth. 2:24; 6:6). This is part of a major pattern woven throughout the Book of Mormon: outcasts of the world — who always consider themselves strangers and pilgrims (see Jac. 7:26; Alma 13:23) — wander through the wilderness or through darkness to escape destruction and to find a promised land (consider the Jaredites, Lehites, Zeniff, Limhi, Alma, and Ammon); they are miraculously brought through darkness and tribulation or are released from prison or servitude in a process that can also bring repentance; the darkness or death-in-life is several times described as lasting three days, notably the vapor of darkness following the great earthquake in 3 Nephi 8; there may be a voice out of heaven which calls for repentance and promises new life (see Hel. 5:29; 3 Ne. 9:1); then the "wanderers in a strange land," whether they have been on an actual journey or not, are delivered in an action involving light and fertility in a promised land. (See 1 Ne. 18:24 in which the Lehites plant seeds in the new land and bring forth the abundance of the earth.) The ultimate journey, of which this is a type, is to the heavenly promised land.

Although not a literal object or event, the whole tree of life complex contains the basic pattern of Book of Mormon typological events.[10] Lehi finds himself in a dark and dreary wilderness; through prayer and faith, however, plus leadership by a man in a white robe (a Moses-Christ figure), he is led to the tree of life (akin to the heavenly destination). Many are drowned in the depths of the fountain or lost in the mists of darkness, connected for Nephi with the "mist of darkness on the face of the land of promise," which was part of the great destruction preceding the appearance of the Lamb of God (1 Ne. 12:4). The vision foretells the antitype of Christ's appearance, being in himself a fruit white and pure, upon which, Alma says in his version of the tree of life, "ye shall feast . . . even until ye are filled, that ye hunger not, neither shall ye thirst" (Alma 32:42; see John 6:35). The vision also projects figuratively the destruction of the Nephite people as a result of pride and temptations, but the full sweep of history on the promised land leads to the restoration of other scripture and to Christ manifesting himself to all nations (see 1 Ne. 12:17-19; 13:38-42).

As with the fruit of the tree of life, the Book of Mormon itself is considered of great worth. Indeed, as the word of God, it figures Christ the Word. It is also a treasure, typifying Christ "in whom are hid all the treasures of wisdom and knowledge" (Col. 2:3). In the beginning of the book, Laman and Lemuel

represent the unbelievers who lament leaving "their gold, and
their silver, and their precious things, to perish in the wilderness" (or so they suppose), while Nephi is willing to give up the
family's material treasures to try to obtain the heavenly treasure
represented by the contents of the brass plates (see 1 Ne. 2:11).
When he is finally successful in obtaining the plates, he appro-
priately finds them in the treasury. Later, Nephi's younger
brother Jacob admonishes the rich whose hearts are set upon
their treasures that "their treasure shall perish with them" (2 Ne.
9:30). The same lesson is preached by Samuel the Lamanite.
Treasures hidden up not unto the Lord are lost; the riches are
cursed, says Samuel, "because ye have set your hearts upon
them, and have not hearkened unto the *words* of him who gave
them unto you" (Hel. 13:21; italics added). The capstone instruction is given by Christ himself in 3 Nephi 13:19-21. The
book ends with Moroni hiding up — unto the Lord — the words
of life, an echo of the Lord's instruction to the brother of Jared
to "treasure up the things which ye have seen and heard" (Eth.
3:21). With an awareness that Christ is the ultimate treasure,
Moroni admonishes his future readers to "come unto Christ,
and lay hold upon every good gift, and touch not the evil gift"
(Moro. 10:30). Thus one framing element of the Book of Mormon is that of treasures of earth versus treasures of heaven.
Joseph Smith first had to recognize the precious golden plates as
spiritual treasure before being permitted to receive them. And
as an ideal type themselves, the plates are firmly established as
real ("We have seen and hefted [them]," testified the Eight
Witnesses) and simultaneously of spiritual import ("It is by the
grace of God the Father, and our Lord Jesus Christ, that we
beheld and bear record that these things are true," affirmed the
Three Witnesses). For us, as modern readers of the golden book,
we would do well to see its pervasive typology in order to value
more fully its treasure.

NOTES

1. Samuel Mather, *The Figures or Types of the Old Testament*, 2nd ed.
(London, 1705), p. 52, reprinted in *Series in American Studies* (Johnson

Reprint Corporation, 1969), italics omitted; introduction and notes by Mason I. Lowance, Jr. Sacvan Bercovitch provides 152 pages of bibliography on typology in his "Selective Check-list on Typology," *Early American Literature* 5 (Spring 1970), and "Selective Check-list on Typology: Part II," *EAL* 6 (Fall 1971), paginated separately from journal.

2. Clear references to typology are found in the following New Testament scriptures: Matt. 12:40; 26:61; John 3:14; 6:26-58; 7:37-38; 8:12; 19:31-33; Rom. 1:20; 5:14; 1 Cor. 5:6-8; 10:1-4, 11; 15:45; 2 Cor. 3:12-14; Gal. 4:22-5:1; Col. 2:12, 16-17; 1 Pet. 1:18-19; 2:5; 3:20-21; Heb., the entire book, esp. 8:2, 5; 9:6-14, 24; 10:1; 13:11-12; Rev. 2:17; 5:5-10.

3. Perry Miller, ed., "Introduction," *Images or Shadows of Divine Things by Jonathan Edwards* (New Haven: Yale University Press, 1948), p. 6.

4. Ursula Brumm, *American Thought and Religious Typology* (New Brunswick, N.J.: Rutgers University Press, 1970), p. 24.

5. Van Mildert, *An Inquiry into the General Principles of Scripture-Interpretation* (Oxford, 1815), quoted in the *Encyclopaedia of Religion and Ethics*, James Hastings ed., 12 vols. (New York: Charles Scribner's Sons, 1958), 12:500.

6. Mason I. Lowance, Jr., "Images or Shadows of Divine Things: The Typology of Jonathan Edwards," *Early American Literature* 5 (Spring 1970): 141. (This is a special typology issue of *EAL*.)

7. Jonathan Edwards, "Types of the Messiah," *The Works of President Edwards* (1847; reprint ed., New York: Burt Franklin, 1968), 9:493.

8. The exceptions surely include Bruce R. McConkie, *The Promised Messiah: The First Coming of Christ* (Salt Lake City: Deseret Book, 1978), chs. 21-24; Hugh Nibley, especially *Since Cumorah, The Book of Mormon in the Modern World* (Salt Lake City: Deseret Book, 1967); "The Expanding Gospel," *Brigham Young University Studies* 7 (1965-1966):3-27; and "Treasures in the Heavens: Some Early Christian Insights into the Organizing of Worlds," *Dialogue* 8 (Autumn/Winter 1974):76-98; Bruce W. Jorgensen and George S. Tate in this volume, and Lenet Hadley Read, "Symbols of the Harvest: Old Testament Holy Days and the Lord's Ministry," *Ensign,* Jan. 1975, pp. 32, 36; "The Ark of the Covenant: Symbol of Triumph," *Ensign,* June 1980, pp. 20-24.

9. This is somewhat akin to Mircea Eliade's point in *The Myth of the Eternal Return*, trans. Willard R. Trask (1949; reprint ed., New York: Pantheon Books for Bollingen Foundation, 1954); or *Cosmos and History* (Princeton, N.J.: Princeton University Press, 1971), p. 34, that in primitive societies the importance of an object or an act is that it imitates or repeats an archetype.

10. See Bruce W. Jorgensen, "The Dark Way to the Tree: Typological Unity in the Book of Mormon," in this volume.

13

George S. Tate

The Typology
of the Exodus Pattern
in the Book of Mormon

George S. Tate graduated from Brigham Young University, majoring in English, and then pursued graduate studies in comparative literature, receiving his PhD from Cornell University in medieval studies (English, Scandinavian, and German). Recipient of many academic honors, he numbers among them a Fulbright fellowship to Iceland in 1971-1972 and a Marshall fellowship to Denmark in 1973. Now associate professor of comparative literature and graduate coordinator of the Department of Humanities, Classics, and Comparative Literature at Brigham Young University, he has published articles on Old English and Old Norse literature and has done other studies in Mormon literature, including an examination of Nobel Prize-winning

This paper was originally delivered at the Association for Mormon Letters session of the conference of the Rocky Mountain Modern Language Association in October 1979.

writer Halldór Laxness who used the Mormons' proselyting and emigration efforts as the basis for an ambitious novel, Paradise Reclaimed *("Halldór Laxness, The Mormons, and the Promised Land,"* Dialogue *11 [Summer 1978]:25-37; also in Icelandic translation as the cover article in the literary supplement of the newspaper* Morgunblaðið, *5 May 1979).*

Professor Tate draws on his background in medieval and patristic studies to find the theme of Exodus typology as prominent and important — indeed, as central — to the Book of Mormon as other scholars have found it to be in Old and New Testament studies. Not only do the events of Lehi's family recapitulate those of the Exodus, but as Professor Tate points out, Nephi himself, the narrator and recorder of those events, is conscious of the parallels and uses them in a powerful way to unify his people and to persuade their compliance to the Lord's pattern.

Nor is Nephi alone, Professor Tate argues, in perceiving the echoes of the Exodus pattern. His brother Jacob alludes unmistakably to Exodus typology as does Alma the Younger. And just as the typological pattern in the Old Testament finds its fulfillment in the New, so does the Exodus type in the Book of Mormon find explicit and eloquent fulfillment in the visit of Christ to the Nephites, recorded in 3 Nephi.

Typology has received considerable attention in recent years; critical and historical studies have explored its implications for historiography and literature, both sacred and secular, ranging from early Christian through medieval to twentieth-century applications.[1] Although there are minor variations and refinements of definition in each instance, the basic features of typology are clear. Deriving from three New Testament uses of τύπος (type) — Adam as the type of Christ, the crossing of the Red Sea as the type of baptism, and baptism as the ἀντίτυπος (antitype or figural fulfillment) of the Flood — the term denotes a relationship between events of sacred history (see Rom. 5:14; 1 Cor. 10:6; 1 Pet. 3:21).

In his seminal essay "Figura," Erich Auerbach concisely defines typological or figural understanding of history as the establishing of "a connection between two events or persons, the first of which signifies not only itself but also the second, while the second encompasses or fulfills the first. The two poles of the figure are separate in time, but both, being real events or figures, are within time, within the stream of historical life."[2] For example, Moses' raising of the brazen serpent on the pole, though indeed a self-sufficient historical event, points ahead to the crucifixion of Christ, which in turn looks back to and meaningfully encompasses the earlier event (see Num. 21:8-9; John 3:14-15). The brazen serpent is thus a type or figure or shadow (the three terms are synonymous) of the healing power of the crucifixion. Typology understood in this sense posits the belief that such correspondences are neither accidental nor arbitrary but that they constitute a significant system of intelligible coordinates in the gradual unfolding of God's historical design. Typological interpretation thus establishes not a meaning of words but a meaning of events and their attendant details, and it does so principally by grounding meaning in the central moment of sacred history, the incarnation of Christ.

In *The Anatomy of Criticism* Northrup Frye writes: "We cannot trace the Bible back, even historically, to a time when its materials were not being shaped into a typological unity, and if the Bible is to be regarded as inspired in any sense, sacred or secular, its editorial and redacting processes must be regarded as inspired too."[3] Like the Bible, the Book of Mormon is figural narrative, and its structure is perhaps most fruitfully approached through typological criticism. The technical terms, *type* and *shadow*, appear both singly and as a pair in the text, especially in Mosiah and Alma. This fact and other indicators have prompted three Mormon literary scholars—Richard Dilworth Rust, Bruce Jorgensen, and myself—to simultaneous investigations of the implications of typology for the interpretation of the Book of Mormon. Rust approaches the text from the perspective of Puritan typologizing, especially Samuel Mather's *The Figures or Types of the Old Testament* (1683, 2nd ed. 1705). His principal contribution is in identifying scattered occurrences of various figures and classifying them according to

Mather's categories.[4] In the finest literary essay on the Book of Mormon to date, Jorgensen, another Americanist, uses typology as a means of understanding the richly suggestive dream of the Tree of Life and its implications for the unity of the whole narrative. In doing so, he, like Frye, commingles type and archetype.[5] I approach the text as a medievalist with some training in patristics. This paper will examine the typology of the Exodus pattern in the Book of Mormon, demonstrating ways in which it unifies the work structurally and thematically.[6]

We may do well to remind ourselves at the outset how important the Exodus is to the structure of the Bible. In *The God of Exodus*, James Plastaras writes: "It was the . . . exodus which shaped all of Israel's understanding of history. It was only in light of the exodus that Israel was able to look back into the past and piece together her earlier history. It was also the exodus which provided the prophets with a key to the understanding of Israel's future. In this sense, the exodus stands at the center of Israel's history."[7] And after examining recurrences of the pattern in the Old Testament following the original Exodus, David Daube comments that "by being fashioned on the exodus, later deliverances became manifestations of this eternal, certainty-giving relationship between God and his people."[8] In fact, we will see how it is primarily through Exodus typology that the Old and New Testaments are drawn together into a figural unity. But at this point I simply call attention to the first two columns of the table listing some Old Testament details of the pattern with their corresponding New Testament fulfillments.

The Book of Mormon opens with an exodus. The narrator, Nephi, seems naturally and strikingly drawn to exegesis: he provides occasional etymologies ("Irreantum, which, being interpreted, is many waters," 1 Ne. 17:5); he glosses passages from Isaiah in targumic manner ("out of the waters of Judah, *or out of the waters of baptism*," 1 Ne. 20:1; italics added); with angelic guidance he provides a full spiritual explication of his father's dream (see 1 Ne. 11-15); and he expounds scripture to his brothers who — grumblers though they be — are conditioned enough to interpretive method to inquire whether Isaiah's prophecies are to be construed literally or spiritually: "What meaneth these things which ye have read? Behold, are they to be understood according to things which are spiritual, which shall come to pass according to the spirit and not the flesh?" (1 Ne. 22:1). Like his father, Lehi, who upon reading about his progenitors in the plates of Laban begins at once to prophesy about his own descendants, Nephi is keenly aware of his distinct moment in history. When this exegete-narrator says, as he does several times, "I did liken all scriptures unto us," we can be quite sure he is not speaking of apothegms or proof texts (1 Ne. 19:23; see also 2 Ne. 11:2, 8; and Jacob's similar statement in 2 Ne. 6:5). Nephi senses that he and his family are reenacting a sacred and symbolic pattern that looks back to Israel and forward to Christ — the pattern of Exodus.

Notice how many details of the early narrative conform to this pattern (see table, column 3). Nephi and his family depart out of Jerusalem into the wilderness, "deliver[ed] . . . from destruction" (1 Ne. 17:14). In what might be called a paschal vision — referring fifty-six times to the Lamb (Lamb of God, blood of the Lamb, etc.) — Nephi's interpretive revelation on his father's dream recalls the passover lamb of Exodus as it figures Christ (chs. 11-15). While a pillar of light rested upon a rock, Lehi had been warned to flee; and the Lord now provides miraculous guidance in the form of a compass-ball, the Liahona, and assures them, "I will also be your light in the wilderness; and I will prepare the way before you" (1 Ne. 1:6; 16:10; 17:13). When the family begins to murmur from hunger as had the Israelites before receiving manna, Nephi obtains food miraculously at the Lord's direction (see 1 Ne. 16:23, 31). He repeatedly receives instruction from the Lord on a mountain (see 1 Ne. 16:30; 17:7) and builds a ship not "after the manner of men; but . . . after the manner which the Lord had shown unto me" just as Moses had received the design for the tabernacle (see 1 Ne. 18:1-3; Exod. 26). (Both ship and tabernacle are types of the church in Christian typology.) Nephi and his family bear with them a sacred text, the plates of Laban, containing the law of Moses in the Pentateuch, and other prophets including Isaiah (see 1 Ne. 5:11, 13, 23). The Lord had promised them: "Inasmuch as ye shall keep my commandments ye shall be led towards the promised land; and ye shall know that it is by me that ye are led" (1 Ne. 17:13). And indeed the party crosses the ocean and reaches this land of promise, learning after their arrival that Jerusalem has been destroyed (see 2 Ne. 6:8).

Though the correspondences between the exodus of the Israelites and this exodus are compelling, Nephi's conscious sense of reenacting the pattern is even more striking. Early in the narrative when faced with the assignment of getting the plates from Laban, he exhorts his brothers: "Let us be strong like unto Moses; for he truly spake unto the waters of the Red Sea and they divided hither and thither, and our fathers came through, out of captivity, on dry ground, and the armies of Pharaoh did follow and were drowned in the waters of the Red Sea" (1 Ne. 4:2). But at this point he cannot have known how apt the allusion really is. This is Nephi before he has the text in hand as a means of glossing his experience, before he realizes in what detail his own family will replicate the Exodus. As his awareness grows, he alludes with increasing frequency to the Exodus (see table, parenthetical references column 3). After the miraculous provision of food, he reminds his brothers that the Israelites "were fed with manna in the wilderness" (1 Ne. 17:28). When the Lord tells Nephi, "I will . . . be your light in the wilderness," Nephi reminds his brothers that the God of the Israelites went before them, "leading them by day and giving light unto them by night" (1 Ne. 17:13, 30).

Laman and Lemuel prove as fickle in observance as the recalcitrant Israelites before them. They do not share Nephi's sense of history; neither the reenactment of the pattern nor the shared text unites them in community, and they seek Nephi's life in the promised land (see 2 Ne. 5:2). Nephi and those who choose his name flee again into the wilderness bearing the ball of guidance and the text whose "statutes" they observe (2 Ne. 5:12, 10; see table, column 4). The Lord causes "a sore cursing" to come upon their enemies, the Lamanites (2 Ne. 5:21). Where Moses had built a tabernacle, Nephi builds a temple (see 2 Ne. 5:16). And after describing the prosperity of the people in the new land, he ends his account by noting that forty years have passed since their departure from Jerusalem (see 2 Ne. 5:34).

Typological thinking has long been observed in the prophets, especially in Isaiah, who several times prophesies of a new exodus. Of this Jean Daniélou writes:

> The Prophets, in the very heart of the Old Testament, are the first who have dwelt on the significance of the Exodus, and their work is of primary importance, for it makes clear that the principles of typology were to be found already among these Prophets. . . . When the New Testament shows that the life of Christ is the truth and fulfillment of all that was outlined and typified in the Exodus it is only taking up and continuing the typology outlined by the Prophets. The basic difference does not lie in the typology, but in the fact that what is presented by the Prophets as something yet to come is shown by the New Testament writers as fulfilled in Jesus Christ. . . . Prophecy, which thus becomes the first degree in the evolution of typology, is seen as establishing a relationship between the New Testament and the Exodus. The organic relation between typology and prophecy, τύπος and λόγος is quite clear, for so far from being distinct categories, prophecy is the typological interpretation of history.[9]

It is worth noting that Nephi's own typological reading of history proceeds not only from the Pentateuch but from his reading of Isaiah; and the chapters that he and his brother Jacob quote from contain such allusions to the new exodus as:

> The Lord shall set his hand again the second time to recover the remnant of his people. . . . And the Lord shall utterly destroy the tongue of the Egyptian sea; and with his mighty wind he shall shake his hand over the river, and shall smite it in the seven streams, and make men go over dry shod . . . like as it was to Israel in the day that he came up out of the land of Egypt. The Lord will create . . . upon her assemblies, a cloud and smoke by day and the shining of a flaming fire by night (2 Ne. 21:11, 15-16; 14:5; compare Isa. 11:11, 15-16; 4:5).

After Jacob cites chapters 49-51 of Isaiah, Nephi says, "I will liken his [Isaiah's] words unto my people. . . . All things which have been given of God from the beginning of the world, unto man, are the typifying of him," and he refers to God's "eternal plan of deliverance from death" (2 Ne. 6-8; 11:2, 4, 5). Then Nephi quotes an additional thirteen chapters, Isaiah 2-14 in 2 Nephi 12-24, and adds eloquently:

> And as the Lord God liveth that brought Israel up out of the land of Egypt, and gave unto Moses power that he should heal the nations after they had been bitten by the poisonous serpents, if they would cast their eyes unto the serpent which he did raise up before them, and also gave him power that he should smite the rock and the water should come forth; yea, behold I say unto you, that as these things are true, and as the Lord God liveth, there is none other name given under heaven save it be this Jesus Christ, of which I have spoken, whereby man can be saved (2 Ne. 25:20).

Nephi's own prophecy of the gentiles (or pilgrims) is cast in Exodus terms (see table, column 5). Led by the Spirit, they cross "many waters" and are delivered out of captivity as God's wrath is kindled against their enemies; they bear with them a sacred text "like unto the . . . plates of brass" containing "the covenants of the Lord . . . [with] the house of Israel"; and they obtain a "land of promise . . . for their inheritance" (1 Ne. 13:12-15, 18-19, 23). This account is consonant with the Puritans' own typological view of their history. As Ursula Brumm has noted: "The ever-present type for the New England Puritans' view of their own destiny was the exodus of the children of Israel from Egypt into the wilderness and then to the promised land. . . . This basic idea is found in many variations in all the New England writers, and it also dominates Cotton Mather's *Magnalia*."[10] She then cites many instances, including such unfortunate details as their identifying Indians with the serpents of the wilderness.

Whatever conclusions one may draw about this correspondence, it is clear that Nephi is conscious of replicating Exodus and that he reads texts and visions figurally. His doing so informs the remainder of the Book of Mormon as the Exodus pattern recurs several times before the coming of Christ in 3 Nephi. In Mosiah, for example, Alma and his followers depart into the "borders of the land" (Mosiah 18:31; see table, column 6). Here the crossing of the Red Sea is replaced by a communal baptism — the fulfillment of the type;[11] they flee into the wilderness, and their enemy, King Noah, is slain along with many of his followers (see Mosiah 18:14-17, 34; 19:10, 20). Alma, like Moses who had appointed captains over every thousand, hundred, fifty, and ten, establishes governance by ordaining one priest to preside over every fifty people (see Mosiah 18:18). In the subsequent lawgiving, Alma, inspired by God, gives commandments to his people in seven verses, each beginning with the authoritative formula: "he commanded them saying" (18:19-24, 27).

Other instances of the pattern are equally evocative. Alma's people are divinely delivered from the Lamanites (see Mosiah 24); so are the people of Limhi (see Mosiah 22); even earlier, the Jaredites depart across "many waters"; the Lord stands in a cloud, speaks on a mountain, and provides light as they pass through the sea towards the "promised land" after "many years" in the wilderness (Eth. 2:4-6, 14; 3:1; 6:2-3, 5; 3:3).

The recurrence of this pattern through the Book of Mormon, with each instance pointing back to the original Exodus and adumbrating the fulfillment of each type in Christ, has implications beyond the meaningful patterning of community in history. As Christian commentators from the Fathers to the present have consistently pointed out, each individual conversion reenacts the Exodus: under spiritual prompting, the person abandons worldliness (Egypt), experiences a rebirth involving the death of the "old man" (baptism), and wanders patiently while tried in the wilderness until proven worthy to enter the promised land.[12] In the Old Testament itself, one notes that the hundreds of times the verb "to deliver" (especially the Hebrew *natsal* and *malat*) appears after the Israelite exodus refer not only to community (e.g., "delivered us from the hand of the enemy," Ezra 8:31) but also, especially in the Psalms, to the individual ("he hath delivered me out of all trouble," "thou hast delivered my soul from death," "he delivered me from my strong enemy," Ps. 54:7; 56:13; 18:17). The verb constantly evokes Exodus.

The relationship between community redemption and individual redemption is dramatically suggested in the account of the conversion of Alma the Younger, who like Paul had persecuted the church. Notice the oblique allusions to Exodus: An angel appears "as it were in a *cloud*," his voice causing the earth to tremble (Mosiah 27:11; italics added). He commands Alma to "*go*, and remember the captivity of thy fathers . . . and remember how great things [the Lord] has done for them; for they were in bondage, and he has delivered them" (Mosiah 27:16). Struck dumb, Alma lies in a trance for "three days and . . . three nights," then sees a marvelous "*light*," arises (note the imagery of baptism and resurrection), and says, "Behold I am born of the Spirit" (Alma 36:16, 20; Mosiah 27:24). He speaks of "*wandering* through much tribulation" while in the trance and says that his soul has been "redeemed from the . . . *bonds* of iniquity" (Mosiah 27:28-29; italics added). Alma then sets about physically repeating the wandering of his trance, "*traveling* round about through the land . . . preaching the word of God in much tribulation, . . . exhorting [the people] with *longsuffering* and much travail to keep the *commandments* of God" (Mosiah 27:32-33; italics added). He refers in the course of his teaching to previous communal deliverances, to the Lamb of God, to the law as a "type of [Christ's] coming," to the Liahona as a "type" of the words of Christ which guide us to a "far better promised land," and to the brazen serpent: "Behold [Christ] was spoken of by Moses; yea, and behold a type was raised up in the wilderness that whosoever would look upon it might live" (Alma 7:14; 25:15; 37:45; 33:19). And toward the end of his life, Alma summarizes the whole direction — individual and communal — of the Old Testament portion of the book:

> God has delivered me from prison, and from bonds, and from death; yea, and I do put my trust in him, and he will still deliver me. . . . For he has brought our fathers out of Egypt, and he has swallowed up the Egyptians in the Red Sea; and he led them by his power into the promised land; yea, and he has delivered them out of bondage and captivity from time to time. Yea, and he

has also brought our fathers out of the land of Jerusalem; and he has also, by his everlasting power, delivered them out of bondage and captivity, from time to time even down to the present day; and I have always retained in remembrance their captivity; yea, and ye also ought to retain in remembrance, as I have done, their captivity (Alma 36:27-29).

One need only consult the George Reynolds *Complete Concordance to the Book of Mormon* (Salt Lake City: George Reynolds, 1900) under the headwords *deliver, deliverance,* and *bondage* to appreciate that it is not only Alma whose memory is alive with recollection of the Exodus.

No less impressive is the fulfillment of the Exodus types in the New Testament portion of the book where the appearance of the resurrected Christ to the Nephites is recounted in 3 Nephi. Each of the synoptic Gospels, in its own way, is concerned with demonstrating a relationship between Christ and Exodus.[13] John the Baptist is the herald who announces the new exodus Isaiah had prophesied (see Matt. 3:3; Isa. 40:3; compare John 1:23). After Jesus is baptized (remember the significance of the Red Sea), he is "led up of the Spirit into the wilderness" where he sojourns for forty days (Matt. 4:1). His temptations correspond to specific failures of the first Exodus, to which he alludes in his responses to the devil. For example, Moses had said to the Israelites: "God led thee these forty years in the wilderness, to humble thee, and to prove thee. . . . And he . . . suffered thee to hunger, and fed thee with manna, . . . that he might make thee know that man doth not live by bread alone, but by every word that proceedeth out of the mouth of the Lord" (Deut. 8:2). To the temptation to change stones to bread after having fasted for forty days, Christ responds with these same words (see Matt. 5:4). Christ is both the new exodus and the new Moses of whom the first was a type. The Sermon on the Mount is the lawgiving of the new covenant. As Daniélou observes, the number of apostles, twelve, "demonstrates that the community founded by Jesus is the true Israel," and "the parallel between Moses and Christ terminates in the Transfiguration, with its numerous references to the Exodus: Moses himself, the cloud, the Divine

voice, the tabernacles."[14] These and other details show Jesus ful-
filling the types by reenacting Exodus.

But it is in the Gospel of John that we encounter the most
concentrated Exodus typology. Indeed, Plastaras has written,
"There is hardly a page of this Gospel which does not contain at
least one allusion to the exodus story."[15] The evangelist writes
that the Word became flesh and "pitched his tent among us"
(Greek, John 1:14); he has John the Baptist proclaim Jesus to
be the "Lamb of God" (1:29); he describes the crucifixion in
terms of Moses' outstretched arms supported by Aaron and Hur
(see John 19:18; Exod. 17:12); and like the paschal lamb,
Christ's legs are not broken (see John 19:33; Exod. 12:46). But
the feature that most distinguishes John from the other Gospels
is the overt, spoken comparisons Christ makes between himself
and details of the Exodus: "As Moses lifted up the serpent in the
wilderness, even so must the Son of Man be lifted up"; "I am the
light of the world"; "I am the bread which came down from
heaven" (John 3:14; 8:12; 12:46; 6:41).

Krister Stendahl has recently called attention to the Johannine quality of the account of Christ's visit to the Nephites.[16] In
this section of 3 Nephi one again encounters overt statements in
the Johannine manner: "I am the law"; "I am the light" (3 Ne.
15:9; 9:18). But since this event occurs after the Resurrection, 3
Nephi does not narrate the details of Christ's earthly actions
which the evangelists had seen as replicating Exodus. Rather it
addresses the typology more indirectly through structuring the
narrative of Christ's ministry and teachings to the Nephites in
such a way as to approximate the pattern (see table, column 7).

The account opens with the apocalyptic destruction of the
wicked cities accompanying the crucifixion of the Lamb of God
(see 3 Ne. 8-9). Christ, the paschal offering, appears and shows
the multitude the marks of the crucifixion and immediately
instructs them in baptism, a detail that has always struck me as
abrupt (see 3 Ne. 11:14, 21). But I would suggest that this seem-
ing abruptness is conditioned by the sequence of the Exodus to
fit the approximate position of the crossing of the Red Sea,
which prefigures baptism. As in the New Testament, Christ
then calls twelve disciples, corresponding to the twelve tribes

and pointing, as Daniélou notes, to the true Israel (see 3 Ne. 11:18-22). Christ then gives the Sermon on the Mount, announcing that he is "come . . . to fulfill" the law, and more directly, "I am the law" (3 Ne. 12:17; 15:9). Whereas Moses had raised the brazen serpent in the wilderness for the healing of all who would look upon it, Christ says, "Look unto me, and endure to the end" (3 Ne. 15:9); shortly thereafter, he heals the sick (see 3 Ne. 17:9). The ministration of angels that accompanies this act of compassion may well evoke the angels of the ark of the covenant that flank the mercy seat (see 3 Ne. 17:24; Exod. 36:8). He then instructs the people in the sacrament of the Lord's Supper, and the bread and wine—like manna—are miraculously provided on the second day (see 3 Ne. 18:1-7, 20:6). As he gives the twelve power to bestow the Holy Ghost "there came a cloud [a type of the Holy Ghost[17]] and overshadowed the multitude" (3 Ne. 18:38). Earlier we observed that Nephi and Jacob derive some of their figural thinking from Isaiah's prophecies of the new exodus. Christ here twice quotes Isaiah 52:12, one of the key passages concerning the glorious new exodus: "For ye shall not go out with haste nor go by flight; for the Lord will go before you, and the God of Israel shall be your rearward" (3 Ne. 20:42; 21:29). And finally as the outer frame of his teachings to the Nephites, Christ gives the people "this land, for your inheritance," speaks of the New Jerusalem, and names the Church whose heavenly counterpart the promised land of Exodus adumbrates (3 Ne. 20:14, 22; 27:8).

To summarize, in the Old Testament portion of the Book of Mormon, the Exodus pattern recurs in greater concentration than in the Bible, and its typology is more conscious because the narrators are understood to possess the Christological key to the fulfillment of the types from Nephi's vision forward, a fulfillment underscored by the patterning of 3 Nephi around the Exodus. The Exodus reverberates through the book, not only as theme but as pattern; and the overall design of the book generalizes the patterning of community in history while at the same time concentrating the Exodus in individual conversion. Exodus is the pattern and message of the text.

TABLE

COLUMN 1 Exodus	COLUMN 2 Christian Fulfillment	COLUMN 3 1 Nephi	COLUMN 4 Nephi's Minor Exodus (2 Nephi)	COLUMN 5 Nephi's Prophecy of Gentiles (1 Nephi)	COLUMN 6 Alma from Noah (Mosiah 18-19)	COLUMN 7 Christ's Appearance (3 Nephi)
Passover lamb	Christ, crucifixion John 1:29, 36; Rev., esp. chs. 5, 6, 7, 14, 21.	(N's paschal vision 11-14. Lamb of God, blood of the Lamb, gospel of the Lamb, etc. [56 refs.])	(N refers to Lamb of God 31:4-6)			Christ appears, shows people marks of crucifixion 11:14
flee bondage into wilderness	world/sin	flee Jerusalem into wilderness (N refers to Israel's exodus 4:2; 17:26)	flees Lamanites into wilderness 5:5, 7	gone out of captivity, delivered 13:19	people flee to borders of land 18:31, into wilderness 18:34	
guidance light/cloud	Christ John 8:12 (Cloud/Holy Spirit)	Lehi sees pillar of fire on rock. 1:6. Lord as light 17:13 Liahona 16:10 (N refers to Exodus light 17:30)	bears Liahona 5:12	led by Spirit 13:12		"I am the light" 9:18; 15:9; 18:24; "I am God of Israel" 11:14; Cloud settles on people 18:38
water	baptism 1 Cor. 10:1-2	Cross ocean (N refers to Red Sea 17:26)	(N speaks of baptism of Lamb of God 31:4-6)	cross ocean 13:12-13	baptism 18:14-17	instructs in baptism 11
enemies destroyed	liberation from sin	Jerusalem destroyed 2 Ne. 6:8 (N refers to destruction of Egyptian host 17:27)	Lamanites cursed 5:21	God's wrath against their enemies 13:14, 18	Noah slain 19:20, his people slain or captured 19:10	apocalyptic destruction of wicked cities 8-9

manna	Christ, eucharist John 6:41, 1 Cor. 10.	food miraculously provided 16:23, 31 (N refers to manna 17:28, in vision: fruit of tree of life 11:8)			"fountain of pure water" 18:5	instructs in sacrament 18, bread and wine miraculously provided 20:6
water from rock	Christ John 7:37-40; 19:34; 1 Cor. 10:4	(N refers to water from rock, 17:29)	(N refers to water from rock 25:20)			
mountain/law	Sermon on Mount Law (grace) John 1:17	Nephi instructed on mountain 16:30; 17:7; 18:3	Nephites observe "statutes" 5:10		lawgiving 18:19-24, 27 "he commanded them" repeated seven times	Sermon on Mount 12-14, come to fulfill law 12:17; "I am the law" 15:9
text (ark)	New Testament	plates (Pentateuch and Isaiah) 5:11	plates 5:12, N makes additional plates 5:31, (law a type of Christ 11:4)	a book of covenants 12:20, 23		ministration of angels 17:24; see angels of ark and mercy seat Exod. 36:8 (Christ refers to Moses, 20:23; quotes Isaiah in 20:36 ff [new exodus text, Isa. 52:12 twice])
tabernacle	church	builds ship according to Lord's instruction 17:8; 18:2	N builds temple 5:16		ordains priests, 1 per 50, 18:18	calls 12, 12:1
order/governance	12 apostles	(in vision: 12 apostles 12:9)				
brazen serpent	Christ, crucifixion John 3:14-15		(N refers to brazen serpent 25:20 prophesies healing 26:9)			"Look unto me and endure to the end" 15:9; heals people 17:9
promised land	(heaven, grace)	led to promised land 5:5 (N refers to crossing Jordan 17:32)	Nephites prosper in land (N notes that 40 years have passed since they fled Jerusalem 5:34)	promised land 13:15; compare U. Brumm, P. Miller, Bercovitch, Mather on Puritan typology		Father commanded me to give you this land 20:14; New Jerusalem 20:22; I will be in your midst 21:25; names church 27:8

NOTES

1. See, for example, such essay collections as Earl R. Miner, ed., *Literary Uses of Typology: From the Late Middle Ages to the Present* (Princeton: Princeton University Press, 1977); Sacvan Bercovitch, ed., *Typology and Early American Literature* (Amherst: University of Massachusetts Press, 1972); and Hugh T. Kennan, ed., *Typology and Medieval Literature, a* special issue of *Studies in the Literary Imagination* 8 (Spring 1975).

2. "Figura," trans. Ralph Manheim, in *Scenes from the Drama of European Literature, Six Essays* (New York: Meridian Books, 1959), p. 53; additional general studies of typology are Jean Daniélou, *From Shadows to Reality: Studies in the Biblical Typology of the Fathers*, trans. Dom Wulstan Hibberd (Westminster, Md.: Newman Press, 1960); and A. C. Charity, *Events and Their Afterlife: The Dialectics of Christian Typology in the Bible and Dante* (Cambridge: Cambridge University Press, 1966).

3. *Anatomy of Criticism* (Princeton: Princeton University Press, 1957), p. 315.

4. " 'All Things Which Have Been Given of God . . . Are the Typifying of Him': Typology in the Book of Mormon," in *Proceedings of the Symposia of the Association for Mormon Letters, 1978-79*, pp. 113-29; reprinted in this volume.

5. "The Dark Way to the Tree: Typological Unity in the Book of Mormon," *Encyclia* 54, pt. 2 (1977): 16-24; reprinted in this volume. Frye describes the Bible as a "typological unity," but also as "a definitive myth, a single archetypal structure" (p. 315).

6. The recurrence of a deliverance pattern in the Book of Mormon has been noted by Hugh Nibley (*An Approach to the Book of Mormon* [Salt Lake City: Church of Jesus Christ of Latter-day Saints, 1957], pp. 113-42) and Richard L. Bushman ("The Book of Mormon and the American Revolution," *Brigham Young University Studies* 17 [Autumn 1976]: 7-10, 17). Neither approaches the Exodus from the standpoint of typology.

7. *The God of Exodus: The Theology of the Exodus Narratives* (Milwaukee: Bruce Publishing, 1966), p. 7.

8. *The Exodus Pattern in the Bible*, All Souls Studies monograph series, 2 (London: Faber and Faber, 1963), p. 14.

9. *From Shadows to Reality*, pp. 156-57. See also Gerhard von Rad, "Typological Interpretation of the Old Testament," trans. John Bright, pp. 17-39, and Walter Eichrodt, "Is Typological Exegesis an Appropriate Method?" trans. James Barr, pp. 224-45 (esp. 234-35), in Claus Westermann, ed., *Essays on Old Testament Hermeneutics* (Atlanta: John Knox Press, 1963).

10. *American Thought and Religious Typology*, trans. John Hoaglund (New Brunswick, N.J.: Rutgers University Press, 1970), pp. 46-47; see also Bercovitch, *Typology and Early American Literature*. Another correspon-

dence is the fact that the somewhat unusual pairing of the technical terms "type and shadow" in the Book of Mormon (Mosiah 3:15; 13:10) is also found in the basic Puritan handbook of typology, Samuel Mather's *The Figures and Types of the Old Testament,* 2nd ed. (London, 1705; reprint ed., New York: Johnson Reprint Company, 1969), which speaks of "Types and Shadows of the Old Testament," "Types and Shadows of the Law," "[L]egal Types and Shadows," etc. (pp. xi, 10, 14). Since these technical terms, which occur both individually and as a pair only in the Old Testament portion of the Book of Mormon, have no basis in Hebrew, and since *type* is extra-biblical if one is limited to the King James Version (which uses *figure*) without reference to the Greek as Joseph Smith was (see Stendahl, note 16 below, p. 142), I suspect that Joseph Smith became acquainted with the terms through the weakened continuation of the typological sermon tradition of the Puritans into the nineteenth century. As such, they constitute translator anachronisms of the sort discussed by Hugh Nibley (e.g., "church," "synagogue," "Christians") in *Since Cumorah: The Book of Mormon in the Modern World* (Salt Lake City: Deseret Book Company, 1967), pp. 187-91.

11. Daniélou's discussion of a Jewish baptismal rite is of interest in the context of this pre-Incarnation baptism: "Furthermore, the relationship of the Crossing of the Red Sea and of Baptism as brought out by St. Paul [1 Cor. 10:1-2] seems to be according to a line of interpretation belonging to the Judaism of his time. For we know that at the beginning of the Christian era, the initiation of proselytes into the Jewish community included, besides circumcision, a baptism. This baptism, as G. Foote-Moore writes [*Judaism,* I, p. 334], was 'a purification that was neither real nor symbolic, but essentially a rite of initiation.' And the purpose of this initiation was to cause the proselyte to go through the sacrament received by the people at the time of the crossing of the Red Sea. The baptism of the proselytes was, then, a kind of imitation of the Exodus. This is important in showing us that the link between Baptism and the crossing of the Red Sea existed already in Judaism and that therefore it gives us the true symbolism of Baptism, as being not primarily a purification, but a deliverance and a creation," *The Bible and the Liturgy* (Notre Dame, Ind.: University of Notre Dame Press, 1956), pp. 88-89.

12. An excellent introduction to this pervasive interpretation of Exodus is Charles S. Singleton's "In Exitu Israel de Aegypto," *78th Annual Report of the Dante Society of America* (1960), rpt. in John Freccero, ed., *Dante: A Collection of Critical Essays* (Englewood Cliffs, N.J.: Prentice-Hall, 1965), pp. 102-21. As a point of departure, Singleton uses Dante's letter to Can Grande, in which the poet explains that the departure of Israel from Egypt is "in the moral sense, 'the conversion of the soul from the grief and misery of sin to the state of grace.' " See Robert S. Haller, ed. and trans., *Literary Criticism of Dante Alighieri* (Lincoln: University of Nebraska Press, 1973), p. 99.

13. For full discussions of this aspect of the gospels and the New Testament generally, see Plastaras, ch. 14, Daniélou, *From Shadows to Reality,* Bk. IV, and *The Bible and the Liturgy,* especially chs. 5, 9, 10, and 19.

14. *From Shadows to Reality*, p. 160.

15. *The God of Exodus*, p. 325.

16. See "The Sermon on the Mount and Third Nephi," in Truman G. Madsen, ed., *Reflections on Mormonism: Judaeo-Christian Parallels*, Brigham Young University Religious Studies Monograph Series, vol. 4 (Salt Lake City: Religious Studies Center, 1978), p. 150.

17. See Daniélou, *The Bible and the Liturgy*, p. 91, on this tradition.

Index